COUNTED OUT

COUNTED OUT

SAME-SEX RELATIONS AND AMERICANS' DEFINITIONS OF FAMILY

BRIAN POWELL, CATHERINE BOLZENDAHL, CLAUDIA GEIST, AND LALA CARR STEELMAN

A Volume in the American Sociological Association's
Rose Series in Sociology

Russell Sage Foundation • New York

Library of Congress Cataloging-in-Publication Data

Counted out : same-sex relations and Americans' definitions of family / Brian Powell ... [et al.].
    p. cm. — (American Sociological Association's Rose series in sociology)
Includes bibliographical references and index.
ISBN 978-0-87154-687-6 (hardcover)   ISBN 978-0-87154-688-3 (paperback)
  1. Families—United States.   2. Gay couples—United States.   3. Gays—Family relationships—United States.   I. Powell, Brian, 1954–
    HQ536.C7575 2010
    306.85086'640973—dc22   2010015513

The paper used in this publication meets the minimum requirements of American National Standard for Information Sciences—Permanence of Paper for Printed Library Materials. ANSI Z39.48-1992.

Text design by Suzanne Nichols.

RUSSELL SAGE FOUNDATION
112 East 64th Street, New York, New York 10065
10 9 8 7 6 5 4 3 2 1

The Russell Sage Foundation

The Russell Sage Foundation, one of the oldest of America's general purpose foundations, was established in 1907 by Mrs. Margaret Olivia Sage for "the improvement of social and living conditions in the United States." The Foundation seeks to fulfill this mandate by fostering the development and dissemination of knowledge about the country's political, social, and economic problems. While the Foundation endeavors to assure the accuracy and objectivity of each book it publishes, the conclusions and interpretations in Russell Sage Foundation publications are those of the authors and not of the Foundation, its Trustees, or its staff. Publication by Russell Sage, therefore, does not imply Foundation endorsement.

Previous Volumes in the Series

═══ Forthcoming Titles ═══

══ The Rose Series ══ in Sociology

T he American Sociological Association's Rose Series in Sociology publishes books that integrate knowledge and address controversies from a sociological perspective. Books in the Rose Series are at the forefront of sociological knowledge. They are lively and often involve timely and fundamental issues on significant social concerns. The series is intended for broad dissemination throughout sociology, across social science and other professional communities, and to policy audiences. The series was established in 1967 by a bequest to ASA from Arnold and Caroline Rose to support innovations in scholarly publishing.

DIANE BARTHEL-BOUCHIER
CYNTHIA J. BOGARD
MICHAEL KIMMEL
DANIEL LEVY
TIMOHY P. MORAN
NAOMI ROSENTHAL
MICHAEL SCHWARTZ
GILDA ZWERMAN

EDITORS

To our families, as we define and embrace them

Contents

═ About the Authors ═

Brian Powell is James H. Rudy Professor of Sociology at Indiana University.

Catherine Bolzendahl is assistant professor of sociology at the University of California, Irvine.

Claudia Geist is assistant professor of sociology at the University of Utah.

Lala Carr Steelman is professor of sociology at the University of South Carolina.

═ Acknowledgments ═

This book is about family—in particular, which living arrangements are counted in Americans' definitions of family, and which ones are counted out. In thinking about the support, advice, and assistance we received while completing this book, we recognize that a great number of people and organizations must be counted in.

This project began as part of the Indiana University Sociological Research Practicum (SRP), which provides undergraduate and graduate students with the opportunity to participate in a large-scale, ongoing, faculty-directed research project. We are indebted to Indiana University's Department of Sociology, College of Arts and Sciences, and the Karl Schuessler Institute for Social Research, which annually sponsor the SRP, as well as the Center for Survey Research, which provided indispensable guidance to the research team in fielding the project. The number of student interviewers and transcribers are too numerous to name here, but their hard work and indomitable spirit were crucial to the success of the project and are very much appreciated. From the Center for Survey Research, we are especially grateful to John Kennedy, whose knowledge regarding interviewing and whose patience with sociologists who know a great deal less about interviewing are second to none. From the Karl Schuessler Institute for Social Research, we also thank Louise Brown, who kept us on budget, and Cher Jamison, who kept us on track. But to say that Cher merely kept us on track is an understatement. Without her meticulous attention to every aspect of the data collection and coding, the project would never have been completed.

We also owe a special debt to Danielle Fettes and Laura Hamilton. Not only did they contribute to chapters (in Danielle's case, chapter 5; in Laura's case, chapter 7, of which she is the lead author), they also were involved in the development of the Constructing the Family Surveys and served as interview supervisors. We are beneficiaries of their insightful comments and suggestions in framing this book. Danielle and Laura are joined by a larger group of SRP research associates, including Kyle Dodson, Emily Fairchild, Yasmiyn Irizarry, Evie Perry, Tiffani Saunders, Amely Schmitt, and Brian Starks. Oren (David) Pizmony-Levy deserves credit for his work on the numerous charts, graphs, and tables in this book. Together this terrifically talented group of young scholars helped to shape this study and facilitate its completion.

Even upon completing the 2003 interviews, we did not anticipate that this project would result in a book. Our plans changed, thanks to the highly persuasive and extraordinarily encouraging Naomi Gerstel and Joya Misra, then part of the American Sociological Association Rose Series editorial team from the University of Massachusetts. The subsequent ASA Rose Series editorial group from Stony Brook University—in particular, Cynthia Bogard—gently shepherded us through the publication process. We are especially lucky that our manuscript was in the remarkably accomplished hands of Suzanne Nichols, April Rondeau, and Cynthia Buck from the Russell Sage Foundation.

We were given the opportunity to try out many of the ideas in this book at presentations at Ball State University, Dartmouth College, Emory University, Florida State University, Harvard Law School, Kent State, Ohio State University, Purdue University, University of California–Irvine, University of Chicago, University of Georgia, University of Mannheim, University of South Carolina, University of Texas, Wake Forest University, and Washington State University. Comments from our colleagues at these universities, along with the generous and incisive feedback from Jerry Jacobs, Suzanne Bianchi, Clem Brooks, Simon Cheng, Kathryn Lively, Patricia McManus, Robin Simon, Regina Werum, and anonymous reviewers of the manuscript, challenged and inspired us and compelled us to reassess some of our own assumptions. In addition, we value the support lent by Art Alderson, Elizabeth Armstrong, Philip Cohen, Tom Gieryn, Carol Hostetter, Jack Martin, Jane McLeod, Patricia McManus, Eliza Pavalko, Lisa Pearce, Bernice Pescosolido, Rob Robinson, Martin Weinberg, and members of the Department of Sociology and the Center for Advanced Social Science Research at New York University, where Brian Powell spent his sabbatical year while revising this manuscript. Financial support provided by Indiana University, University of California–Irvine School of Social Sciences, Carolina Population Center, University of Utah, and University of South Carolina also is greatly appreciated. We are delighted that funding from the National Science Foundation, the National Center for Family and Marriage Research, and Indiana University for a third wave of the Constructing the Family Survey will allow us to address unanswered questions that arose from the 2003 and 2006 waves.

No list of acknowledgements would be complete without thanking our families, in the most inclusive sense of the word. It includes an army of friends and relatives—among them, Sarah Brauner-Otto, Jo Dixon, Christina Ek, David Esposito, Olivia Esposito, Rinaldo Esposito, Roberta Esposito, Scott Kimberly, Dean Krechevsky, Sigrun Olafsdottir, Barbara Pelly, Brea Perry, Glenn Powell, Jay Powell, Mel Powell, Aileen Schulte, Brian Shoot, Karen Shoot, Jim Simon, Joseph Steelman, Brian Sweeney, Amanda Thompson, and Laurie Young—many of whom doggedly cajoled and guilted us into finally completing this manuscript. And, of course, it includes our partners—Robert Fulk, Brandon Konda, Rachel Tharpe, and Carl Ek—who humored us, suffered with us, and fed us through this endeavor. We thank all those in our lives who have shown what family really means and who inspired us to explore and explain the same in American society today.

= Chapter 1 =

Family Counts

AMILY counts. That is, a family counts for its members and for its
inextricable ties to other institutions. It counts for society at large
because it represents a major conduit through which cultural
knowledge flows from one generation to the next and beyond, and because it is a means by which necessary goods are distributed to members of society. Family and society are so interwoven that arguably,
without family, we would have no society. Virtually all socialization
theories see familial influence as pivotal from childhood to adulthood.
Inequality also has deep roots within family. Scholars representing diverse theoretical leanings agree that family confers advantages and disadvantages that are difficult to erase (Becker 1980; Bourdieu and Passeron 1977; Coleman 1988; Featherman and Hauser 1978). In addition,
family is the group that people often turn to in moments of triumph
and moments of failure. An abundant literature dating back at least to
the sociologist Émile Durkheim (1897/1977) contends that family is a
primary institution into which people feel socially integrated and that
this connectedness is consequential for the well-being of family members and the well-being of society.

Although we should be careful not to valorize family reflexively, we
cannot deny the major role that family plays in fulfilling objectives that
range from sheer survival to personal well-being—or the failure to do
so. The appreciation of family as a societal cornerstone is one reason
why the academic and public debate over "family decline" or "family
change" is so spirited and controversial. The numerous realms in which
it matters make the study of family a genuinely interdisciplinary arena.
Scholars who study it come from the arts and humanities, public health,
psychology, anthropology, political science, economics, communication, sociology, evolutionary sciences, and beyond. The scholarship
across disciplines on the impact of family underscores its relevance in
virtually every corner of social life. In other words, family counts.

There is another way in which "family" counts: what we collectively

1

define and accept as family has far-reaching implications. The boundaries that we—and others—make between family and nonfamily play both subtle and not-so-subtle roles in our daily lives. Imagine, for example, a recently married couple who plan to host their first Thanksgiving dinner, only to be told by their parents that they will not attend this dinner because the married couple is "not yet a family"—a signal that they consider children a requirement to become a family, and perhaps less than subtle hint that they expect grandchildren. Or consider a gay male couple who have lived together for fifteen years and who find themselves unsure about how to complete the question "number of family members traveling with you" on a customs declaration form while traveling abroad. Or imagine a lesbian who has requested a bereavement fare from an airline to attend the funeral for her partner's mother being told that it is unclear whether she qualifies as a "family member." Or picture an empty-nest married heterosexual couple who are contemplating a move from their large house in a "single-family residential zone" to a smaller condominium because they no longer need so much room, let alone a "family room."

These scenarios—some based on our own experiences—are far from unique. References to family and various implied or explicit definitions of family are ubiquitous in our everyday lives—from signs for "family" restrooms in public buildings (typically portraying a stick-figure family of a man, a woman, and one or more children) to brochures describing "family" care or benefits at universities and other workplaces (some prominently displaying a prototypical father-mother-child family and others offering a more varied visual representation of family). These depictions often embody and perpetuate what some scholars refer to as heteronormative conceptions of "the family" that privilege marriage, the presence of children, gendered roles, and especially heterosexual relationships (Berkowitz 2009; Bernstein and Reimann 2001b). This representation of the Standard North American Family (SNAF)—as characterized by the Canadian sociologist Dorothy Smith (1993)—serves as a yardstick against which other living arrangements are measured and consequently are seen as "lesser" families, or not as family at all.

Messages about family are heard in various venues. We hear of "family hour" on television; "family day," "family vacations," and "family night" at restaurants; "family visitation hours" at hospitals; "family-friendly" governmental policies; "pro-family" advocacy groups; and "family values." These messages give preference not only to family but also to particular definitions of family that include certain living arrangements—often those constituting the SNAF—and exclude others, even if those in the excluded categories see themselves as family. We also hear of initiatives to "build strong families" as a means to slow down the rate of "family decline" or "family dissolution"; family in this context takes on a circumscribed operationalization. And we hear of emotionally charged debates regarding the extension of various rights and obligations to same-sex couples, with each side of the dispute attempting to take ownership of the word "family"—one promoting a traditionally bounded definition and the other side advocating a more all-encompassing definition that challenges a narrow, hegemonic vision of family. In other words, "family"—what we define as family—counts.

Both families themselves and our definitions of "family" count, but we do not know enough about what Americans count as family. Although scholars have amassed abundant and persuasive evidence of the relevance of family in virtually every aspect of individuals' lives and written extensively on Americans' views regarding an array of family-related topics (for example, the work-family imbalance, the division of labor in the home, and prescribed gender expectations in families), they mostly have bypassed public definitions of family. Social scientists have not, however, avoided defining families themselves. To be sure, at least since the early 1900s family scholars have debated among themselves over the meaning of family; however, these debates have relied primarily on academicians' own definitions of family—which we briefly discuss later in this chapter—and not on those of laypeople. Some scholars have written about the ways in which people think about or define their own families; much of this scholarship explores the experiences of marginalized groups (for example, African Americans' inclusion of extended or fictive kin as part of their family, or the efforts of same-sex couples to construct and reaffirm their identity as family) (Carrington 1995; Hill 1999; Sullivan 2001; Weston 1991). But missing from the literature, with the exception of some insightful but limited college student surveys (Ford et al. 1996; see also Weigel 2008), are analyses of the parameters that Americans set in defining other people's families.[1]

The distinction between what people define as their own family and what they define as family in general is not minor. Understanding how people broadly define family and why they do so matters a great deal. Subjective assessments of family have meaning and consequences, not only for individual interactions with others but also for potential social change. Public opinion certainly is not the only factor that drives social and policy change. But recent ballot initiatives regarding gay marriage, adoption, and foster care accentuate the importance of public views and definitions. These votes confirm that policies are not created exclusively in a top-down fashion, and they point to the danger of underestimating the power of popular opinion. In Arkansas, for example, a

strong majority (57 percent) voted in 2008 in favor of a statute that pro-
hibits a minor from being adopted or placed in a foster home "if the
individual seeking to adopt or to serve as a foster parent is cohabiting
with a sexual partner outside of a marriage which is valid under the
constitution and laws of this state."[2] The law did not explicitly differentiate between same-sex and heterosexual cohabiting couples, but commentators often characterized it as a "gay adoption ban" in which the
restrictions on all unmarried couples—instead of only same-sex couples—were added so that the law would survive court scrutiny (DeMillo 2008; Miller 2008). In the same year, in a tightly contested referendum, Californians voted in favor of Proposition 8, which amended the
state constitution to restrict marriage to opposite-sex couples. Super-
seding a 2008 California Supreme Court decision that permitted same-
sex marriage (*In re Marriage Cases*), Proposition 8 prevented the extension of the rights and benefits of marriage to gay and lesbian couples;
its supporters and opponents anticipate that legal appeals regarding
this proposition may ultimately reach the United States Supreme Court.
In the following year, voters in Maine decided to repeal one of the very
few state laws in the United States that allowed same-sex marriage.
The referenda in Arkansas, California, and Maine—along with others
in multiple states especially in the past decade—underscore the centrality of public opinion in delineating the boundaries of family. These
votes also speak to the pivotal role that issues surrounding same-sex
couples assume in contemporary debates about the definitions of family.

Given the slim margin of victories in California and Maine and the
possibility that the boundaries the public makes between family and
nonfamily are porous and fluid, understanding Americans' definitions
of family is critical. And identifying the factors that could alter these
definitions should be fundamental for both advocates and opponents
of more expansive definitions of family.

This book reports on results from the Constructing the Family Surveys of 2003 and 2006, in which 712 and 815 Americans (including nationally representative subsamples and a smaller subsample of Indiana
residents), respectively, were interviewed about their stances regarding
same-sex couples, cohabiting couples, gay marriage, gay adoption, the
extension of certain marital/family rights to gay and cohabiting couples, and, most importantly, what counts as family. These interviews
also covered a variety of other family-related topics, including some
that have mostly been ignored by social scientists—among them, public views regarding the relative influence of biological and social factors
on children's development, whether boys (or girls) in single-parent
households are better off living with their fathers or mothers, and
whether women should assume their husband's last name upon mar-

riage. In addition, these interviews solicited sociodemographic information and items regarding religious ideology that enable us to explore quantitatively the distribution of responses, identify social cleavages in the responses, and examine how these responses link to other ideological standpoints. The inclusion of open-ended questions (for example, respondents were asked why they believed that certain living arrangements do or do not count as a family) also offers a unique glimpse into how people explain their views regarding family, how they discuss their beliefs regarding gender and sexuality, and how these positions are intertwined.[3] These are, to our knowledge, the first sociological surveys of this scope that explicitly tap into Americans' definitions of family and the rationale behind their definitions.

Given the contemporary debates, the impetus for both this book and the Constructing the Family Surveys is simple. Few would deny that the public and academic discourse regarding the meaning of family has become more intense in the past few years. The language typically used to describe "family" (or "the family"), often based on assumptions about traditional family roles and composition, increasingly has been contested in academic scholarship (for example, in studies of divorce, cohabitation, gay and lesbian couples, and single parenthood) and in the public sphere. Some lament what they see as the weakening, or destruction, of "the family." But others—often relying on theoretical and empirical developments in sexuality and family studies that also engage issues of class, race, gender, and sexuality—celebrate the mounting diversity of family forms and the challenge they present to hegemonic family ideals. Changes in the visibility of these "new" families and reactions to these changes purportedly were pivotal in recent elections in the aforementioned referenda regarding adoption and foster care among cohabiting gay and heterosexual couples in Arkansas and gay marriage in California, as well as in similar ballot initiatives throughout the United States. It is not a stretch to predict that conflict over who counts as family will continue and perhaps become even more acrimonious. The general question of what defines a family—and in particular, whether same-sex couples should be counted in or counted out of the definition—is at the forefront of what some refer to as a cultural divide, or even an escalating culture war, in the United States.

Yet we do not know how Americans define family or how they distinguish between family and nonfamily. The overriding objective of this book, then, is to explore people's definitions of family—not who they consider to be their own family, but who they believe fits under the abstract umbrella of "family." More specifically, our goals are to explore the degree of consensus or disagreement over the definition of family—and in particular, to determine whether same-sex couples are counted in or counted out of this definition; consider how Americans talk about the definition of family; identify the extent to which these definitions vary along sociodemographic lines, including age or co-hort, gender, education, race, and religion; examine how these defini-tions are linked to beliefs regarding the etiology of children's behavior and traits, in particular the causes of sexual preference; and assess how these definitions are intertwined with gender ideology—more specifically, with views about parenting and marital name change practices.

In meeting these goals, we seek not only to understand how people are making sense of—and in some cases struggling with—changes in living arrangements in the United States, but also to make admittedly cautious predictions regarding the future. For example, to what extent and in what direction do the social cleavages in attitudes regarding the meaning of family forebode changes in these attitudes? Which types of frames or arguments are most resonant and potentially most influen-tial in directing people toward a more inclusive (or more exclusive) definition of family that accommodates (or leaves out) same-sex house-holds? How likely is it that Americans will reassess their definitions of family? A collateral goal of this book is to encourage a reassessment of assumptions that continue to be held by a number of sociologists and other social scientists—for example, the view that family and marriage are intrinsically sexist and harmful institutions or the apparent as-sumption that all genetic explanations are inherently conservative or reactionary.

We now turn to an examination of the theories, actors, and frames shaping the debate over family and its definition. We first briefly sum-marize various family scholars' treatments of the term "family" and then introduce recent theoretical and empirical developments, most notably by sexuality scholars, that present formidable challenges to prevailing assumptions regarding family.

Academic Accounts: Social Scientific Definitions of Family

Across the social sciences, definitions of family are quite easy to come by, but they can be difficult to reconcile. Family is the focal point of much scholarly activity—so much so that we cannot do justice to this vast body of scholarship here. Rather than offering a lengthy review, we highlight key examples of the varied scholarly definitions used in research and of the often competing and quarrelsome nature of these definitions. Two strands of scholarship inform this approach: first, lit-erature that deliberates over the meaning and definition of family, coming mostly from family scholars, and second, writings, often from sexuality and gender scholars, that are more recent and use a more critical lens to explore how family and views regarding family reflect and perpetuate what these scholars describe as heteronormative, gendered, and racialized ideology.

Family Scholars: Defining Family and Debating Family Diversity

Even in the early part of the twentieth century, scholars provided markedly different versions of what a family is and where its boundaries lie. The sociologist Ernest Burgess (1926, 3) conceptualized family not as a particular structural entity but instead as a "unity of interacting personalities":

> By a unity of interacting personalities is meant a living, changing, growing thing. . . . The actual unity of family life has its existence not in any legal conception, nor in any formal contract, but in the interaction of its members. For the family does not depend for its survival on the harmonious relations of its members, nor does it necessarily disintegrate as a result of conflicts between its members. The family lives as long as interaction is taking place and dies only when it ceases.

Others elaborated on this interactionist approach to family (Waller 1938), although most social scientists relied on more structural definitions that restricted "the family" to certain living arrangements. Along these lines, the anthropologist George Murdock (1949, 1) specified several conditions for a group to qualify as a family, which he defined as "a social group characterized by common residence, economic cooperation and reproduction. It includes adults of both sexes, at least two of whom maintain a socially approved relationship, and one or more children, own or adopted, of the sexually cohabiting adults." Murdock's definition relies to a great extent on the functions that family performs, and it explicitly or implicitly permits adoption, polygamy, and extended families. Sexually cohabiting adults, however, cannot be the same sex to meet the criteria for this particular definition. Indeed, many social-scientific definitions of family have relied on structural parameters similar to those provided by Murdock, though more restrictive in some cases and less restrictive in others. The communication studies scholars Ascan Koerner and Mary Ann Fitzpatrick (2004) note that structural definitions of family have been highly visible—and arguably dominant—in the academic community, thus privileging the presence of particular "family members" and ignoring or downplaying the roles or economic, instrumental, or socioemotional functions that families serve. Consequently, groups that do not meet these structural prerequisites for family status are seen as defective families, as invalid families, or simply as not families at all—even if their members meet the needs that families are expected to fulfill (Bernstein and Reimann 2001b).

Some scholars call for a move away from definitions that rely on either structure or function. One perspective that has been gaining momentum is a social constructionist approach, as exemplified by the following comments by the sociologists James Holstein and Jaber Gubrium (1999, 5):

> Traditional approaches typically assume that *the* [emphasis in original] family . . . exist[s] as part of everyday reality in some objective condition. . . . Research typically attempts to describe and explain what goes on in and around the family unit. . . . The constructionist approach, in contrast, considers family to be an idea of configuration of meanings, thus problematizing the experiential reality.

Other social scientists also challenge the idea of a monolithic standard for defining family (Aldous 1999; Settles 1999), some taking this challenge so far that they recommend expunging the term "family" (or at least "the family") from academic discourse (Bernardes 1999).

Some social scientists agree that reaching a resolution regarding the meaning of family may be a futile effort but nevertheless offer definitions that may be palatable to at least a large segment of the scholarly community. For example, although the Swedish sociologist Jan Trost (1988, 301) has written that "there is no possibility of defining the family," he still proposes a fairly inclusive structural-based definition that recognizes any living arrangement that includes at minimum a parent-child unit or a spousal or cohabitational unit.[4]

We concur with Trost's position, as do others, that a working definition of family would be useful but is tricky to reach agreement over. Without a shared operational definition of family, it is difficult to arbitrate among key debates regarding family.[5] For example, those scholars who lament "the decline of the family" often equate family decline with societal decline and are alarmed about future prospects for this country, as well as for other countries—most notably Western European ones—in which family putatively is on the decline (Glenn 1993; Glenn et al. 2002; Popenoe 1993; Waite and Gallagher 2000). But how do we know whether or not family is in decline if scholars cannot agree what is family and if we do not know what the public defines as family?

Those who bemoan family decline seem to rely on a more restrictive definition of family (for example, defining it as a nuclear family with a father, a mother, and children) than do those who see not family decline per se but rather a diversification of family forms. The former group includes "pro-marriage scholars" who chide other social scientists for their sanguine attitudes about family changes and what these changes may promote. Instead, their views to some degree harken back to the depiction by the sociologist Talcott Parsons (1954, 1955) of "the American family" as a happily married husband, wife, and multiple children. They express concern regarding family definitions that use a kitchen-sink approach or that include a laundry list of various living arrangements. Although this group might contend that it acknowledges that other forms of living arrangements count as family, their usage of terms or phrases like "family decline," "family dissolution," "family breakdown," "intact family," "broken family," "unbroken family," "the family in crisis," and "death of the family" often conflates "family" or "the family" with a particular and preferred family form.[6]

In contrast, another group of scholars—a group that currently appears to comprise the plurality of social scientists—sees family in terms that are more consistent with a broader operationalization of family (Coleman and Ganong 2004; Coontz 1992; Demo, Allen, and Fine 2000).[7] Members of this group challenge the idea that the alternative to "traditional family" is "no family." Instead, they favor a far-reaching vision that is consonant with the proliferation of scholarship that explores—and finds great strengths and resiliency among—"atypical," "alternative," "transgressive," and "postmodern" family forms (Cheng and Powell 2005; Rosenfeld 2007, forthcoming; Stacey 1996; Stacey and Biblarz 2001). Although this group may not fully agree over which living arrangements count as family—or even whether reaching agreement is a worthy endeavor—its members do agree that scholars should move away from provincial notions of "the family." As a result, postsecondary family sociology and family studies textbooks and readers typically eschew the use of "the family" in their titles and instead refer to "families," often in tandem with "diversity" (for example, *Diversity in Families*; *Marriage and Families: Intimacy, Diversity, and Strengths*; and *Marriages and Families: Diversity and Change*).

Responsiveness to a more inclusive conceptualization of family also precipitated the change in the title of the flagship journal of the National Council of Family Relations from *Journal of Marriage and the Family* (emphasis ours) to *Journal of Marriage and Family*. That said, it is telling that in this journal marriage is paired with family, just as love often is paired with marriage ("love and marriage"), thus perpetuating—unintentionally or not—the idea that marriage is (or should be) a precondition for family just as love is (or should be) a precondition for marriage.

"Diversity defenders"—as described by the sociologist Andrew Cherlin (2003)—have enjoyed great success in expanding the scope of the scholarship that currently is subsumed under the topic "family." This shift suggests some real progress in the efforts among many members of the academy to relax the definition of family. Still, some academicians wonder how much progress actually has transpired. They note how difficult it is for scholars—even those who resolutely believe that boundaries between families are and should be porous and dynamic— to fully and consistently escape from a narrow definition of family in their writings (Allen 2000; Cheal 1991; Seltzer 2000).

This difficulty is exemplified by the treatment of same-sex couples in family scholarship. More than a decade ago, the human development and family studies scholars Katherine Allen and David Demo (1995) lamented the virtual invisibility of gay men and lesbians in family research. They viewed the study of same-sex-couple families as a "new frontier" that few scholars had yet traveled and that would add much needed vitality to the field. Family scholars' failure to study same-sex couples may have been due to various factors—among them, inertia, compliance with scholarly norms and definitions commonly featured in family research, or the sheer difficulty of obtaining strong data on this topic (especially quantitative data, the modal form of data in family scholarship).

Much has changed since Allen and Demo's entreaties to expand family studies. Given the growing number of family studies on gay couples and gay parenting, the term "new frontier" arguably is no longer operative (for two comprehensive reviews, see Berkowitz 2009 and Goldberg 2009). Indeed, some of these studies have received a great deal of public attention. For example, the sociologists Judith Stacey and Tim Biblarz (2001; Biblarz and Stacey 2010) have used insights from both family and gender theories to question commonly held assumptions regarding the influence of same-sex parents on their children—an issue that many believe is central to Americans' ambivalence toward or devaluation of same-sex families. Similarly, the sociologist Michael Rosenfeld (2007) has explored the commonality of the experiences of gay couples and interracial couples—a topic that had previously received a great deal of speculation but little empirical evidence. Nevertheless, even those who applaud the increasing visibility of same-sex families in family scholarship express concern over the continued marginalization of same-sex families in empirical analyses, as well as the methodological limitations typical of these studies (Patterson 2000).

Others point to theoretical opportunities missed—in particular, theories of race, gender, and sexuality (Berkowitz 2009).

Sexuality and Gender Scholars: Exploring Chosen Families

Family scholars have mostly lagged behind their counterparts who focus on gender and sexuality in recognizing and studying gay and lesbian households. At least by the early 1990s, sexuality and gender scholars had embraced the idea that same-sex couples, as well as other coresidential (and non-coresidential) groups, count as family. The anthropologist Kath Weston (1991), for example, asks the question: "Is 'straight' to 'gay' as 'family' is to 'no family'?" Her answer is no. Instead, Weston's ethnographic account of "families we choose" examines how families are formed in multiple configurations in the gay community. She describes how gay men and lesbians navigate their lives with chosen families (some made up of gay romantic partners, some made up of friends) alongside their lives with unchosen families (that is, their parents, siblings, and other "blood" relatives). She also discusses how these chosen families challenge long-held heteronormative views of family that privilege marriage, biological parenthood, gender-specific roles, and heterosexuality. These four factors are irrelevant (or at least less relevant) to members of the "new" family forms and instead are supplanted in importance by what families do: provide material support, create emotional ties, and give a sense of connectedness. The mainstream public may show some willingness to appreciate these familial functions, as suggested by the popularity of television shows such as *The Golden Girls*, *Friends*, and *Will and Grace*, all of which underscored the connectedness of their characters, who, regardless of kinship tie, considered themselves family. Nevertheless, Weston does not discount the high level of public resistance to gay families—resistance that occurs in part because gay families purportedly threaten the hegemonic, heterosexual family form and undermine societally prescribed, traditional norms regarding gender and sexuality.

Other sexuality and gender scholars have echoed Weston's comments and explored the experiences of self-described gay and lesbian families, the strategies they adopt to construct meaning so that they are seen as "family," their views regarding efforts to legitimize same-sex relations, and their interactions with their relatives and the community at large—more broadly, the struggles they face (see, for example, various chapters covering these issues in Bernstein and Reimann 2001a). The sociologists Mary Bernstein and Renate Reimann (2001b), among others, emphasize the subversive power that gay and lesbian families wield in that they challenge predominant conceptions of gender and sexuality. Bernstein and Reimann also call attention to the heterogeneity of these families, which comprise racial minorities, nonromantic couples, gay male couples with children, and lesbian couples without children, among others; these authors note that such families contribute to a critical reassessment of familial norms and, more broadly, the meaning of family.

Incongruously missing from this scholarship is the public's definition of family. Of course, sexuality scholars have explored attitudes toward homosexuality—often conceptualized as homophobia, heterosexism, homonegativism, and sexual prejudice, among others (Herek 1990, 2000; Hudson and Ricketts 1980; Weinberg 1972)—and they have identified the correlates and antecedents of these attitudes, among them, gender, age, education, region, urban residence, and religiosity (Anderson and Fetner 2008; Britton 1990; Herek 1988, 2000; Kurdek 1988; LaMar and Kite 1998; Loftus 2001). Social scientists also have documented how views regarding homosexuality are interconnected with gender attitudes, homosociality (the preference to associate with members of the same sex and, by extension, the privileging of father-son and mother-daughter relationships), and contact with gay men and lesbians (Britton 1990; Herek and Capitanio 1996). Others—for example, the sociologist Arlene Stein (2001)—have conducted rich ethnographies to explore the battle lines drawn between advocates and opponents of gay rights and the meanings that both sides give to questions of sexuality. Still others—among them the sociologist Kathleen Hull (2006)— have used various sources (such as the letters to the editor that appear in newspapers) to infer public views regarding same-sex marriage and whether these views mesh with the arguments promoted by gay rights or "pro-family" elites.

It is indeed remarkable how much and how broadly scholarship on this topic has emerged in a fairly short period of time. The insights from these studies represent a huge and welcome increment in the understanding of same-sex couples and of public attitudes. As will be seen in subsequent chapters in this book, these insights greatly inform our project. Yet, despite all of the information that can be gleaned from these studies, none of them address what we contend is a fundamental question: *which living arrangements are counted by mainstream Americans as family and which are counted out?* Just as sexuality scholars have noted the centrality of appreciating how same-sex couples—and other "transgressive" living arrangements—navigate or attempt to take ownership of the concept of "family," we contend that it is as important, if not even more so, to understand what Americans define as family, why they hold these particular definitions, and how their views of family intersect with their background, life experiences, and social attitudes.

The Structure of the Book

In chapter 2, we examine responses to a series of closed-ended questions about what constitutes a family. More specifically, we presented the interviewees with descriptions of eleven living arrangements—some that included same-sex couples—and asked them whether they personally thought that these arrangements count as family. The description of the patterns begins simply with presentations of the specific distributions of responses (the percentage of respondents who believed that each living arrangement is a family). We then use a variety of techniques to determine how responses and respondents are clustered. Among these techniques are a mechanical identification of each response combination, a narrowing of the combinations to ten, and finally, latent class models, which allow us to identify three ideal types of clustered responses. We also assess the degree of change in these responses in a fairly short but critical period of time—between 2003 and 2006. We conclude this chapter by showing that belonging to one of these three types—which we label "exclusionists," "moderates," and "inclusionists"—is implicated in views regarding the extension of various rights (such as marriage and adoption) to same-sex couples.

In chapter 3, we complement the discussion from the previous chapter with an examination of how Americans describe "what determines whether a living arrangement is a family." We explore the common themes as well as points of departure within and among the exclusionists, moderates, and inclusionists in our sample. We consider the different frames used in their definitions—including whether they emphasized the structure or functions of family; whether they privileged cultural scripts, functional tasks or roles, emotional or affective ties, and the presence of children; and whether they employed institutional themes such as legal recognition and religious beliefs. In addition, we point to seeming inconsistencies—or what may be alternatively described as ambivalences, complexities, or nuances—in the responses and to variations in how unwavering or how tentative individuals were in their views and, in turn, how susceptible they were to future changes in their positions regarding family definitions, especially their position on whether same-sex couples are to be counted in these definitions.

We examine how Americans' social location shapes their definition of what is and what is not family in chapter 4. We highlight differences (or similarities) by age and cohort, education, race, family background, contact with gays and lesbians, gender, region, urban residence, and religion. The chapter concludes by identifying parallels between contemporary resistance to same-sex couples and earlier views regarding interracial marriage and by extrapolating from these patterns to predict changes in Americans' definitions of family in the future.

As noted earlier in this chapter, scholarship that invokes the concept of heteronormativity posits that views regarding gender and sexuality are inextricably enmeshed in views regarding same-sex couples and family. In the next three chapters, we explore this proposition by considering how Americans' attitudes regarding other aspects of gender, sexuality, and socialization are implicated in the boundaries they make between family and nonfamily. Americans' beliefs regarding the causes of sexual preference are the focus of chapter 5, which covers two debates: the "nature-nurture" debate, that is, the extent to which human behavior is a function of biological ("nature") or of social ("nurture") factors; and the science-religion debate—the extent to which scientific and religious explanations are diametric or compatible. After briefly describing the ongoing academic and public dialogue regarding the etiology of human behavior and traits, we report on responses to a set of questions that asked Americans to identify the most important factor in the development of these behaviors and traits—most notably, sexual preference. We then explore whether knowing individuals' responses gives us greater analytical leverage in understanding, or even predicting, their definitions of family. The chapter closes with a discussion of the ramifications of key findings for sociological assumptions regarding the politics of explanations that invoke "science" or "God's will."

Gender ideology and views of parenthood form the crux of chapter 6. We report on Americans' closed- and open-ended responses regarding child custody—in particular, whether in single-parent households a boy is better off living with his mother or father and whether a girl is better off living with her mother or father. Americans' explanations for their preferences open a window on their views about gender, homosociality, "appropriate" parenting, and, in turn, whether same-sex couples count as family.

We consider gender ideology from a different lens in chapter 7. Specifically, we delve into Americans' stances regarding a topic that has been virtually ignored by gender and family scholars: women's and men's last-name change upon marriage. At first glance, the question of marital name change may seem to have little to do with the overall topic of this book (definitions of family). Closer inspection, however, suggests otherwise. We examine the extent to which views regarding the practice of marital name change—which we contend speak to views regarding both gender and family identity—map onto the boundaries that Americans make between families and nonfamilies.

In chapter 8, we close by revisiting the major and consistent patterns and recurrent themes from the previous chapters and gauging what these patterns presage for social constructions of family. Because some of the patterns we discerned led us to reconsider some of our own positions, we would encourage other social scientists to contemplate how these patterns offer alternatives to mainstream sociological and social-scientific assumptions regarding, among other topics, family, gender, and the fundamental causes of human behavior. We make cautious predictions about whether public opinion will hit a certain threshold culminating in a relaxation of the resistance to nontraditional family forms. We conclude that it is just a matter of time before same-sex couples are no longer counted out.

═ Chapter 2 ═

Who Counts as Family?

W HO DO Americans count as family? Do they see family through the lens of nostalgia or through conventions that favor traditional forms? Alternatively, does public opinion indicate movement toward greater acceptance of various nontraditional living arrangements, most notably same-sex couples? Or do public views appear so jumbled that they lack any consistency?

Finding consensus among existing definitions of family is not easy. The disagreement even among academicians is evident from the brief overview presented in chapter 1. It has been common for social scientists to express or reinforce—often inadvertently—a heteronormative orientation in their writings regarding "family" or "the family." Others, however, have begun to steer away from this circumscribed definition. Instead, they now focus on broader conceptions of cohabitation arrangements that include same-sex living arrangements, among others (Berkowitz 2009; Bernstein and Reimann 2001a; Trost 1988, 1990) and offer constructionist accounts that allow for more fluidity (Holstein and Gubrium 1999); some have given up altogether on a unified concept of "family" or "the family" (Bernardes 1999; Settles 1999).

Competing visions of the meaning of family come from other places as well. *The American Heritage Dictionary*, for example, offers two definitions of family that speak to different themes: "A fundamental social group in society typically consisting of one or two parents and their children"; and "Two or more people who share goals and values, have long-term commitments to one another and reside usually in the same dwelling place." Note that the first definition privileges the presence of children (a biological connection), while the latter highlights mutual intimacy between at least two persons (an affective connection).[1] The U.S. census definition of family—"a group of two people or more (one of whom is the householder) related by birth, marriage, or adoption and residing together"—corresponds more closely with the first definition. This definition disqualifies childless same-sex couples from family status, but places same-sex couples with children in the paradoxical position of being in both the category "family" (one or both adults being legal parents) and the category "nonfamily" (the adults not being related by birth or married), even if they live in a state that recognizes same-sex marriage (such as Massachusetts).[2] Media depictions of family waver between unquestioningly celebrating the nuclear heterosexual family and challenging—sometimes forcefully, sometimes equivocally—the traditional forms. Similarly, political parties and self-identified family advocacy organizations advance disparate portrayals of family. The Alliance for Children and Families characterizes family by the "intimacy, intensity, continuity, and commitment among their members," and Parents, Families, and Friends of Lesbians and Gays (PFLAG) explicitly "rejects that GLBT persons exist independent of the institution of family." In contrast, the Alliance Defense Fund sees marriage as a prerequisite to family and contends that "God has defined marriage as one man married to one woman." The question, then, of who counts as family—and in particular, whether same-sex couples should be seen as family—is at the center of contemporary debate over families and family policy. How families are defined has far-reaching policy implications, including but certainly not restricted to determining who makes decisions about the end of life, who is responsible for caring for others, who has medical proxies, who is eligible for family benefits, who is entitled to alimony and child support, and who is to receive assets upon an individual's death. Who is counted in the definition of family and who is counted out tell us which personal relationships we value and which ones we do not.

Although we can appreciate or debate the merits and influence of the various discussions and definitions of family described here and in chapter 1, most of these descriptions share a common limitation: few of them take into account how the public defines family. To be sure, some studies have considered how certain groups (for example, same-sex couples or African Americans) define their own families (see, for example, Weston 1997). But these analyses cannot tell us about the public at large. Nor can they tell us which living arrangements Americans characterize as family overall, regardless of how they define their own family. Nonetheless, such studies do tell us that to a great extent the meaning of family is normative and is derived from people themselves rather than from directives imposed on them by the government, advocacy groups, the media, or academicians. Considered collectively, prior work highlights the relevance of public opinion. Americans' distinctions between families and nonfamilies may or may not dovetail with the boundaries constructed by various actors in public debates. Some elite pronouncements regarding family may resonate with the public,

while others may not. These issues typify the questions that can best—
or only—be addressed by asking people themselves.

To understand the circumstances under which Americans label
groups of people as family, we analyze a series of questions that we
asked of the more than 1,500 interviewees in the Constructing the Family Surveys of 2003 and 2006 (see appendices 1.A and 1.B). More specifically, we asked:

> People these days have differing opinions of what counts as a family.
> Next, I will read you a number of living arrangements and I will ask you
> whether you personally think this arrangement counts as a family.
>
> First, a husband and a wife living together with one or more of their
> children. Would you consider this group of people to be a family?

In addition to this traditional family form, we asked about ten other
living arrangements.[3] Among heterosexual couples:

- A man and woman living together as an unmarried couple, with
  one or more of their children
- A husband and wife living together who have no children
- A man and a woman living together as an unmarried couple who
  have no children

Among homosexual couples:

- Two women living together as a couple with one or more of their
  children
- Two men living together as a couple with one or more of their chil-
  dren
- Two men living together as a couple who have no children
- Two women living together as a couple who have no children

With single parents, respondents were asked about the following arrangements:

- A man living alone with one or more of his children
- A woman living alone with one or more of her children

And finally, respondents were asked whether housemates could be
considered family under the following definition: two people living to-

gether as housemates who are not living as a couple and have no children. Interviewees also were asked to elaborate on their own definitions of family; we discuss these open-ended responses in chapter 3.

These living arrangements reflect several dimensions by which family (or nonfamily) can vary: by marital status, by presence of children, by number of adults, and by the (presumed) sexuality of adults. This abridged selection of living arrangements cannot fully capture the myriad of living arrangements that could be considered family (for example, spouses living apart, siblings living together, extended family members living together).[4] In addition, other information about a living arrangement, such as level of commitment, may influence whether it is deemed a family—a point we return to in chapter 3. These caveats aside, responses to our questions offer what we believe is a much-needed glimpse into the boundaries that Americans draw between families and nonfamilies. And as we demonstrate later in this chapter, these responses powerfully map onto views regarding family policy. Indeed, it is our contention that adopting a more expansive definition of family is typically a necessary—although insufficient—condition of endorsement of more egalitarian family policies, such as health care benefits for same-sex and heterosexual cohabiting couples.

Our aim in this chapter, then, is to get a general sense of the nature of opinion regarding the meaning of family and the dimensions that matter most in shaping the public's definitions of family. We accomplish this goal in several steps. First, we explore the distribution of responses in the 2003 survey regarding each of the eleven arrangements that we asked about. Second, we examine how many and which combinations of arrangements individuals saw as family, identifying the ten most frequently used clusters of arrangements. Third, we use these data to collapse all responses into three categorical latent variables and then calculate the percentage of responses that fall into each of these categories. These three "latent classes" correspond closely with the most popular combinations and allow us to link these data more easily to other issues addressed in later chapters. Fourth, we take advantage of the data collected in a later wave (2006) to see whether the boundaries between families and nonfamilies have changed during a period of time in which public debates about family (most notably around the issue of same-sex marriage) were highly visible and contentious. Fifth, and finally, we briefly examine whether public definitions of family—and in particular the three broad categories from the latent class analysis—are implicated in views regarding same-sex marriage and other family policies. Together this information draws a clearer picture of Americans' definitions of family.

Which Living Arrangements
Count as Family?

Figure 2.1 displays the percentage of respondents in the 2003 survey who viewed each living arrangement as a family. Not surprisingly—and reflecting the heteronormativity in definitions of family (Bernstein and Reimann 2001b; Ryan and Berkowitz 2009; Stein 2001; Weston 1991)—the most-agreed-upon arrangement was a husband, a wife, and their children. Indeed, every respondent in 2003 stipulated that this type is a family—in effect affirming the "Standard North American Family" (Smith 1993) as the benchmark against which other living arrangements were compared.[5] In contrast, a slightly smaller percentage—albeit a difference that is statistically significant—agreed that living arrangements including a single father with children (94.2 percent), a single mother with children (94 percent), and a married couple without children (93.1 percent) constitute families.[6] These differences may seem minor, but they do suggest that the most-agreed-upon family forms tend to rely on at least one of two prerequisites: the presence in the home of a child, and a legal heterosexual relationship—or, more precisely, a relationship that is not a same-sex relationship or a cohabiting heterosexual one. These conditions mirror in part the changing nature of American families—for example, the high divorce rate that often results in single parenthood. Further, since the majority of married couples eventually have children, respondents may have assumed that the legal, legitimating status of marriage is soon accompanied by parenthood, unless a couple is infertile.

There was considerably less agreement regarding unmarried heterosexual couples with children. Compared to views regarding married couples with children, approximately 20 percent fewer respondents (78.7 percent) were willing to define cohabiting couples with children as a family. Of note, cohabiting-parent households were perceived differently, and less favorably, than single-parent households. Open-ended responses indicate that our interviewees assumed (or as one respondent explained, were willing to give single parents "the benefit of the doubt") that single parents had once been married and did not have the option of marrying again. In other words, respondents were disinclined to penalize the unmarried single parent because that parent's reason for being single is ambiguous. In contrast, cohabiting couples were more likely to be penalized and less likely to be afforded family status because respondents interpreted cohabitation as a sign of moral weakness or weak commitment between heterosexual partners and their children. This pattern also suggests that, at least for a large number of respondents, the mere presence of children is not enough in and of itself to confer family status on a living arrangement.

Figure 2.1   Which Living Arrangements Count as Family?

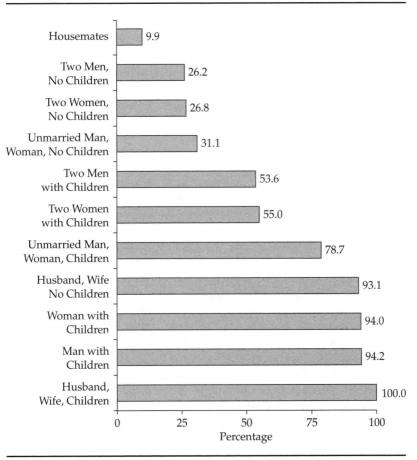

Source: Constructing the Family Survey (Powell 2003).

These suggestions are further borne out when we turn to the respondents' attitudes toward same-sex parents. Slightly more than half of the respondents said that two women (55 percent) or two men (53.6 percent) living as a couple with children are a family. Americans seem quite torn over the legitimacy of such living arrangements. As we will see in the next chapter, for some respondents parenthood trumped a same-sex relationship. For other interviewees, same-sex unions were seen as equivalent to cohabiting couples or married couples. For still others, the presence of children was insufficient to counterbalance the presence of a legally unsanctioned relationship (similar to an unmarried man and woman with children) or a same-sex one.[7] Clearly, homosexual living arrangements were granted less legitimacy than heterosexual ones. That said, it is noteworthy—and, we believe, a sign of the future—that the number of Americans who count same-sex couples with children as family now surpasses the number of those who do not.

When it comes to same-sex and cohabiting couples, children are a pivotal factor in legitimizing nontraditional living arrangements as family. Although children may not be the only factor in defining a family, they go a long way in some people's minds toward reinforcing the image of a family. Conversely, the absence of children among same-sex and cohabiting couples translates into a precipitous decline in the percentage of interviewees who saw these couples as family. More specifically, whereas nearly four-fifths considered a heterosexual cohabiting couple with children a family, fewer than one-third (31.1 percent) saw similar couples without children as family. Slightly over one-fourth of respondents saw same-sex couples without children as family (26.8 percent for lesbians and 26.2 percent for gay men). Glancing across levels of support for unmarried heterosexual couples and homosexual couples without children, the difference is fairly small (or at least smaller than that observed when comparing cohabiting and same-sex couples with children). Although this is apparently some form of "homosexual penalty" (as compared to heterosexual cohabiting couples), the penalty is greater when children are involved.

The last living arrangement considered is that of "two people living together as housemates who are not living as a couple and have no children." Approximately one in ten respondents (9.9 percent) accept this type of unit as a family, suggesting widespread agreement that families must have legal, romantic, or parental ties. In other words, although several popular television shows have introduced—and even promoted—the idea of "chosen families" that comprise nonromantic friends (for example, as mentioned in chapter 1, *The Golden Girls*, *Friends*, and *Will and Grace*), the vast majority of Americans are unprepared to include these arrangements under the rubric of "family." Because this living arrangement is so rarely deemed a family, it is not considered in the remainder of this chapter (although we briefly return to it in chapter 4).

Patterns in Family Definitions

The previous section paints a broad picture of views regarding family, but it is far from complete. If we look at individual living arrangements only, it is difficult to say how a respondent defined family *overall*. Did respondents who considered unmarried heterosexual parents a family also accept same-sex parents as a family? Did marital status alone count for some respondents, while for others only parental status mattered? In other words, how do we categorize Americans' definitions of the family?

Because each item is binary (respondents said that the particular living arrangement is or is not a family), it is theoretically possible to yield over one thousand combinations of responses. The full distribution of the actual patterns of response is presented in appendix 2.A.[8] Overall, our interviewees recognized thirty-five sets of living arrangements as family. The ten most frequently used configurations capture over 90 percent of the respondents' definitions of family living arrangements. These categories are summarized in table 2.1.

The top four categories capture over two-thirds (70.7 percent) of respondents' definitions of family. Virtually tied for the two most popular categories of responses are: (1) all living arrangements count as a family (19.5 percent) and (2) all living arrangements with children or with a legal marital relationship count as a family (19.2 percent).[9] Thus, nearly two-fifths of our interviewees provided open—arguably, remarkably open—definitions of family, especially compared to the next two groups. The third group, constituting approximately one-sixth (17.0 percent) of our sample, did not define any of the same-sex couples as a family, regardless of the presence of children. This same group did, however, grant cohabiting couples with children the status of family. The fourth group (15.0 percent) did not distinguish between same-sex and cohabiting couples: neither were considered family, even with children in the household. Moving down from the top four categories, we see groups that placed increasing restraints on what counts as a family, from total inclusiveness to exclusiveness.

Although table 2.1 shows that fewer respondents subscribed to any of the remaining six patterns, these combinations suggest even more complexity in how individuals define family. For example, 5.2 percent of the respondents included all but one living arrangement in their definition of family, the exception being cohabiting heterosexual couples without children. From the perspective of this group, having a child or being married *if one is legally allowed to do so* is a prerequisite for family status. Interestingly, respondents in the sixth category (4.4 percent) also characterized nearly all living arrangements as family. The exceptions here, however, are in precisely the opposite direction of the former group: same-sex couples without children are excluded from consideration as family. To this group of interviewees, having a child or being heterosexual is a precondition for designation as family. Whereas this group saw parenthood as a means by which same-sex couples can warrant family status, the seventh group (4.1 percent) did not. According

Table 2.1 Cross-Classification of Living Arrangements Defined as Family

	Percentage (N) of Respondents	Husband, Wife, Children	Man with Children	Woman with Children	Husband, Wife, No Children	Unmarried Man, Woman, Children	Two Women with Children	Two Men with Children	Unmarried Man, Woman, No Children	Two Women, No Children	Two Men, No Children
1.	19.5% (132)	Yes	Yes	Yes	Yes	Yes	Yes	Yes	Yes	Yes	Yes
2.	19.2 (130)	Yes	Yes	Yes	Yes	Yes	Yes	Yes	No	No	No
3.	17.0 (115)	Yes	Yes	Yes	Yes	Yes	No	No	No	No	No
4.	15.0 (102)	Yes	Yes	Yes	Yes	No	No	No	No	No	No
5.	5.2 (35)	Yes	Yes	Yes	Yes	Yes	Yes	Yes	Yes	Yes	Yes
6.	4.4 (30)	Yes	Yes	Yes	Yes	Yes	Yes	Yes	Yes	No	No
7.	4.1 (28)	Yes	Yes	Yes	Yes	Yes	No	No	Yes	No	No
8.	2.8 (19)	Yes	Yes	Yes	No	Yes	Yes	Yes	No	No	No
9.	1.9 (13)	Yes	Yes	Yes	No	Yes	No	No	No	No	No
10.	1.8 (12)	Yes	No	No	Yes	No	No	No	No	No	No
11. to 35.	9.1 (62)	—	—	—	—	—	—	—	—	—	—
Sum	100 (678)	100%	94.2%	94.0%	93.1%	78.7%	55.0%	53.6%	31.1%	26.8%	26.2%

Source: Constructing the Family Survey (Powell 2003).
1. All arrangements count.
2. Must have children or be married.
3. Cohabiting couples without children and homosexual couples do not count.
4. Homosexual couples and cohabiting couples do not count.
5. Everyone but cohabiting heterosexuals.
6. Everyone but homosexual couples without children.
7. Everyone but homosexual couples (with or without children).
8. Must have children.
9. Must have children and not be homosexual couples.
10. Must be married (with or without children).
11. to 35. All other answer combinations.

to this group, no same-sex relationship counts as family, but all other living arrangements do.

Roughly 7 percent of respondents are in one of the last three sets of response categories. For the eighth group, parenthood is an absolute—and the only—requirement; thus, even a married couple with no children was not considered a family by these respondents. Although few Americans subscribe to this categorization, in our concluding chapter we briefly describe how it may be more commonly endorsed elsewhere, most notably in Germany. Married couples without children also are excluded in the ninth group's definition of family, as are other childless couples (same-sex and heterosexual) and same-sex couples with children. In other words, to these respondents, one must be a parent and not be in a same-sex relationship to qualify as family. In this category, the definition is restricted to heterosexual parents with children and to single parents; again, childless married couples do not count. Finally, the tenth category consists of respondents who believed that only married couples are family.

Theoretical Categories: Latent Classes

As seen earlier, Americans apparently rely on various logics when setting boundaries between families and nonfamilies. Given the complexity of these responses, we initially explored how each of the various configurations is shaped by sociodemographic factors (for example, age, education, religious affiliation) and intertwined with other attitudes (toward, for instance, parenting, child development, or gender). In doing these preliminary analyses, we became frustrated by the unwieldiness of so many clusters of responses, as well as by the difficulties in assessing the approximately 10 percent of interviewees who did not fit neatly into any of the ten most recurrent responses. At the same time, we were beginning to identify commonalities across some of these groups. Consequently, we sought to collapse this constellation of responses into a smaller, but still meaningful, set of categories.

To meet this challenge, we turned to a statistical procedure to identify categories of sets of responses. This approach, latent class analysis, allows us to partition commonly grouped responses by determining the underlying dimensions (latent classes) of responses.[10] These predicted latent classes can be construed as the "ideal types" for defining family. Although latent class analysis may obscure some of the heterogeneity outlined earlier in this chapter, extensive supplementary analysis shows that, with few exceptions, the use of these broader categories yields not only useful but statistically defensible results.

Table 2.2 shows how responses to each item fall into our three latent classes, which can best be thought of as indicating the broad conditions under which Americans define a living arrangement as a family.[11] We label these classes as:

1. *Exclusionists* (45.3 percent of the sample): Exclusionists, the plurality of the sample, strongly privileged the traditional heterosexual family (especially those with children) and appeared willing to compromise this view only for situations in which people may have been involuntarily removed from it—for example, through divorce or widowhood (a single man with children or a single woman with children). Exclusionists expressed greater ambivalence about unmarried heterosexual couples with children (only 56.5 percent agreed that this living arrangement falls under the rubric of family), but were resolutely resistant to same-sex couples (with or without children) and cohabiting couples without children, believing that these arrangements should be counted out of any definition of family.

2. *Moderates* (29.3 percent of the sample): Moderates placed even more primacy on children, extending family status to any arrangement with children. Indeed, they were slightly more likely to see same-sex partners with children as family (100 percent and 94.7 percent for lesbian and gay male couples, respectively) than married couples without children (90.7 percent). Still, they were sufficiently swayed by the legal status of marriage to differentiate strongly between married couples without children and other couples without children. For this group, a living arrangement must have children or a legal bond (marriage) to be a family.

3. *Inclusionists* (25.4 percent of the sample): This group had such a broad conception of family that they saw each of the ten living arrangements as a family.[12]

Continuity and Change in Family Definitions: 2003 to 2006

Major disputes over the legal status of same-sex couples—and correspondingly, the meaning of family—have occurred since the early 1970s, starting with the case of *Baker v. Nelson*, in which the Minnesota Supreme Court ruled that there was no constitutional right for two people of the same sex to marry. During the next two decades, the rights of same-sex couples were further limited in some ways, but advanced in others; among these, *Braschi v. Stahl Associates*, a 1989 ruling by the New York State Court of Appeals, affirmed the family status of

Table 2.2   Three Latent Classes of Family Definitions: Conditional
Probabilities of Item Responses (N=678)

Family Definition Dimensions [a]	Exclusionist (45.3 percent)		Moderate (29.3 percent)		Inclusionist (25.4 percent)	
Husband, wife, children	Yes	(1.000)	Yes	(1.000)	Yes	(1.000)
Man with children	Yes	(0.872)	Yes	(1.000)	Yes	(1.000)
Woman with children	Yes	(0.872)	Yes	(0.995)	Yes	(1.000)
Husband, wife, no children	Yes	(0.907)	Yes	(0.907)	Yes	(0.994)
Unmarried man, woman, children	Yes	(0.565)	Yes	(0.975)	Yes	(1.000)
Two women with children	No	(0.989)	Yes	(1.000)	Yes	(1.000)
Two men with children	No	(0.987)	Yes	(0.947)	Yes	(1.000)
Unmarried man, woman, no children	No	(0.881)	No	(0.820)	Yes	(0.802)
Two women, no children	No	(0.993)	No	(0.984)	Yes	(1.000)
Two men, no children	No	(0.990)	No	(0.969)	Yes	(1.000)

Source: Constructing the Family Survey (Powell 2003).
[a] As described in the chapter, the category "two people living together as housemates" is excluded because so few Americans included this living arrangement as family.

certain same-sex couples for the purposes of rent control, in particular tenant succession rights. But it was not until the early 1990s that the legal question of same-sex marriage was revitalized with the case of *Baehr v. Lewin*, in which the Hawaiian Supreme Court ruled that the prohibition against same-sex marriage was unconstitutional unless the state could establish a compelling interest for the ban. This ruling, along with other actions that further moved same-sex couples in the direction of legal acceptance and family status, precipitated a series of counteractions, including the congressional vote in favor of the Defense of Marriage Act (DOMA), which defines marriage as the "legal union between one man and one woman as husband and wife," and the passage in several states of laws that explicitly ban same-sex marriage, even if the marriage was entered into in another state that allowed it.

Although civil unions already were legal in one state (Vermont) before our 2003 survey, public discourse regarding same-sex couples arguably did not reach its peak until after November 2003, with the case of *Goodridge v. Massachusetts Department of Public Health*, in which the Massachusetts Judicial Supreme Court ruled that the state prohibition of same-sex marriage violated the state constitution. Six months later, same-sex couples from Massachusetts were allowed to file for marriage licenses. With this court case, the option of same-sex marriage emerged as a bona-fide possibility—and for many as an imminent danger—not only in Massachusetts but in other states. The actions by the Massachusetts court prompted officials in localities in California, New Mexico, New York, and Oregon to issue marriage licenses to gay and lesbian couples and to perform same-sex weddings. These actions not only triggered a series of lawsuits intended to expand the rights of same-sex couples but also provoked vehement opposition, as evidenced by the approval in 2004 of constitutional bans on same-sex marriage in thirteen states: Arkansas, Georgia, Kentucky, Louisiana, Michigan, Mississippi, Missouri, Montana, North Dakota, Ohio, Oklahoma, Oregon, and Utah.[13]

As noted in chapter 1, we conducted an abridged version of the Constructing the Family Survey in 2006. The time between our two surveys was a critical and politically contentious period, especially regarding rights for same-sex individuals and couples.[14] In fact, many believe that the escalating concern regarding same-sex marriage (and its accompanying "assault" on traditional marriage) resulted in a backlash in attitudes toward the rights of same-sex couples and played an influential role in the 2004 presidential election (Campbell and Monson 2008; Cooperman and Edall 2004; Greenberger 2005; for a differing interpretation, see Burden 2004). Some political commentators, sociologists, and gay advocates, in fact, have questioned whether the much-lauded gains in Massachusetts outweighed the losses coming from a presumed decline in public support and from an increasingly angry and organized opposition (Hull 2006; Zimmerman 2008).

Our analysis indicates, however, that such fears are unwarranted. If a backlash following the events in Massachusetts occurred (as suggested by various polls, such as Pew Research Center for the People and the Press 2006), it was short-lived. That is, even if anti-gay sentiment increased after *Goodridge v. Massachusetts Department of Public Health*, by the summer of 2006 the level of support for same-sex couples—as well as for other "transgressive" couples (such as cohabiting heterosexual couples)—had returned to its 2003 level and in fact was even greater. This change is illustrated in figure 2.2.[15] From this figure, we see a notable—and, as confirmed by bivariate and multivariate analyses (both t-tests and logistic regression analyses), a statistically significant—increase in the percentage of Americans who saw same-

Figure 2.2   Which Living Arrangements Count as Family? Changes Between 2003 and 2006

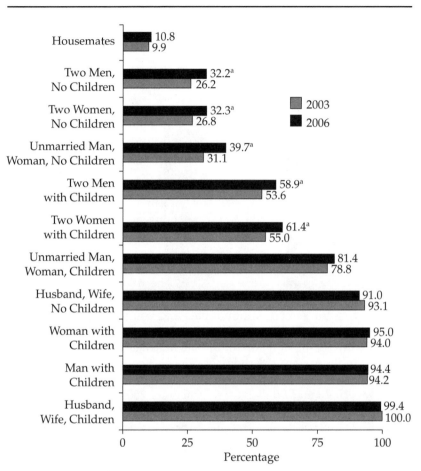

Source: *Constructing the Family Survey* (Powell 2003, 2006).
[a] Indicates a significant change between 2003 and 2006 ($p \leq 0.05$).

sex couples with children as family: from 55.0 percent in 2003 to 61.4 percent in 2006 for lesbian couples with children, and from 53.6 percent to 58.9 percent for gay male couples with children. Figure 2.3 shows an unambiguous and statistically significant decline in exclusionists (from 45.3 percent to 38.1 percent) and a corresponding increase in inclusionists (from 25.4 percent to 32.4 percent).[16]

Some gay rights advocates might be disappointed that the change in attitudes is not even greater. But the key point here is that there *has*

Figure 2.3   Family Definition Clusters: Changes Between 2003 and 2006

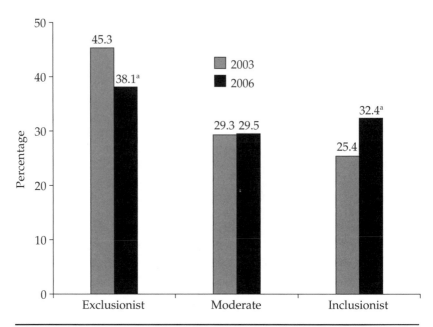

Source: Constructing the Family Survey (Powell 2003, 2006).
[a] Indicates a significant change between 2003 and 2006 (p ≤ 0.05).

been change toward greater acceptance of family diversity, even during a period of time when others had predicted weakening support for same-sex rights. It is unclear whether we have reached a tipping point in the movement toward inclusivity, but it is clear that over three-fifths (61.9 percent) of Americans currently express a willingness to accept some forms of same-sex relationships as family. Our goal here is not to explicitly identify the sources that precipitated these changes. Our interviews, however, point to a pivotal factor: the greater openness in public and especially private discourse (whether positive *or* negative) that was prompted in part by legal challenges to current marital law. We return to this issue in chapter 4.

Public Definitions of Family and Views on Social Policy

So far we have described Americans' definitions of family, identifying a typology that clusters the variation of responses into three groups: exclusionists, moderates, and inclusionists. The question, however, that some readers may still have is this: what does this typology actually tell us? Or even more pointedly, what does it matter if some Americans define certain living arrangements (such as same-sex and cohabiting couples) as family, while others do not? We contend that identification of this typology is not an engaging but ultimately fruitless exercise. Instead, we concur with the conclusion of the political sociologists Clem Brooks and Jeff Manza (Brooks and Manza 2007; Manza and Brooks 1999a), along with the conclusions of the sociologist Paul Burstein and the political scientists Benjamin Page and Robert Shapiro (Burstein 1998, 2003; Page and Shapiro 1983, 1992; see also Erikson, MacKuen, and Stimson 2002; Stimson, MacKuen, and Erikson 1995), all of whom contend that changes in public policy are responsive to changes in public opinion. Put simply, public opinion matters.[17]

But do public definitions of family translate into views regarding family policy? To answer this question, we asked our respondents whether they agreed or disagreed with statements regarding an array of family policy issues, among them same-sex marriage ("Gay and lesbian couples should be allowed to marry"), same-sex adoption ("Gay and lesbian couples who have been living in a long-term stable relationship should be allowed to adopt children"), and the extension of various rights and benefits to same-sex and heterosexual cohabiting couples (for example, "A man and woman living together as an unmarried couple who have no children should have benefits such as health insurance for the partner," and, "Two men living together as a couple, or two women living together as a couple, who have no children should have benefits such as health insurance for the partner"). Demonstrating the utility of our tripartite taxonomy of families, figure 2.4 compares the views of inclusionists, moderates, and exclusionists on same-sex marriage and same-sex adoption (using the 2003 survey).

The distinctions among these three groups are dramatic. More than 80 percent of inclusionists either strongly support (50.8 percent) or somewhat support (35.7 percent) the right of same-sex couples to marry. Moderates are torn, with almost 50 percent in agreement (16.5 percent strongly in favor and 33.3 percent somewhat in favor). Meanwhile, more than 90 percent of exclusionists oppose same-sex marriage, with 78.5 percent strongly opposed. Similar patterns are observed for views regarding same-sex adoption, although support among moderates now exceeds 50 percent (54.6 percent), a signal that moderates privilege children in their conceptualization of family.[18]

The dissimilarity between inclusionists, moderates, and exclusionists extends beyond their views on same-sex couples. As seen in figure 2.5, of the three groups, inclusionists are the most amenable to the provision of benefits to cohabiting heterosexual couples: nearly 75 percent

Figure 2.4   Support for Same-Sex Marriage and Same-Sex Adoption: Exclusionists, Moderates, and Inclusionists

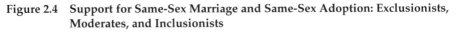

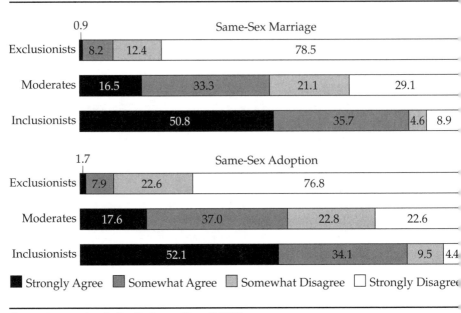

Source: *Constructing the Family Survey* (Powell 2003).

of inclusionists (74.6 percent) are in agreement. Tellingly, however, inclusionists are even more likely to support extending these benefits to same-sex couples (81.1 percent). The strength of their support is greater for same-sex couples as well, with 45.9 percent strongly in favor (compared to 34.1 percent for cohabiting heterosexual couples).

Paralleling their views regarding same-sex marriage, moderates are almost evenly split in their support of benefits to same-sex couples (48.1 percent in favor and 52.0 percent opposed), and slightly more opposed when asked about heterosexual couples (42.4 percent in favor and 57.6 percent opposed). That being said, moderates do not generally distinguish much between cohabiting heterosexual and gay couples.

In contrast, exclusionists are firmly resistant to granting benefits to same-sex couples (86.2 percent), with over two-thirds (68.6 percent) strongly opposed. In contrast, a minuscule number (1.7 percent) are strongly in favor. Cohabiting heterosexual couples do not fare well either, although the level (77.8 percent) and intensity (49.8 percent strongly disagree) of opposition is less than that directed toward same-sex couples. In other words, exclusionists are strongly opposed to granting rights and benefits to both types of couples; however, their

Figure 2.5   Support for Benefits Such as Health Insurance for Cohabiting Heterosexual and Same-Sex Couples Without Children: Exclusionists, Moderates, and Inclusionists

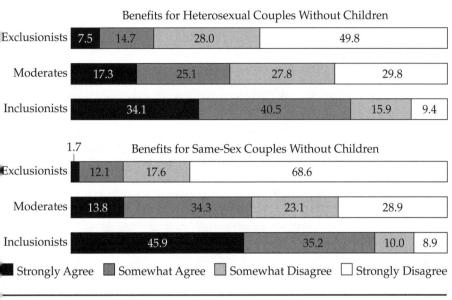

Benefits for Heterosexual Couples Without Children

	Strongly Agree	Somewhat Agree	Somewhat Disagree	Strongly Disagree
Exclusionists	7.5	14.7	28.0	49.8
Moderates	17.3	25.1	27.8	29.8
Inclusionists	34.1	40.5	15.9	9.4

1.7   Benefits for Same-Sex Couples Without Children

	Strongly Agree	Somewhat Agree	Somewhat Disagree	Strongly Disagree
Exclusionists	1.7	12.1	17.6	68.6
Moderates	13.8	34.3	23.1	28.9
Inclusionists	45.9	35.2	10.0	8.9

■ Strongly Agree ■ Somewhat Agree ■ Somewhat Disagree ☐ Strongly Disagree

Source: Constructing the Family Survey (Powell 2003).

opposition is much stronger when aimed at same-sex couples. One cannot help notice how exclusionists' responses are the mirror image of those provided by inclusionists, who overwhelmingly support the extension of rights and benefits across both living arrangements, but express greater support for same-sex couples than for unmarried heterosexual ones. The rationale behind these differences is further explored in the next chapter.

These patterns offer compelling evidence that the boundaries that individuals draw between families and nonfamilies map onto their views regarding family policy. It should come as no surprise that fewer than 1 percent of exclusionists are strongly in favor of same-sex marriage: if one does not believe that any type of same-sex couple counts as family, then how could one support marital rights for them? It appears that agreement that some same-sex couples are family is a necessary step toward seeing same-sex couples as worthy of the legal and social recognition granted to married couples. It is not a sufficient step, however, as demonstrated by the huge variation among moderates in reactions to same-sex marriage. Nonetheless, the implication of these findings, that the number of inclusionists has increased in the past few years (and, as we predict later in this chapter, will continue to do so in the foreseeable future), while there has been a commensurate decrease in exclusionists, bodes well for same-sex and cohabiting heterosexual couples.

Conclusion

However difficult it is to disentangle definitions of the family—more specifically, to identify the parameters that distinguish families from nonfamilies in American society—it is important and consequential to do so. The importance of these definitions has not gone unnoticed by scholars and other elite commentators who try to privilege and promulgate particular conceptualizations of family. Attempts to draw boundaries are motivated in part by the recognition that definitions of the family have meaning at both the private and public levels (Cherlin 2004). At the private level, these definitions affect who is and who is not considered a family in day-to-day interactions. At the broader, more public level, they have consequences for who is and who is not treated as a family in the legal systems, with all the rights and obligations that are legitimated by these definitions. The extent to which definitions of family are amenable to change also may foreshadow legal and social change. Yet, despite the presence of the various competing definitions floated in the public arena, the very simple question "How do Americans define family?" has been mostly ignored. This gap is perplexing because the ways in which people draw boundaries around the units they accept as families may ultimately sway public views on social and legal policies.

In this chapter, we begin to fill this gap. We do so by giving a broad overview of the distinctions that Americans make between families and nonfamilies and analyzing a unique data set that asked survey respondents a series of questions about whether they agreed or disagreed that a particular living arrangement is a family. Although our list of living arrangements is by no means exhaustive, it includes the key living arrangements that go to the heart of contemporary discourse on family rights and obligations.

The extent to which Americans accept specific living arrangements as family differs dramatically. At one end of the spectrum, Americans fully agree that married heterosexual couples with children count as family. At the other end of the spectrum, there is almost universal rejection of the idea that housemates living together constitute family. To us, however, the most informative and notable categories are in between. More specifically, assessments of cohabiting heterosexual, gay, and lesbian couples do not evoke such clear consensus. That over half of our sample sees some types of same-sex—and cohabiting heterosexual—couples as family is telling. Many Americans use homosexuality or cohabitation as a disqualifier for family status. But the presence of children in the home is used by a larger portion as the main axis around which to form judgments about what constitutes a family, thus serving to counteract this disqualifier.

Overall, this information brings us much closer to understanding the meaning of family in modern American society. Some fault lines are vividly clear. Differences between inclusionists, moderates, and exclusionists seem to be large. At first glance, it might appear that moderates are right in the middle of the continuum between exclusionists and inclusionists. After all, moderates mostly agree with exclusionists that same-sex couples without children are not family, but also mostly agree with inclusionists that same-sex couples with children are. Still, we believe that the distance between moderates and exclusionists is wider and less reconcilable than the distance between moderates and inclusionists.

On what basis do we make such an assertion? Acceptance of any same-sex couples as family constitutes a quantum leap in tolerance considering how such arrangements have been traditionally thought of in American society. The fact that moderates and inclusionists share the belief that, at the very least, some same-sex partnerships should count as families suggests a growing acceptance of same-sex unions. Further, as we will see in the chapters that follow, social constructions based on emotional ties are also common strategies in defining family. We therefore predict that the distance between moderates and exclusionists will not only be maintained but may even widen, while the gap between moderates and inclusionists will concomitantly narrow. If our predictions are accurate, then American society may well be at the precipice of even greater acceptance of a variety of family forms. A convergence between moderates and inclusionists might lead to social policy change that moves us ever closer to the extension of the rights and privileges that accompany family membership to same-sex couples. There are hints in the data—both in this chapter and in later ones—that portend such a conclusion.

In making predictions about the future, it is difficult to imagine that inclusionists will become less expansive in their views regarding family. In addition, we are agnostic about the prospect that most exclusionists will relinquish their firmly held traditional views of family, at least in the near future. That said, we observed a reduction in the percentage of exclusionists between 2003 and 2006. These patterns are particularly striking given the brevity of the time between the surveys as well as claims of a concurrent backlash in attitudes toward same-sex couples during this time period. Instead, we contend that the room for the most change lies with the moderates. A focus on same-sex couples with children provides an opening for increased acceptance of such living arrangements as family, and by extension the rights and responsibilities that accompany family status. So the moderates, who accept same-sex unions more readily when the living arrangement includes children, represent the most amenable and potentially transformative group. The directions in which American society goes with respect to embracing different types of living arrangements as family therefore most probably lie in the hands of moderates.

Other lessons are to be learned from our analysis for both advocates and opponents of same-sex rights and benefits. The patterns suggest that optimal strategies for the promotion of either approval or disapproval of these rights and benefits may rest on how the argument is framed (Hull 2006). Often advocates emphasize the theme of individual rights in their campaigns to promote equality. Although this strategy may sway some people, our results indicate that a more successful strategy would emphasize the presence of children in same-sex households. Conversely, those who oppose the extension of same-sex rights have often decried the problems faced by the children of same-sex (and cohabiting) couples. This strategy ironically may be counterproductive because it reminds the American public that same-sex couples and heterosexual cohabiting couples live with their children, and that reminder, in turn, increases the likelihood that people will see same-sex couples as families.

We covered a great deal of ground in this chapter. Still, our analysis to this point raises as many questions as it addresses. How do people justify the particular boundaries they make between families and nonfamilies? That is, what frames are more common and resonant for exclusionists, moderates, and inclusionists? Do exclusionists, moderates, and inclusionists vary along sociodemographic lines, and if so, what do these differences portend for future definitions of family? To what extent do exclusionists, moderates, and inclusionists vary in other attitudes—in particular, in their views on child development, parenting, and gender? In the ensuing chapters, we answer these questions with the goal of making predictions about the future of American definitions of family.

=Chapter 3 =

Family Accounts: How Americans Talk About Family

I N THE previous chapter, we identified the living arrangements that Americans count or do not count as family. We found deep disagreement, especially regarding same-sex couples and childless heterosexual cohabiting couples. From their responses, we also discovered that Americans belong to three broad but distinct categories: exclusionists, moderates, or inclusionists. We speculated on the commonalities and distinctions in the reasons for the boundaries between family and nonfamily that these three groups make. Still, our speculation is just that: mere speculation based on inferences from the closed-ended questions. Answers to these questions are useful, but they do not tell us why Americans are either so willing to endorse an inclusive definition of family or so resistant to doing so.

To better understand the rationale behind Americans' boundary-making between family and nonfamily, we must rely on how Americans talk about family. To accomplish this goal, we report in this chapter on Americans' responses in 2003 to this open-ended question:

> In thinking about your answers to the past few questions about what counts as family, what determines for you whether you think a living arrangement is a family?

How exclusionists, moderates, and inclusionists answer this question gives us important insight into Americans' attitudes regarding family that responses to the closed-end questions cannot convey by themselves. To be sure, the answers to this question echo some themes that we posited in the last chapter. But they add new insight by showing the struggles and complexities that Americans face when defining family and by identifying the arguments that are most resonant and potentially most influential in effecting change. They also take us in new directions that bring up new questions—questions that we subsequently posed in 2006.[1]

In Their Own Words: Exclusionists

As described in the previous chapter, exclusionists—who constituted 45.3 percent and 38.1 percent of our 2003 and 2006 samples, respectively—adhere to a more circumscribed definition of family that privileges married heterosexual couples, permits exceptions in the case of single parents, shows ambivalence about cohabiting heterosexual couples with children, and categorically disallows other living arrangements, most notably those of same-sex couples. Figure 3.1 covers the major themes that exclusionists invoked when asked in their own words to explain why they believed that certain living arrangements count or do not count as family.[2]

Marriage As Fundamental

Clearly, the most common theme, offered by over half of the exclusionists (56 percent), is the primacy of marriage. Indeed, most exclusionists' key requirement for family status is a marital ceremony or other explicit legal arrangement. The transcripts of our interviews are replete with phrases such as "the marriage vow," "the marriage covenant," "ceremonial arrangements," "legal marriage," "legal connection," and "legally binding." In their references to marriage, exclusionists also often mentioned the gender of the marital partners—most notably specifying them as "man and wife," "man and wife living together," or "marriage between a man and a woman"—thus making it explicit that their definition excluded gay and lesbian couples. Still others discussed marriage in conjunction with children—for example, "a married couple and their children"—but more often than not exclusionists squarely emphasized marital status.

This sentiment was echoed repeatedly in our interviews, even by exclusionists who could be characterized as less than traditional in their own behaviors. A divorced man in his late forties noted: "The marriage . . . I feel pretty strongly about this because I've been married twice, and I've been in a few of these situations. So I think the marriage part makes it a family whether we want it to be or not sometimes."[3]

Interestingly, some exclusionists advocated an explicitly legalistic stance toward family, arguing that if the government does not confer family status—and consequently, familial rights and obligations—to groups other than marital couples, then nonmarital living arrange-

Figure 3.1   Themes Used By Exclusionists

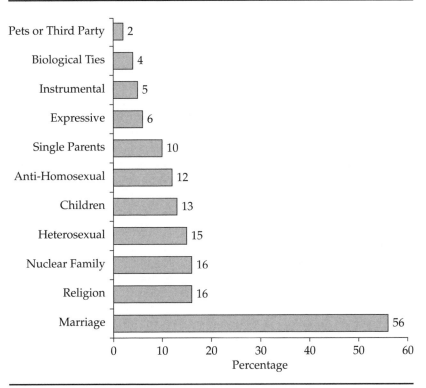

Source: Constructing the Family Survey (Powell 2003).

ments by definition cannot be families. In explaining why same-sex couples do not count as family, a woman in her forties observed:

> If you got two males or two females, and they're living as a couple, [and] you go to insurance purposes, you cannot get the benefits from a person's job or from insurance. Or if the person dies, it's going to always ask for the next of what? Kin. So under this umbrella, I'm going on that standard. Because if someone dies, they ask you for the next of kin. And if they're not married, they couldn't be considered family.

Similarly, a young woman from Texas justified her exclusion of same-sex couples from her definition of family: "In Texas I don't think it's legal for gay people to get married, if you know what I'm saying. So I don't think that's a family."

In the last chapter, we contended that if Americans see a particular living arrangement as a family, they typically are more predisposed to grant familial rights and benefits to that group than to others. That is, their definitions usually precede their endorsement of familial rights. Thus, reconfiguring the line between families and nonfamilies—a line that is very difficult to cross for most exclusionists—should be a critical factor in the public's advocacy of the expansion of familial rights. But as suggested in the last two quotes and in several similarly phrased responses, it appears that for some exclusionists the legal prohibition of rights to certain groups helps shape the boundaries they make between families and nonfamilies.[4] If exclusionists' explanations accurately portray their viewpoint (instead of merely being a rationalization for their position), this suggests that some exclusionists could move toward inclusivity. That is, if legal and other rights become increasingly conferred on unmarried couples, then some exclusionists' intransigence in their definitions of families and their non-acceptance of family rights for unmarried couples might dissipate. We should emphasize the word "some," however, since the modal reaction by exclusionists indicates that their positions are obdurately held and less receptive to change.

Children As "Blood" Ties

Approximately one-third of the exclusionists explicitly referred to children (13 percent), biological ties with children (4 percent), or the nuclear family (16 percent)—often in tandem with a discussion of marital status. Typical of this coupling of marriage and parenthood are the following two comments:

> If you're united in marriage and it's also—how am I going to say this—if you're united in marriage through church or through ceremony and not through love but through procreation. United in marriage and procreation of children.

> Well, I mean, basically when you get married, you become a family because you become united and one. And then when you have children, that's an extension of yourself. So, you know, when you're married, you're united, and then you have children that become the family. I mean, whether the partner, when you become divorced, I mean, that is unfortunately a decision you end up making, but you still are a family with your children. But, I mean, that's what I consider a family. People just living together are not really a family because they're not united and [haven't] made that commitment.

The concept of "blood" ties, or consanguinity, often was conflated with children ("they're all blood-related," "tied by blood," "one is related by blood," "marriage or blood relation," "blood relationship and marriage"). Marriage may still be paramount, but the "blood connection" offers a value-added component to the family, as illustrated by the explanation of a woman in her seventies:

> A family is a married couple with children. A man and a woman, husband and wife, and children, or not children. But I think the marriage is what makes the family, it makes it legal, because you have blood to be a family if the children carry the blood. Of course, the husband and wife don't. They have separate blood, but I consider that a family, and I don't consider the other arrangements where there isn't a legal commitment a family.

We will return to the issue of "blood" relations when we explore moderates' explanations for their definitions of family. But it is telling that exclusionists' use of the concept of blood in effect establishes another fault line: one between biological children ("blood ties") and children who typically are not related by blood, that is, adoptive children. In contrast to moderates, who more frequently mentioned adoption—although often as an afterthought or as, in the words of the sociologist Allen Fisher (2003), "still not quite as good as having your own"[5]—exclusionists typically do not even consider adoption in their discussions of parenthood. Put another way, the focus on blood indicates that, for exclusionists, it is not children per se who help make a family, but biological children.

Single and Cohabiting Parents

It might appear difficult to reconcile exclusionists' adamant focus on marriage and the nuclear family with their expressed willingness to count households with a single parent and child as family. Yet accommodating references to single parents were straightforwardly made in the responses and were fairly numerous (10 percent). Exclusionists often, in the words of one respondent, "give the benefit of the doubt" by assuming that the parent was not single at the birth of the child and that single parenthood was instead due to divorce ("Well, it's like people that are married. Or like, if a person's divorced and they have a child with them") or the death of the other parent:

> I would say a married couple with or without children, or in particular, if one or the other of their spouses has died, is gone, and they would be

raising their children on their own . . . that probably would be my idea that could be a family.

By mostly ignoring the possibility that the child was "born out of wed-lock," the overwhelming majority of exclusionists could justify the inclusion of single parents with children as family without being compelled to rethink their overall beliefs regarding the primacy of marriage.

Cohabiting heterosexual couples with children, however, posed a more serious threat to these strongly held beliefs. Consequently, exclusionists were split in their assessment of cohabiting heterosexual couples. Many were unwilling to compromise on the importance of a legal marriage contract. As an elderly woman proclaimed: "I don't believe in shackin', as you call it. I don't think that's right."

Others expressed ambivalence but still believed that the presence of children and the heterosexuality of the adults makes such a union a sufficiently legitimate family. A man in his fifties explained his reason for counting a heterosexual cohabiting couple with children as family:

> Well, marriage is one thing—although I think I said one couple was, [and] they weren't married, but they had children together. So I think, in my mind, them having children together makes them married even though they don't have the real certificate. So I guess it would be either a marriage or sharing children.

Reservations about cohabiting couples often were accompanied by a willingness to accept the evolving nature of relationships—at least for heterosexual cohabiting couples. A woman in her sixties reluctantly included heterosexual cohabiting couples with children as family by explaining:

> I was brought up that you were married. Now that changes. Time goes by, I guess. For years I didn't like the idea of people living together not being married, but things change. People change. That I can deal with. But I was brought up believing in marriage.

Thus, heterosexual cohabiting couples with children represent the focal point for exclusionists' struggle in their own definition of family. Some exclusionists continue to debate the wisdom of moving the boundary between families and nonfamilies to include heterosexual couples with children. In contrast, where there is little struggle or debate among exclusionists is in their position on same-sex couples: exclusionists were virtually unanimous in setting a clear, unambiguous fault line that did not include same-sex couples.

Privileging Heterosexuality and Censuring Homosexuality

To exclusionists, same-sex couples, regardless of the presence of children, or "blood," are categorically not family. Over one-fourth of our interviewees addressed the issue of same-sex couples—some (15 percent) implicitly by couching their response in terms of the need for partners to be heterosexual and some (12 percent) explicitly by pronouncing that homosexuality disqualifies a same-sex couple from achieving family status. Some responses simultaneously privileged heterosexual relations and censured same-sex ones, as illustrated by the comments of a man in his thirties who listed the types of living arrangements he counted as family: "Husband and wife, children, or husband and wife, no children. Or, in what seems to be a couple living together—a heterosexual couple anyway. I'm not partial to the two-women-or-two-men-together-as-couple type of thing."

The use of "I'm not partial" is characteristic of the many respondents who showed discomfort with the idea of same-sex couples, or with homosexuality more specifically, but still used phrasing that ranged in tone from mild to harsh in discussing their uneasiness or disapproval. For example, "I'm not with lesbian- and gay-type couples," "That's just how I feel," "I just don't believe in it," "I don't agree with those,"or "I'm sorry, but I just cannot agree with it." Interestingly, some interviewees appeared to purposefully avoid using the terms "gay," "lesbian," and "same-sex" and instead used "it" or "those," while others lowered their voice (sometimes to a whisper) when referring to same-sex couples or homosexuality. These are clear verbal signals of discomfort with something that exclusionists may well consider a taboo.

More striking, however, are the comments of exclusionists who showed no reticence in voicing a more explicitly hostile reaction to gay and lesbian couples. Some of these comments are brief, but revealing:

Are they a family? Hell, no!

All gays and lesbians should be shot.

Others expressed frustration over attempts to "normalize" same-sex relations, as seen in the angry tone and comments of an elderly man:

Well, if they're lesbians, then it isn't a family. I know a lot of them are trying to push that sort of thing nowadays, but most people around here don't agree with that thinking because this is southern Indiana.

Some went even further and contended that homosexuality is a perversion or sickness. A woman in her twenties, for example, described her views about family and homosexuality:

> I would say a husband and wife, which is a man and a woman—not two women and not two men—but a man and a woman who are married, who are committed to each other, who are committed to their children, and are committed to the vows that they made to each other when they got married. Not unless, of course, the husband and wife were together and one of the spouses died and it's just the widower or widow left behind with the children. Then I would also consider that a family. Because that's the way it was intended to be from the beginning of time. Lesbianism and homosexuality is a sickness.

Often views regarding homosexuality and same-sex relations, and to a lesser extent heterosexual marriage and children, were accompanied by—or, more accurately, framed by—comments anchored in religious beliefs (16 percent). For many of these exclusionists, firm—indeed, uncompromising—guidelines that distinguish families from nonfamilies are "ordained by God," "in the eyes of God," "God's law," "God's intention," "in the Bible," "the biblical standard," and "what the Bible says." Religious frames undergirded both mild and stronger opposition to same-sex families. This middle-aged woman was unable to mesh her belief structure with the idea of a homosexual family:

> We are Christians, and so we try really hard to live by Christian values, and it's very hard for me to understand a living arrangement where partners are of the same sex, and I just don't think that that constitutes a family.

The invocation of religious beliefs, however, did not preclude some flexibility—or at least some recognition that living arrangements that presumably violate some religious norms can count as family, but only if the living arrangement is heterosexual. A woman in her fifties explained:

> Well, I'm a Christian, and I believe that a man and woman should be married. And I know there's circumstances when a man and woman may not be married that have children, and to them, they still could be a family. But two men living together? No, not what I consider a family. Or two women living together, whatever.

Others who relied on religious imagery appeared even less receptive to same-sex couples. In the following response, a middle-aged woman drew on her religious beliefs, but then added a new category of family member:

> I see a family as . . . a husband and wife or a single person with or without a child or children, because they were ordained by God. And with Sodom and Gomorrah, God destroyed Sodom and Gomorrah, each of those cities from ancient times, because all the sodomy and relationships that weren't right, that could not be called family.

When asked whether she wanted to add anything else, she replied: "Not especially, although I'd say a single person with a pet is a family."

Her response may have been singular in its explicit contrast between gay couples and pets, but it spurred us to include a closed-ended question in 2006 that asked whether "pets should be counted as family members."[6] Approximately half of the Americans we interviewed (51 percent) were inclusive in this regard. Figure 3.2 more specifically juxtaposes their inclusivity concerning pets with their position on gay couples without children. Quite tellingly, roughly one-third (30 percent) of our sample, and an even higher proportion of exclusionists (approximately 20 percent greater), believed that pets count as family while gay couples do not.[7]

In listening to exclusionist comments about gay and lesbian couples, we were reminded of parallels to racial discourse, especially from the mid- to late twentieth century. Some exclusionists were uncomfortable even saying the words "gay," "lesbian," and "homosexual," as seen by the pauses in their speech, the lowering of their voices, and their roundabout answers. Others said that they "really don't want to talk about that." Others expressed revulsion at the idea of homosexuality, same-sex relationships, and same-sex parents. Others showed indignation toward attempts by same-sex couples to "push their way" onto society, while others employed religious frames to justify exclusion. Of course, the comments of some exclusionists were not characterized by any of these qualities. But it is striking that some simply were worried that they would say something wrong, while others neither hesitated nor showed remorse about articulating what inclusionists and moderates might see as hateful or intolerant views—for example, the opinion that the status of gays and lesbians should be lower than that of an animal (a pet). In these ways, the comments of some exclusionists were reminiscent of the comments that racial majorities have voiced about racial minorities, a point we return to later in this chapter.

Figure 3.2   Do Gay Couples and Pets Count as Family?

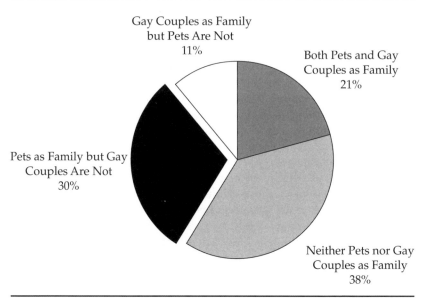

Gay Couples as Family
but Pets Are Not
11%

Both Pets and Gay
Couples as Family
21%

Pets as Family but Gay
Couples Are Not
30%

Neither Pets nor Gay
Couples as Family
38%

Source: Constructing the Family Survey (Powell 2006).

Exceptions and Contradictions

As mentioned earlier, excerpts from the interviews give a clear picture of the predominant themes that exclusionists used to describe the boundaries they make between families and nonfamilies. Most exclusionists emphasized marital structure—and to a lesser degree, parental structure, the importance of heterosexual bonds, and correspondingly the dangers and immorality of same-sex relationships. Still, given the sheer number of interviews we conducted, it would be surprising if we did not also find exceptions. For example, what families actually do— that is, how families function—appeared to be secondary to structural concerns, or at least it was not mentioned by approximately nine out of ten exclusionists. In contrast, 6 percent discussed emotional ties (for example, love, caring, and happiness), and 5 percent pointed to instrumental tasks (such as working together, paying bills, or handling the family's economic needs) (see figure 3.1). The concepts of expressive and instrumental functions, popularized by the sociologists Talcott Parsons and Robert Bales over fifty years ago, often have been criticized by contemporary sociologists as old-fashioned and sexist in their justification of gendered roles of families (Parsons and Bales 1955; for a brief critique, see Budig 2007). Yet, ironically, among exclusionists—certainly among the most conservative and traditional group that we interviewed—discussions of either or both instrumental and expressive functions were outnumbered by references to the legitimate structure of family. In other words, to exclusionists a family is defined, with few exceptions, by its structure and less so by its presumed functions. As we will see in chapter 6, however, exclusionists might not mention instrumental and expressive functions when defining family, but still hold very closely to a strict gendered division of labor in the household and a gendered notion of appropriate feminine and masculine behavior.

The exclusionists who focused on relationship quality or familial functions were exceptions in a second way: they were more likely to offer open-ended discussions of family that were at odds with their closed-ended responses. A man in his forties, for example, presented a definition that at face value did not seem limited to heterosexual couples: "I would say the way they act. If they're doing things together with significant other/partner and children, that's to me familial." Yet, in the closed-ended questions, he excluded same-sex couples with and without children. This seeming contradiction, in effect, emerges for nearly all exclusionists who mentioned instrumental or emotional bonds in relationships.[8] Most, however, did not acknowledge any contradiction here, perhaps because they could not envision same-sex couples having the requisite instrumental and expressive bonds that constitute a family.

The rarer exception was the exclusionist who did recognize this apparent tension, as in the case of a woman in her forties who emphasized the emotional quality of a relationship: "Well, I believe that a loving. . . . [pauses] Well, you know, actually two men or women could actually be a family in a sense because it's just a loving two people or a household that is a very loving nurturing household." After wondering whether it was possible to change her closed-ended questions, she concluded:

> Well, technically, no, that's not really a family. But you know, I'm saying where [I'm] coming from. I don't know. It's a tricky question there. No, I'd rather you not change it, but my real view on it is, a loving family, you know, a loving household.

This ambivalence suggests a potential window that opens the way for exclusionists who conceptualize family in terms of caring, commitment, love, and "what families do" to expand their definition of family. However, the fact that even exclusionists who saw the contradiction in their responses held on to a narrow list of living arrangements as family suggests that this window is barely open—or is certainly more closed than for moderates.

In Their Own Words: Moderates

Recall from chapter 2 that fewer than one-third (29 percent) of our interviewees fell into the moderate category. As an ideal type, moderates define living arrangements that include children (regardless of marital status) or married couples as family. The most important distinction between moderates' and exclusionists' closed-ended responses, as reported in chapter 2, is the pivotal role that children play in legitimating relationships as family. That is, exclusionists do not see same-sex couples with children as family, but moderates do. Yet, like exclusionists, moderates include married couples in their conception of family, regardless of the presence of children, but not childless unmarried heterosexual or same-sex couples.

In explaining their definitions of family, moderates further accentuate their commonalities with and dissimilarities from exclusionists. Figure 3.3 presents the common themes expressed by moderates in their interviews.

Children As Fundamental

As more than half (59 percent) of the moderates explained, the presence of children is the sine qua non of "family":

Children is a family.

I think you need children to be a real family.

I would say people living together in the same household raising children. I guess that's all there is.

Since the presence of a child supersedes all else, marriage is secondary, if not irrelevant. To be sure, marriage was still mentioned, but by a much smaller percentage of moderate respondents (28 percent) and more often than not in tandem with a discussion of children. When marriage and children were conjointly mentioned, it is notable that children typically were given precedence, as indicated by the greater attention given to children than to marriage in their answers. These comments by a woman in her thirties underscore the relative importance of children:

Figure 3.3   Themes Used by Moderates

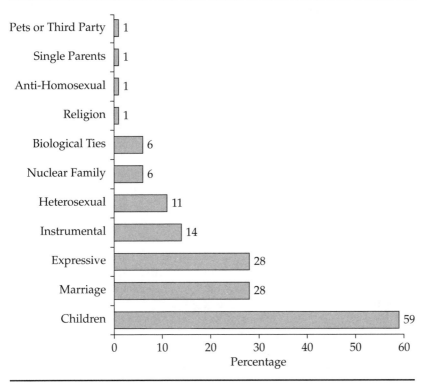

Source: *Constructing the Family Survey* (Powell 2003).

Well, I guess I would have to say, there have to be children involved or marriage. I mean, any two people can live together. I don't think that makes them a family; I think that makes them friends. I think to be a family there needs to be some kind of blood relation there. I'm not necessarily concerned that the mother and the father, or that the same-sex couples, aren't married if they're raising children together. But if there's no kids and they're not married, that doesn't, to me—there needs to be either marriage or some kind of blood relation for that to be family, I guess.

Note that marriage also played a role in this respondent's determination of what counts as family, but that it was secondary to the presence of children in the household. As long as there are children—that is, a "blood relation"—in the household, marriage is not required for family status. By the same token, the gender and sexuality of the parents were inconsequential for this woman. This is the case for many moderates, as exemplified by these remarks from a man in his thirties and a woman in her seventies, respectively:

> Two people living together are just roommates to me. As soon as there are kids involved, then it's a family, whether they're both the same sex or not.

> I guess it would be a couple with children. A man and a woman, a boy and girl, girl and girl, whatever. If it's a family, there are two adults and children.

Some moderates privileged children or "blood" ties to the point that they were ambivalent about granting family status to married couples without children. A middle-aged woman began by including childless married couples in her definition, but then shifted her position:

> Well, I think you should be related some way, by marriage or, I don't know, a family to me can be a man, two women and a couple kids. I mean, I don't think, I don't consider just a man [and] a wife with no kids a family, I don't know why. Maybe that's wrong. I don't know. It's an awful small family, and they are not really related. [*laughs*] I mean, they're related by marriage, but they are not blood, you know. I think family is blood, the same genes. [*sighs*] I don't know. I just think of families as being relations.

Her reference to genes and blood mirrors the exclusionists' comments mentioned earlier (as well as those of the moderate who discussed the "blood relation"). But unlike exclusionists, she, along with other moderates, acknowledged children who are not tied to the parent by "blood." She continued: "Not that there couldn't be a wonderful family adoption thing going on. But that didn't come up. Well, I guess I consider [adoptive children and parents] a family, even though that's not a blood relative."

Her response suggests that she could see beyond biological ties, an ability that other moderates also possessed. The presence of children, then, must connote other requisite qualities of family. To moderates, children are a proxy of two common bonds—the bond between the parent and the child and the bond between the two parents or partners. When we look at the responses given by moderates, it is apparent that they found an observable commitment—to raising children, to a partner, to providing love and support within a set of relationships—to be very important. Moderates were reluctant to call any living arrangement without such priorities a family. Children, therefore, signify responsibility and commitment. A man in his fifties explained it this way:

> I think when both parties share a common interest, such as a child, and they take heart to, you know, come about with the proper provisions for that, like a father was to provide for his family or a mother would provide for the family. You know what I'm saying? It's a goal, it's something. I guess it's the best way I could put it.

Signals of Commitment: Marriage and Same-Sex Couples

Interestingly, moderates did not explicitly use the term "commitment" as frequently as exclusionists did. But over one-third emphasized expressive qualities (28 percent), such as love, caring, and emotional bonds, or instrumental qualities (14 percent), such as taking care of each other, buying a house, and earning income. In fact, moderates referred to these qualities more frequently than they mentioned marriage—an indication that moderates, unlike exclusionists, believe that the quality of the relationship matters more than the structure of the relationship. These views were exemplified by the comments of a woman in her fifties:

> First of all, I mean, that's kind of automatic if someone has, if people living together have children, they're automatically family. And then I would think that intention, especially if it's borne out by any kind of legal or civic ceremony or documents, to prove that the intention's—for it to be long-term. And also the quality of the relationship, the depth of the relationship. So if people treat each other well and really care about each other and pull together, that helps create family.

Despite the fairly broad and inclusive nature of her answer, she did not include same-sex couples without children as family in her closed-ended responses. It appears that, to moderates like this respondent, children, legal status, or some other marker must be present to confer family status. Her response, then, is similar to those of the many moderates who showed a greater willingness to acknowledge some same-sex couples (those with children) but not other same-sex couples (those without children) as family. Some moderates explicitly commented on what some might consider a contradiction by contending that childless same-sex couples lack the bond implicit in either parenthood or marriage. Some specifically seek a sign of a long-term commitment; this young woman discussed what she believed might be missing in a same-sex relationship:

> Oh, God! Okay, to me, it's like people that are planning on being together for a long period of time. Like being together forever. I've heard of best friends moving in together, and they're kind of like family. So, to me, it's two people that are going to be committed to each other for the long haul, not just . . . I don't know.
>
> No, I mean, I'm not saying that two men and two women can't be in it for the long haul, but there's nothing binding them together.

For some moderates, time spent together translates into a committed relationship, as indicated by multiple references to this very issue:

> If they intend it to be a permanent arrangement rather than a passing convenience.

> A commitment that we're together for life.

Duration appears to be a sign of commitment for many moderates. They did not necessarily deny the possibility that same-sex relations can be enduring. But in the absence of a signal or proxy of permanence of relationship (or what one moderate referred to as "a guarantee"), many moderates were reluctant to include childless same-sex couples and, to a lesser extent, childless cohabiting heterosexual couples as families.

Contradictions and Omissions

More so than exclusionists or inclusionists, moderates struggled in their open-ended responses, perhaps because, as part of the muddled middle, they were trying to reconcile traditional views that they might have held for a long time with a willingness to be open to change. It therefore is not unexpected that moderates were more likely than exclusionists or inclusionists to offer positions that appeared incompatible. Moderates—in particular, moderate women—were more likely to voice these inconsistent stances. Moreover, it is telling that in virtually every case in which a moderate recognized his or her own inconsistencies, this person's open-ended responses emphasized the quality of the relationship (for example, love and commitment) and thus suggested a broader interpretation of family than implied by his or her closed-ended responses. Typical of this pattern is a woman in her thirties who responded: "Just two people that love each other. So that kind of contradicts my other answers." Similarly, a woman in her fifties commented:

> Well, if you have two or more individuals living together—and I'm probably contradicting myself—if you have, uh, two individuals living together and married, unmarried, whatever, and if they have children, that, yes, I consider that a family. But then, you know, what really determines what a family is, that's where you get into the full contradiction of everything.

When asked to clarify her position, she added: "Well, personally, I believe that it's two individuals living together, whether they have the kids living there or not, then probably, in a sense, it is a family. So," she said, laughing, "I contradicted everything I said."

Some moderates attributed the contradiction in their responses to the fact that they had "never given it a lot of thought," which suggests their openness to changing how they define family. Social psychologists have long maintained that we experience cognitive dissonance when we hold contradictory positions (Cooper 2007; Festinger 1957). To eliminate the dissonance, we often will shift our positions so that they are more in line with each other. In our interviews, some of the moderates attempted to reconcile their ostensible inconsistencies by indicating that they wanted to change their original closed-ended questions to include same-sex couples without children as family ("erase the no's and put them yes's"). Others did not specifically ask to change their position, but expressed a receptiveness to change in the future, as in the case of a middle-aged woman who commented:

> I hadn't really thought about it. So, to me, I don't want to discriminate against people and to have their rights limited because of that. But I can't answer to know really how. You know, I may change my mind too . . . if that would be a family or not.

In other words, giving people an opportunity to think about the meaning of family opens some of them to the prospect of greater inclusivity. It is possible, nevertheless, that if Americans, especially moderates, are so susceptible to change, the change could be in the direction of a more conservative position—that is, one closer to the exclusionist vision of family. A move in that direction among moderates seems highly doubtful, however, especially if we consider the themes they mostly omitted in their open-ended responses—more specifically, the themes that appeal to anti-gay sentiment and religion.

Moderates may not be fully comfortable with the issue of same-sex relations (many used equivocal language such as "I don't know, I just don't know"), but they also appeared equally if not even more uncomfortable with anti-gay rhetoric. That is, they mostly avoided making explicitly or viscerally anti-gay remarks. In fact, only 1 percent of the moderates offered comments along these lines. A similarly small number (1 percent) of moderates brought up the Bible or religion in their open-ended discussions regarding the definition of family. In other words, anti-gay language and religious justifications—arguably the two most emotionally charged frames that exclusionists strongly resorted to in their explanations of what counts and does not count as family—had limited appeal to moderates. In contrast, appeals to children and observable commitments, along with recognition of the inconsistencies in their own stances, created an opportunity for moderates to move to greater acceptance of nontraditional living arrangements and even closer to the positions of inclusionists, to whom we now turn.

In Their Own Words: Inclusionists

As discussed in chapter 2, inclusionists endorse the most broad-ranging conception of family. Constituting approximately one-fourth (25.4 percent) of our interviewees in 2003 and one-third (32.4 percent) in 2006, inclusionists typically counted each living arrangement included in the interview as family.[9] The only point of disagreement in the closed-ended responses was whether a childless heterosexual cohabiting couple counts as a family: approximately 20 percent of inclusionists did not include this living arrangement as family. The major themes that surfaced in inclusionists' open-ended comments are presented in figure 3.4.

Relationship Quality As Fundamental

One overarching theme emerged in inclusionists' discussions of family. Unlike exclusionists and moderates, inclusionists did not insist on certain structural features of a living arrangement in their definition of family. For inclusionists, the key factor was not religiously or legally sanctioned marriage (as was often raised by exclusionists) or the presence of children (as was typically espoused by moderates). Instead, revealing a remarkably cohesive stance—much more so than was seen among either exclusionists or moderates—nearly all inclusionists focused on the quality of the relationship. How people within a given living arrangement feel about, treat, and interact with each other determines family status. A woman in her thirties explained:

Figure 3.4   Themes Used by Inclusionists

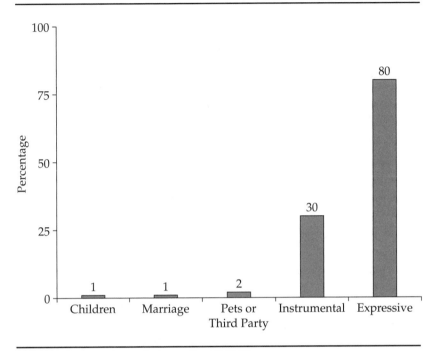

Source: Constructing the Family Survey (Powell 2003).

Basically, because of the feelings, of the level of emotion that are in-volved. As an example, if you have two people living together, not in-volved in a relationship, but just living together . . . that's just two friends living together for maybe financial benefit or something of that nature, but not because they love each other and will be there for each other and share sexual feelings and physical. . . . From a family standpoint, because you consider that person to be your family if you are feeling that way toward them, sexually active with them, loving them, being supportive of them, whether it be financially, emotionally. It doesn't matter, just as you would consider a husband to be a part of your family, a wife to be part of your family. We're dealing with titles here. But just individual people, the way that they feel about the other person: that's what consti-tutes them as a family.

As a man in his thirties put it more directly:

A living arrangement doesn't make a family, period. How the people treat each other makes a family. How the respect between two people or between a group of people. Not just two people, but a group of people. Children as well as adults. How they are treated and how they are brought back together makes a family.[10]

With their focus on the quality of the relationship, the gender of the people in the relationship becomes less relevant to inclusionists. As a middle-aged woman explained: "It doesn't matter who they are. It doesn't matter if it's a man and woman, whatever." In this case, she explicitly referred to "a man and woman" but discounted gender as being of little consequence. Others, however, made the question of gender even more of a non-issue by using nongendered phrasing. A woman in her thirties, for example, bypassed sex-specific references by using the gender-neutral term "people":

> Two people living together who love each other, with kids or not with kids. People who just live together that love each other that are working together to make a household, that's a family. Who love each other. It's got to have love in there to make a family.

Her verbal choice to avoid gendered terms was typical of most inclusionists, who instead referred to "a loving couple" or "a loving, compatible relation" and used language such as: "if you're happy together and love each other," "they're all loving," "two people who love each other," and "two people that love each other—you know, with children, without—no matter their sexuality."[11] In other words, love and other expressive aspects of the household were so consequential— indeed, these were mentioned by 80 percent of all inclusionists—that they relegated gender to a triviality, at least with respect to the meaning of family.

The importance of the relationship between the partners transcended not only gender but also legal status, parenthood (which was mentioned by fewer than 1 percent of the inclusionists), and, relatedly, "blood." A woman in her thirties, for example, weighed affective ties against biological ones: "I just feel like if there's an emotional connection, emotional bonding is sometimes a tighter bond than blood." Still, some inclusionists recognized that their broadly expansive position was at odds with the current social and political climate. A man in his fifties jokingly expressed concern over what he characterized as his "way too liberal" perspective:

> The difference for me is caring for each other or . . . the love they have for each other. It's, you know, it doesn't have to be marriage. Marriage to me

doesn't necessarily define a household. If there were to be two men that are not—it's—unless you go to Vermont or Canada—these days are not allowed to get married. Neither are two women. But that doesn't make it not a household. Did I explain that okay? The care and respect they have for each other is what makes the difference. . . . So something that's not purely economic in nature. Don't tell this to George Bush. I mean, he's not listening, is he?

(His comments proved eerily predictive: two years later, in 2005, the news broke about President Bush's authorization of wiretapping.)

Commitment: Presumptions and Signals

Inextricably connected to emotional ties is the concept of commitment. In identifying the key criterion for family, one young woman defined family as: "Pretty much their commitment to each other. The joy of a family to me is anything that's basically binding two or more people together." Her comments were seconded by other inclusionists who recurrently talked about commitment when discussing the meaning of family: "a sense of commitment to each other," "within a committed relationship," "if there is a real commitment there," "people who commit to each other," and "the commitment that people have with each other."

Certainly, some exclusionists and moderates also emphasized commitment, albeit much less frequently than did inclusionists. But for exclusionists commitment was signified mostly by marriage and legal and ceremonial vows, while for moderates commitment was customarily connoted by children or time together. Inclusionists diverged from both by usually presuming that if there is a relationship, then there is a commitment. In other words, commitment in a relationship requires no additional proof beyond the existence of the relationship.

Although there were some inclusionists who did not automatically presume commitment in some living arrangements without corroborating evidence, these inclusionists, in sharp contrast to moderates and exclusionists, appeared to be less likely to require evidence from same-sex couples (most notably, those without children) than from their cohabiting heterosexual counterparts. In the previous chapter, we speculated that this group—representing one-fifth of inclusionists—were reluctant to accord family status to these heterosexual couples because they have neither made the commitment to have children nor exercised the option to get married—an option unavailable to most same-sex couples in the United States. The comments from a woman in her fifties are consistent with our speculation:

If there's children involved, then I believe it's a family. Or if there's a husband and wife. And as far as the homosexual relationship, they're not allowed to get married, I don't think. So I would say that they were living as a married couple.

Overall, this cluster of inclusionists was more concerned than their fellow inclusionists with "observable" or "guaranteed" signals of commitment. A woman in her thirties explicitly equated heterosexual cohabitation with a lack of commitment:

What I consider a family? Oh, I guess it's more about commitment, that there's commitment there to being together. And the only one I said no to was the boyfriend and girlfriend living together. But I guess it's because that doesn't feel like it's as big of a commitment.

When inclusionists did discuss signals of commitment, they usually relied on one of several categories. Certainly, love or more broadly expressive ties were paramount. But instrumental qualities in the relationship also were seen by some inclusionists as commitment markers. In fact, nearly one-third (30 percent) of inclusionists mentioned instrumental qualities, occasionally in combination with expressive ones, in their definitions of family. Acts of service essentially verify commitment. A young woman, for example, saw instrumental interdependence as a prerequisite for family standing: "If you depend on each other to survive—well, if you're physically, mentally, or financially dependents on someone else—then I would consider them a family." By the same token, a woman in her fifties briefly discussed the importance of working as a unit (a concept mentioned by other inclusionists): "Living, doing all the things a family should do. Sharing a household and income and so on. So I would say they were living as a unit."

Of note, the focus on instrumental relations by inclusionists did not assume a rigid gender division in familial tasks, as is often implied in Parsonian discussions of family dynamics. Rather, there was no reference to gender. Instead, the assumption was that the instrumental functions can be met regardless of the gender of the family members.

Inclusionists also saw intentionality as a basic marker of commitment. The intention to be together and to remain a family was seen as critical. A woman in her fifties specifically defined commitment in these terms: "If they purchased the house together and they intend it to be a permanent arrangement rather than a passing convenience." Her response emphasized an action—purchasing a house—that connotes a sense of permanency. Other inclusionists considered the length of time that people live together as evidence of intentionality, as illustrated by the remarks of a man in his fifties:

I guess for me it almost becomes a time frame of people living for a good period of time and that they have common interests. I guess, well, when it becomes a question of individuals living together for very short periods of time and constantly there was some kind of a change, I guess I would not be as open to that as I would be to people that have done it for extended periods of time.

He did not specify what counts as a "good period of time," but another middle-aged man did:

As long as someone's involved with each other and they're living in the house and they've been over six months to a year, I would consider that a family whether there's kids involved or not. If they're not involved and they're just friends or they're just sort of dating and they're roommates sort of, that's one thing, I would say that's not considered a family. But if the person—man or woman, or woman-woman, man-man, doesn't't matter—if they're a couple and they have been together for quite, for at least six months to a year, I would consider that family.

As mentioned earlier in this chapter, some moderates also regarded the amount of time two individuals had spent together as a proxy for commitment. In contrast to moderates, however, nothing in the inclusionists' comments assumed that commitment, intention to be together, or, in the words of a man in his forties, "permanence and duration" is greater for heterosexual couples than it is for same-sex ones. If anything, some inclusionists' remarks implied the exact opposite assumption—that the markers of commitment are more likely present among childless same-sex couples than among childless heterosexual ones.

What happens, then, if an additional proxy for commitment is included in the description of couples? The frequent references by moderates and inclusionists to relationship length prompted us in 2006 to ask a series of questions that spoke to this issue. We asked whether respondents considered a childless same-sex couple a family "from the moment they move in together as a couple," and if not, whether they deemed this couple a family "if they have lived together as a couple for ten years." We asked the same questions regarding childless cohabiting heterosexual couples and a slightly different pair of questions regarding childless married couples (whether they are a family "from the moment they are married," and if not, "if they have been married for ten years").

As can be seen from figure 3.5, the vast majority of respondents believed that a married couple becomes a family immediately upon marriage (90.2 percent among exclusionists, 86.1 percent among moderates, and 95.8 percent among inclusionists).[12] Given these high per-

Figure 3.5   When Do Married, Cohabiting, and Gay Couples Count as Family?

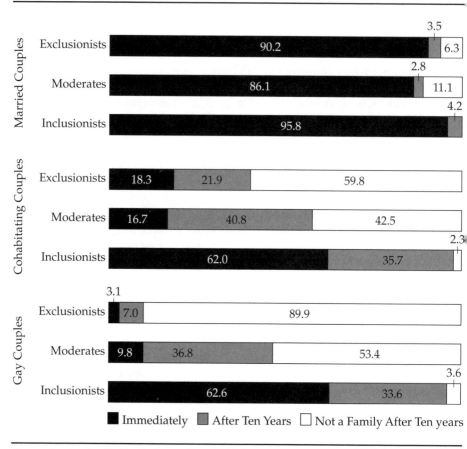

Source: *Constructing the Family Survey* (Powell 2006).

centages, being married for a ten-year time span only slightly increases these figures, although moderates were less open here (88.9 percent) than were exclusionists (93.7 percent) or inclusionists (100 percent).

In contrast, the impact of time as a proxy for commitment—especially for moderates—is brought to light when we look at same-sex or heterosexual cohabiting couples. As described in the last chapter, moderates typically did not include same-sex couples without children as family. But as can be seen in the figure, once the amount of time together is added into the equation, nearly half of all moderates (46.6 percent) believed that a childless same-sex couple living together for ten years is a family. In other words, time together is such a persuasive marker of commitment that it can push many Americans toward a more liberal, inclusive vision of family.

Whatever it Means to Them(WIMTT)

Comments by inclusionists indicated their expansive vision of family, one in which they set broad—and mostly gender-neutral—criteria (such as love and commitment) that facilitate the inclusion of a broad range of living arrangements as family. Some inclusionists, however, went even further. They contended that no one but those in a particular relationship can set the key criteria for their family status. As an illustration, a woman in her sixties placed the responsibility on the prospective family members:

> I think it depends on what the people think they have. If they have a family relationship, then that's family. What you think you are. You know if you're living together as a couple, then that's a family. Probably a lot depends on how these people consider themselves. So, I would say that's the determining factor: what the people think they are.

When they are asked for clarification of a question or concept, a standard protocol for interviewers at survey and interview centers is to respond with "whatever it means to you"—also known by its acronym, WIMTY (Moore 2004). Just as interviewers allow interviewees to use their own definitions, this woman let others define their family on their own terms. Her words were echoed in comments by other inclusionists: for example, "if they perceive themselves as a family," "if they consider themselves a family," and "two people that care about each other and form a relationship that *feels* [our emphasis] familial." In other words, these inclusionists were relying on a similar construction of family, or what we would refer to as the acronym WIMTT: "whatever it means to them."[13] This concept dovetails closely with the idea of "families we choose," popularized by the anthropologist Kath Weston (1997). Individuals who invoked this concept in their discussion were the most inclusionist of the inclusionists. And judging from their comments, they might have been receptive to even more transgressive living arrangements that were not asked about in our interviews—for example, groups of more than two adults living together.

Inclusionists' use of WIMTT can go beyond the definition of family and be extended to putatively legally defined arrangements, such as marriage. As an example, a middle-aged woman who was one of the few inclusionists to state explicitly that family is defined by "probably marriage" offered a decidedly constructionist definition of marriage:

"If they're married or they *think* [our emphasis] they're married, I think that they're a family."

In sum, some inclusionists focused on what a group of people feels about each other, others on what a group of people does for each other, and still others on whether a group actually defines itself as family. Despite some disagreement over the sheer amount of latitude in defining family, inclusionists shared in common an encompassing vision of family that places familial function or familial self-definition above structural constraints.

Words Creating Pictures

As outlined earlier, exclusionists, moderates, and inclusionists rely on strikingly divergent frames when delineating family boundaries. To summarize these differences, we present visual depictions of the most common words used by exclusionists, moderates, and inclusionists in figures 3.6, 3.7, and 3.8, respectively. In these "word clouds," also known as "tag clouds" or "text clouds," the most frequently used words are displayed in larger fonts and are darker. The word clouds visually crystallize the most prominent themes for each group.[14]

Among the words most frequently used by exclusionists—other than "family," which also was mentioned regularly by moderates and inclusionists, no doubt because they were explaining what they believed counts as family—we can see an emphasis on structure ("married," "marriage," "children," "kids"), law or religion ("Bible," "Christian," "God," "legal"), and gender ("husband," "man," "wife," "woman").

Moderates also used words that indicate structure. But the words "children," "child," and "kids" were unmistakably mentioned with greater regularity than were "marriage" or "married," a pattern that is consistent with moderates' privileging the presence of children over marriage. Moderates were decidedly less gendered than exclusionists in the words they used. Sex-specific references to partners ("husband," "wife," "man," "woman") were used less frequently than non-sex-specific terms ("people," "couple"). We also detect the emergence of words among moderates that are absent in the exclusionist word cloud. Several of these words suggest affective or instrumental bonds (for example, "admiration," "care," "feel," and "share").

Inclusionists' choice of words was diametrically opposite from those used by exclusionists. Words connoting structure were secondary to words signifying affective ties. In fact, some words that were prominently used by exclusionists do not even appear in the inclusionist word cloud—most notably "marriage" and "married." Also missing from the inclusionist word cloud are the sex-specific roles of

Figure 3.6   Most Frequently Used Words: Exclusionists

answer arrangement believe Bible blood child children Christian commitment consider couple determines divorce don't either family father God guess heterosexual husband kids legal life living love man marriage married mother people question raising really related relationship religion sex single spouse think together uh um wife woman women

Source: Constructing the Family Survey (Powell 2003).

Figure 3.7   Most Frequently Used Words: Moderates

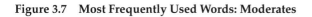

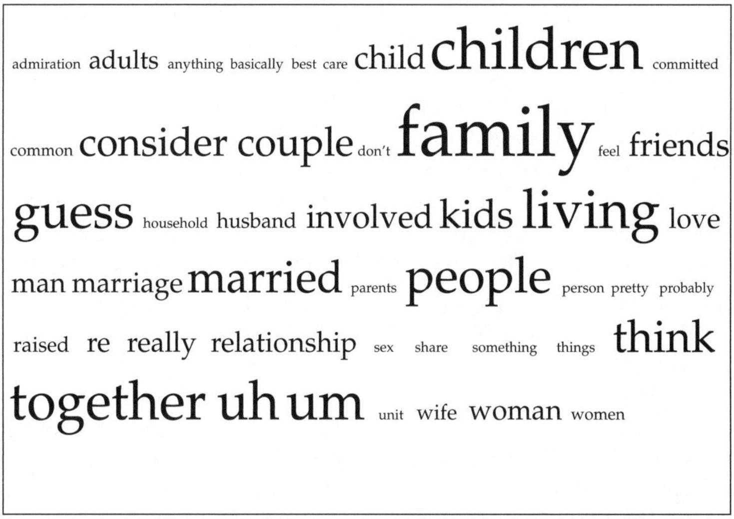

admiration adults anything basically best care child children committed common consider couple don't family feel friends guess household husband involved kids living love man marriage married parents people person pretty probably raised re really relationship sex share something things think together uh um unit wife woman women

Source: Constructing the Family Survey (Powell 2003).

Figure 3.8   Most Frequently Used Words: Inclusionists

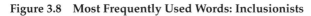

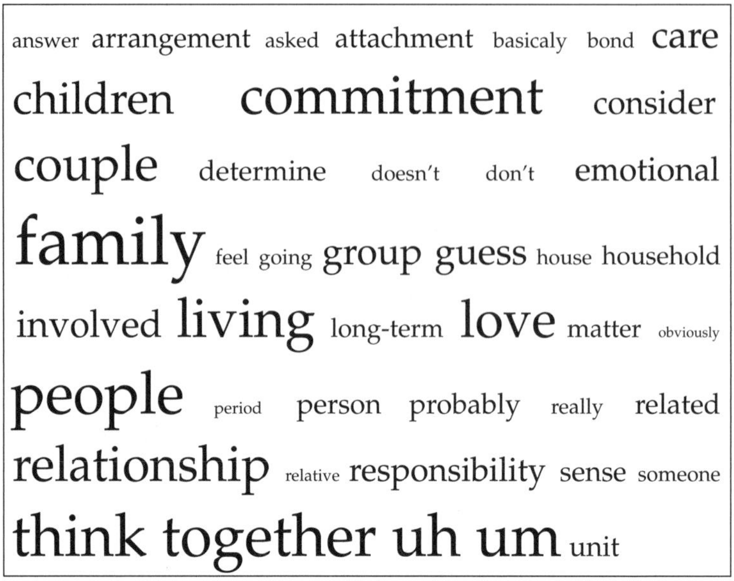

answer arrangement asked attachment basicaly bond care
children **commitment** consider
couple determine doesn't don't emotional
family feel going group guess house household
involved living long-term love matter obviously
people period person probably really related
relationship relative responsibility sense someone
think together uh um unit

Source: Constructing the Family Survey (Powell 2003).

"husband," "wife," "man," and "woman"—a sign that gender is absent in the calculus of most inclusionists' understanding of family. Instead, these words are replaced by words that do not appear in the exclusionist word cloud: "attachment," "bond," "care," "emotional," and "responsibility" (a word that we discuss in greater detail in chapter 4). Perhaps more importantly, both "commitment" and "love" were mentioned by all three groups but were given priority only by inclusionists. Despite the frequent pairing of "love and marriage" in popular music, literature, and quotes, it appears that exclusionists, moderates, and inclusionists by and large decouple them: exclusionists, and to a lesser extent moderates, privileged marriage over love, while inclusionists believed that loves transcend marriage.

Words of (Dis)Comfort

Word clouds typically exclude utterances. In this case, however, we decided to include two of these words: "uh" and "um." These, along with similar words ("ah," "hmm") and other nonverbal cues (such as sighs, laughs, and pauses), were sprinkled throughout our interviews with exclusionists, moderates, and inclusionists. We recognize that these sounds and cues can have multiple meanings, as scholars of linguistics and conversational analysis contend.[15] They could indicate, among other things, that the speaker is trying to recall a word, deciding what to say, or feeling uncomfortable. In listening to our interviews, we found examples of these various meanings, although we were especially intrigued with comments that implied a sense of discomfort or awkwardness in speaking about same-sex relationships and explicitly saying the words "gay," "lesbian," or "homosexual." Exclusionists often showed uneasiness with these terms and found ways to avoid using them, but so did some moderates, as illustrated by the comments of a middle-aged woman:

> Well, they could be married or unmarried. They could be, I mean, um, the same sex. And they're, how can I put this? [laughs] Ah, [laughs] they, well, they could have children, or no children, but they are, um, um, romantically involved? [laughs]

As noted earlier in this chapter, these verbal cues are similar to those often used by racial majorities to describe racial minorities. The parallel between views of same-sex couples and historical views of racial minorities—and, as we discuss later in this book, of interracial couples—led us in 2006 to ask exclusionists, moderates, and inclusionists how "comfortable" they were with having gays and lesbians as neighbors, physicians, or teachers for their children.[16] These closed-ended questions are loosely derived from the social distance scales that historically have been used to study racial attitudes (Bogardus 1932).[17]

Exclusionists, moderates, and inclusionists exhibited stunningly different levels of comfort with gays and lesbians. As shown in figure 3.9, over half of exclusionists strongly (32.0 percent) or somewhat (21.1 percent) disagreed that they would be comfortable having a gay man or lesbian "move in next door."[18] Their discomfort level increased (to 63.1 percent) when asked about a gay or lesbian couple. Unsolicited asides from exclusionists offered additional insight into their views: some used disparaging words to describe these scenarios (for example, "such garbage") or they expressed reluctant acceptance of same-sex couples in their neighborhood, "as long as they're not rolling around the lawn." Resistance to a gay or lesbian teacher (71.0 percent) or a gay or lesbian doctor (65.2 percent) was even greater: over half indicated that they strongly disagreed that they would be comfortable in these situations.[19] Here some exclusionists offered specific criteria under which they would accept a gay or lesbian doctor—for example, "if he is the only doctor alive." In a variation of the "don't ask, don't tell" policies of the

Figure 3.9   Comfort Level Interacting with Gays and Lesbians: Exclusionists, Moderates, and Inclusionists

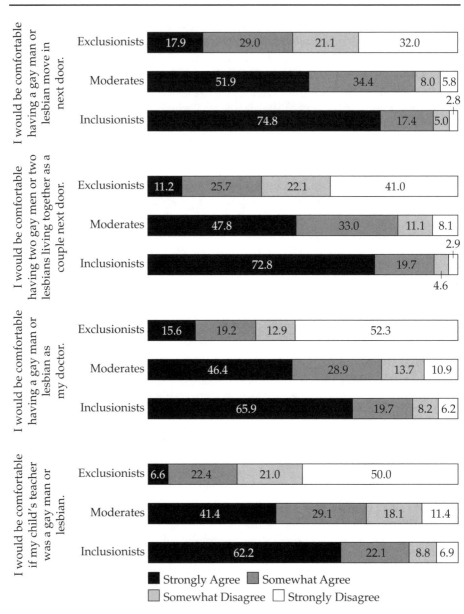

Source: Constructing the Family Survey (Powell 2006).

U.S. military, some exclusionists volunteered that the issue was not homosexuality per se, but rather whether it was public—for example, "if I don't know about it, it's okay with me."

At the other end of the spectrum, over 90 percent of inclusionists reported being comfortable with living next door to a gay man or lesbian (92.2 percent) or a gay or lesbian couple (92.5 percent). Their professed comfort with gay or lesbian doctors (85.6 percent) or teachers (84.3 percent) is almost as high. As one might expect, moderates' reported comfort level lies between that of exclusionists and moderates. But it is revealing that moderates' responses are closer to those of inclusionists. These patterns lend added confidence to our contention that the distance between moderates and inclusionists is smaller than that between moderates and exclusionists. They also bolster our prediction that moderates' potential migration is more likely in the direction of inclusionist than exclusionist positions.

Conclusion

As we examine how Americans talk about family, we see the complexity of their definitions and the difficulties they have with them. Their answers reveal a great deal about how people think about—and sometimes negotiate with themselves regarding—the boundaries between families and nonfamilies and also pinpoint openings where their beliefs are receptive to change. Other scholars have called for paying greater attention to what the public thinks about issues regarding same-sex couples and how they talk about these issues and focusing less on the opinions of elites (especially academic and political elites). Kathleen Hull (2006), for example, contends that activists' inattention to non-elite discourse creates a "missed opportunity"—both for those working to promote marital equality for same-sex couples and for those laboring to prevent it.[20] Such discourse can be useful in identifying themes that resonate with the public and those that do not.

Americans' responses to our 2003 and 2006 survey questions affirm the basic differences between the three groups that were identified by the latent class analysis in the previous chapter (exclusionists, moderates, and inclusionists). But more importantly, they provide richer insights into how people formulate the boundaries they make. Had we relied solely on the closed-ended responses covered in the previous chapter, we would not have observed the refinements and qualifications that underlie and complicate Americans' definitions of family. The richness of their responses affirms what proponents of qualitative scholarship and of mixed methods have long claimed. These responses both corroborate and elaborate the typologies introduced in the last chapter.

With respect to exclusionists, we detect apparently unflinching adherence to definitions based on structure, law, tradition, and religion. These definitions, which are not easily shed, hinge on the primacy of marriage and privilege the traditional nuclear family over other living arrangements. To most exclusionists, structure—marriage and, to a lesser extent, biological parenthood—trumps function, that is, what families actually do. To be sure, comments by some exclusionists allowed for the possibility that certain alternative living arrangements serve the purposes of family. Accordingly, some exclusionists struggle to permit flexibility in their definitions. But this flexibility is limited primarily to single-parent households and cohabiting heterosexual households with children. Missing are same-sex couples, toward whom exclusionists show great resistance, discomfort, or antipathy. In this chapter, we identified some means by which some exclusionists may be amenable to change despite their overall intransigence. Still, mass movement toward acceptance of same-sex couples seems improbable for exclusionists, at least in the short term.

In contrast, we see great potential for movement among moderates. At first, it appears that moderates also rely on straightforward markers that distinguish families from nonfamilies—most notably the presence of children and, secondarily, marriage. But moderates do not value parenthood and marriage merely in structural terms. Instead, they value parenthood and marriage for what they connote: a bond or sense of commitment. Children require financial and social investments that almost by definition mean that family members are committed to and sacrifice for other members. Moderates, then, see children in a household—and marriage—as evidence of real emotional and instrumental ties, or as one interviewee termed it, a "guarantee."

But moderates' comments also revealed that there are other ways to signal commitment—for example, the duration of the relationship. Consequently, we demonstrate that if one brings the length of the relationship into the dialogue, moderates often move away from their strict adherence to parenthood as a necessary requirement of family status for heterosexual and same-sex cohabiting couples. Offering additional signals of commitment among these couples may be a highly effective means to further promote moderates' willingness to endorse a more expansive definition of family. In contrast, we see few arguments that would persuade moderates to turn to a more restrictive definition. Moderates may show some discomfort with same-sex neighbors, teachers, or physicians, but their reactions are much closer to those of inclusionists than those of exclusionists. The sheer absence of references to religion and of anti-gay rhetoric in their comments also suggests that appeals to religion and immorality would be unsuccessful among moderates, if not counterproductive.

What makes us even more confident of moderates' receptiveness to change, however, is their own recognition of the inconsistencies in their reactions. Their remarks were enlightening and showed that moderates are wrestling with their personal conceptions about who counts as family and who is counted out and, in particular, whether family boundaries should be expanded to include gay couples. What strikes us is the extent to which moderates mull over this topic, often challenging their original reasoning and sometimes then changing their minds toward a more inclusive stance. Other moderates grapple with their logic but ultimately remain not ready to confer family status to childless same-sex couples—or at least, not ready yet.

The group that appears most impervious to change are inclusionists. In contrast to exclusionists, inclusionists believe that function trumps structure. In many ways they are romantics because they privilege love and emotional ties over legally defined, traditionally sanctioned, or religiously ordained family structures. But they also are pragmatists, because more so than either exclusionists or moderates, they emphasize what families actually do and how families define themselves. Although it is possible that some inclusionists would eventually reverse their position, their strong consensus over the determinants of family status—in particular, the quality of the relationship regardless of its structure and the functions, interdependencies, and expressiveness among family members—makes it difficult to imagine a marked shift toward exclusionism.

But it also might be difficult for some social scientists to reconcile the finding that inclusionists' reliance—and, to a lesser degree, that of moderates—on functions and interdependencies creates a foundation for liberal views regarding family. Very simply, the most inclusive respondents invoked functionalism, while the most exclusionist ones steered clear of it. That appeals to familial function fuel open-mindedness is an interesting—and for some family scholars, troubling—departure from accepted social-scientific thought. Just as many of our respondents were reassessing their assumptions regarding family, so too should social scientists reevaluate their often reflexive suspicion that functionalism must always be inherently conservative and unable to accommodate social change. Indeed, the Parsonian representation of the "normal American family" with women specializing in expressive, nurturant roles and men in instrumental, breadwinner roles is now widely discarded by social scientists—ourselves included—and seen as obsolete, sexist, and potentially dysfunctional. Nonetheless, from our own ob-

servations of how individuals incorporate functions into their definitions of family, we wonder about the wisdom of the wholesale rejection
of any recognition of familial functions—even when the functions are
distanced from any discussion of gender. It is the focus on family functions that may offer Americans a compelling rationale for greater acceptance of various family forms.

═ Chapter 4 ═

Family Counts Divided: Social Location and Definitions of Family

To THIS point we have outlined Americans' definitions of family and whether same-sex couples are counted in or out of these definitions. Americans splinter into three distinguishable groups that set markedly dissimilar boundaries between family and nonfamily—inclusionists, moderates, and exclusionists. These boundaries are consequential: they are implicated in Americans' views regarding family policy, notably same-sex marriage. And as we saw in chapter 3, these boundaries are accompanied by an assortment of competing justifications—from a concentration on structure to an emphasis on what families actually do.

In this chapter, we take another look at boundaries. But here we explore not only boundaries that people erect between family and nonfamily but also the sociodemographic boundaries, or cleavages, that figure into their constructions. More specifically, we examine whether Americans' inclusion or exclusion of same-sex couples in the definition of family varies by social location—that is, by such sociodemographic factors as gender, age, education, and race. In addition, we consider the influence of physical location, or geographical boundaries—more specifically, urban-rural and regional differences. We also investigate the extent to which family background, religious beliefs, and contact with gays and lesbians are implicated in the definitions of family that Americans supply.

Social scientists have long recognized the importance that social location plays with respect to an array of social attitudes. The application of this insight to views on sexuality, however, is relatively new. Still, the accumulating evidence regarding sociodemographic differences in these attitudes—coming from studies that rely on responses from col-

71

lege students, social workers, police officers, convenience samples, and national samples—points to certain potentially influential factors (Andersen and Fetner 2008; Bernstein and Kostelac 2002; Bernstein, Kostelac, and Gaarder 2003; Black, Oles, and Moore 1998; Britton 1990; Herek and Capitanio 1995, 1996; Herek and Glunt 1993; Jensen, Gambles, and Olsen 1988; Loftus 2001). A primary goal of this chapter, then, is to see whether the social cleavages suggested or found in these analyses are also confirmed in Americans' views regarding which living arrangements count as family and, in particular, whether same-sex couples are counted in or counted out of definitions of family.

To meet this goal, we conducted a series of multivariate analyses— more specifically, multinomial logistic regression—to test the direction, significance, and robustness of the effect of these sociodemographic factors on the likelihood of being an exclusionist, moderate, or inclusionist. Models exploring the effects of gender, age, education, race, family background, marital status, region, urban residence, and religious beliefs are displayed in appendix 4.A.[1] We also conducted multivariate analyses that gauge the influence of social contact—that is, the effects of having a friend or relative who is gay. Appendix 4.B summarizes these effects. With only one exception (discussed later in this chapter), each of these items is consistently and significantly implicated in Americans' definitions of family. The abundance of information that comes from Americans' responses to open-ended questions, as well as their unsolicited comments to closed-ended ones, further enables us to delve more deeply into some of these sociodemographic differences.

Examination of group differences is crucial not only to comprehend the current landscape of public opinion but also to permit us to make some predictions about future conceptualizations of family, another one of our key objectives in this chapter. A better understanding of the influence of sociodemographic differences (in particular, age and education) and of social context (especially contact with gays and lesbians) helps us forecast social changes in the public debate about the meaning of family. It also allows us to consider the parallels between contemporary views on same-sex couples and historical views on interracial couples.

Sociodemographic Influences

Gender Differences

A burgeoning and extensive literature in the social sciences indicates that women are more liberal than men when it comes to views regard-

Figure 4.1   Family Definitions, by Gender

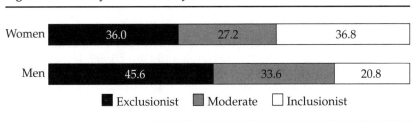

Source: *Constructing the Family Survey* (Powell 2003, 2006).

ing gender and sexuality.[2] Still, the source of gender differences remains in dispute, with explanations originating from sociology, social
psychology, economics, gender studies, and evolutionary psychology
and physiology (see, for example, Bernstein and Kostelac 2002; Herek
1988). Regardless of the derivation of gender differences, we find a similar trend with respect to views about family. Figure 4.1—as well as
other figures in this chapter—displays predicted probabilities derived
from multivariate models that control for other key socioeconomic factors.[3] Women are plainly more inclusive than men in their definitions
of family. Men are over twice as likely to be exclusionist (45.6 percent)
than inclusionist (20.8 percent), while women are equally likely to be
exclusionist (36.0 percent) or inclusionist (36.8 percent).[4]

In chapter 3, we identified various frames that exclusionists, moderates, and inclusionists used in explaining what determined for them
whether a living arrangement was a family. Recall that exclusionists
focused heavily on legal structure (in particular, marriage) and religion, while moderates emphasized the presence of children and inclusionists underscored the importance of the expressive and, to a lesser
degree, instrumental functions of family. When we look at women's
responses separately from men's, we see both similarities and differences in the ways in which women and men talked about family (see
figure 4.2). Both women and men frequently discussed the role of children (especially moderates) and marriage (most notably exclusionists).[5] Moreover, both men and women (mostly inclusionists, but also
some moderates) frequently referred to expressive aspects of the family: for example, "whether the people care enough about each other,"
"a sense of commitment to each other," or simply "love, respect, and
friendship!" That being said, among inclusionists, women were over
twice as likely as men to use the terms "love" or "loving."

The most striking gender difference, however, is the greater emphasis that men put on the instrumental functions of family (22.5 percent)
compared with women (7.0 percent). This sex difference is present

Figure 4.2   Themes, by Gender

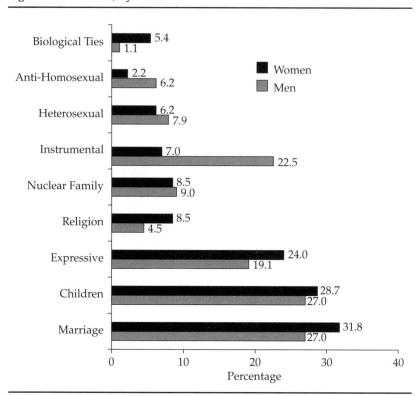

Source: *Constructing the Family Survey* (Powell 2003).
Note: Because some interviewees mentioned more than one theme, the sum of the percentages exceeds 100 percent. In addition, this figure does not include all of the themes mentioned in the interviews.

among exclusionists and moderates but is especially strong among inclusionists. Whereas women privileged the quality of the relationship, for many men, what makes a family a family is providing for family members, sharing financial burdens, and, in the words of a man in his forties, meeting the overall functions of a family: "Participation of all involved persons in contributing to a whole in functioning like a group of people sharing what they have in order to better themselves altogether, and therefore individually." Men often spoke pointedly about "taking responsibility," as illustrated by the comment that "a group of people who take responsibility for each other pretty well counts as a family." As a young man asked and then answered:

What would I call a family? I would say living under the same roof, with appropriate responsibilities. I guess that would be the broadest sense I could throw out there.

Another respondent echoed this view, but also recognized the impor-tance of the expressive role of families:

Well, I feel that really the only substantial thing you need to have a fam-ily is a group of people who live together under the, you know, assump-tion that they are going to stay together. You know, like they're a group of people, who, I guess, are sort of bonded by love and responsibility.

Our qualitative analysis, then, points to a fundamental difference between women and men not only in their definitions of family but also in their rationale for these views. Interestingly, instead of focusing on what family members do for them, men privileged what they often are expected to provide—responsibility and instrumental support—while women emphasized what they typically are expected to offer—love and emotional support.[6] In chapter 2, we noted that political frames that highlight familial commitment resonate with Americans. But the gender patterns outlined here also suggest that the use of themes that appeal to responsibility, and to functionality more broadly, may be a particularly winning strategy if one's objective is to shift men's positions toward a more expansive view of family.

Age and Cohort Differences

We next consider whether definitions of family are shaped by age. As seen in figure 4.3, views regarding family vary dramatically across age groups. Among Americans over the age of sixty-four, more than three-fifths (61.1 percent) were exclusionists, over one-fourth (26.3 percent) were moderates, and approximately one-eighth (12.6 percent) were in-clusionists. But when we look at younger Americans, especially those under the age of thirty, we see a diametric pattern. Over one-third (36.1 percent) took an inclusionist stance, while nearly two-fifths (39.4 per-cent) were moderates and only one-fourth (24.5 percent) were exclu-sionists. Apparently, a clear majority of senior citizens did not see any type of same-sex—or cohabiting—couple (with or without children) as family, while an even larger majority of young adults (75.5 percent) rec-ognized some form of same-sex couples as family. As noted earlier, these predicted probabilities are based on multivariate models that ad-just for other key sociodemographic factors. Previous studies have doc-umented that younger adults express more liberal attitudes regarding

Figure 4.3   Family Definitions, by Age and Cohort

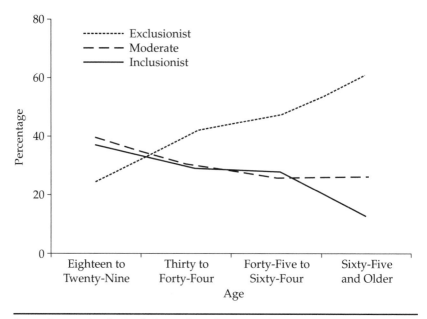

Source: *Constructing the Family Survey* (Powell 2003, 2006).

homosexuality than do their older counterparts; the findings from our analyses suggest that this pattern can be extended to Americans' boundary-making between family and nonfamily (Andersen and Fetner 2008; Britton 1990; Loftus 2001; Wilcox and Wolpert 2000; Yang 1997).

What do these findings imply? Do they suggest inevitable movement toward same-sex rights in the future by virtue of the eventual replacement of the older, more conservative adults with the younger, more liberal ones? Alternatively, do they suggest that younger adults ultimately will become more similar to their older counterparts in their views regarding family as they grow older? Many social conservatives seem to share the view that the generational differences are real—and disquieting. They are concerned that their deeply held traditional views on the meaning of family will become a minority viewpoint, a relic of the past. Their urgency to enact constitutional amendments that would ban gay marriage at the state and federal levels signifies a growing awareness that a more tolerant climate toward same-sex couples may well be on its way. As an illustration, in an interview in 2006, Trent

Lott, former senator from Mississippi, was asked by a reporter to assess the apparent support for same-sex marriage by "kids in their twenties." He responded:

> Frankly, I'm not sure that's a positive commentary . . . about our times and our kids. You know, I don't want to be too judgmental. But it is, you know, an evolving or a different standard from what we've had in the past. I'm troubled by it, quite frankly.

Later in the interview, Lott offered an optimistic—at least in the view of social conservatives—spin that the tendency for younger adults to be more liberal is merely transitory (Lott 2006):

> You know the old argument: When you're young, if you're not liberal, there's something wrong with your head. And when you're older, if you're sixty and you're still liberal, there's something wrong with your mind.

Lott's contradictory responses highlight the difficulty in disentangling the effects of age and cohort—a challenge regularly faced by those who study the life course and aging. How can we separate the effects of age that arise from the experience of living—and especially from coming of age—during particular historical periods from the effects of age that reflect maturity and the aging process?

The effects of cohort can be quite powerful and, as we suggest later, especially influential in shaping contemporary definitions of family. The cohort explanation contends that age differences represent real differences between specific cohorts and not just the effect of maturation on people's views (Brewster and Padavic 2000; Schnittker, Freese, and Powell 2003). Under this argument, people of roughly the same age may be similarly shaped by key social events that they experience and share in adolescence and early adulthood, a time when individuals are still formulating their views and opinions about an assortment of topics. After early adulthood, readiness to adopt new attitudes declines rapidly. Consequently, many beliefs that crystallized during the formative years remain relatively stable over the life course (Alwin and Krosnick 1991). Therefore, one may expect cohorts born around the same time to share many common experiences, which in turn may mold their political and social views across a lifetime (Alwin, McCammon, and Hofer 2004; Mannheim 1928/1952). An impressive body of research corroborates the power of cohort effects by identifying consistent generational differences in such diverse areas as voter turnout (Firebaugh and Chen 1995), feminist self-identification (Schnittker,

Freese, and Powell 2003), and perspectives on marriage and gender roles (Amato and Booth 1997).

Others do not deny the importance of cohort, but express concern that an overreliance on cohort explanations mistakenly downplays the aging process itself. While aging is not a life event by itself, with the exception perhaps of birthdays for very young or very old individuals, it does represent an individual's cumulative experience and likelihood of having experienced a number of critical transitions. Views that seemed appropriate at an earlier stage may take a very different meaning over time—for example, when an individual becomes employed. Marriage and parenthood and the responsibilities that accompany these role transitions are often cited as catalysts behind adults' change in outlooks.[7] Furthermore, advancing age is often associated with economic prosperity, greater community embeddedness, and, relatedly, adherence to the status quo. Thus, although some accounts suggest little change in individuals' attitudes as they age, such consistency may not be the norm. Instead, over the life cycle a series of triggering events may sway individuals to shift, even in their core principles.

Although we find dramatic differences in views regarding families across age groups—with older respondents being less inclusive than younger ones—we cannot state with confidence that these patterns signify an age or a cohort effect. Still, a closer examination of the data may give us some, although admittedly still limited, analytical leverage when trying to reconcile these disparate explanations. We discern some evidence of a genuine age effect (although not for our key question of interest), but more importantly, we also find evidence that suggests a cohort effect for attitudes regarding same-sex and cohabiting couples.

We stumbled on the age effect when we examined individuals' reactions to "two people living together as housemates who are not living as a couple and have no children." As noted in chapter 2, approximately 10 percent of Americans classify this living arrangement as family. We initially expected that the youngest respondents would be the most likely group to think of housemates as family. Our reasoning was simple: younger adults are presumptively the most liberal and expansive in their views regarding family and are more likely than other groups to have recently experienced living in such an arrangement or to have friends who do. We also thought we would find an inverse linear relationship between age and seeing housemates as family.

Put bluntly, we were wrong in our expectations. It is true that those under the age of thirty were more accepting of housemates as family than were their peers between the ages of thirty and forty-four. Interestingly, however, the respondents most likely to label housemates as family—even though the figure still is quite low—were adults sixty-five years of age and older.[8]

This pattern undermines the idea that aging is invariably related to greater conservatism and resistance to new ideas. Instead, there appears to be rather convincing evidence of an age effect that we refer to as the "Golden Girls" effect.[9] Perhaps the living arrangements of today's elderly, more and more of whom share living facilities—and correspondingly fewer of whom grow older near their extended "traditional" family of children and grandchildren—shaped how our elderly sample responded to this question. Cohort explanations are less persuasive: it makes little sense to assume that older respondents—especially those age sixty-five and older—were reared during a time when this type of arrangement was more prevalent or socially acceptable than it is for any of the younger cohorts.[10] Instead, it appears that some individuals adjust their views to fit their different life circumstances as they age. Being faced with the plausibility and even desirability of living in such an environment may render traditionally defined family ties less important.

At the same time—and more importantly—we believe that evidence from our data alternatively offers some support for a cohort account for the greater acceptance of various family forms among our younger respondents. We identify this apparent cohort effect by looking at the predicted probabilities for more differentiated age categories than those studied earlier. Figure 4.4 displays these patterns. We see that individuals between the ages of forty-five and fifty-four were significantly more open in their definitions of family than their counterparts in both of the two age cohorts closest to them—those who were younger (between thirty-five and forty-four) and those who were older (between fifty-five and sixty-four). In other words, this age group deviates from the otherwise consistent pattern that older Americans subscribe to more restrictive definitions of family. This age group falls squarely in the middle of the baby boom generation.[11] This pattern comports with scholarship indicating that baby boomers are more tolerant than their closest age cohorts when it comes to issues concerning race, gender, and family issues (Alwin, McCammon, and Hofer 2004; Firebaugh and Davis 1988; Mason and Lu 1988; Scott 1998, 2000). Coming of age during an era of remarkable political and social change, baby boomers were exposed to vivid public debates about civil rights (especially regarding gender and race), perhaps more so than other cohorts.[12] It therefore makes sense that those in the baby boom cohort tend to take a more liberal view than do the adjacent generations, although their views still are not as open-minded as those of their much younger counterparts.

Figure 4.4   The Baby Boom Exception: Family Definitions, by Detailed Age and Cohort Categories

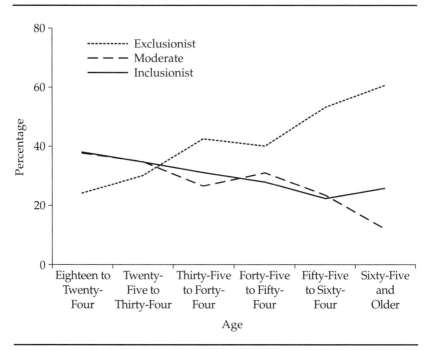

Source: Constructing the Family Survey (Powell 2003, 2006).

The baby boom exception suggests that cohort effects figure into definitions of family. Not unlike the baby boom generation, today's youth and young adults are coming of age, or have already come of age, during a period of greater openness about same-sex partnerships and other less traditional relationships than ever before—indeed, many have been reared in something other than the "standard" mother-father-children household. At the private level, their gay and lesbian relatives and friends apparently are more candid about their relationships, as we discuss later in this chapter. At the public level, the media representation of same-sex individuals and couples has reached an unprecedented level of visibility. Although we may have a long way yet to go, the sheer fact that the topic of homosexuality is no longer as much of a taboo in conversations in both the private and public spheres, as it used to be, speaks to how far we have come. As a result, younger cohorts see smaller distinctions between gay and straight and, in turn, are more likely to espouse an expansive definition of families than are their older peers.

The stark difference in the views of younger and older adults was perhaps most clearly understood by our respondents, especially our older ones, as demonstrated from their open-ended responses to questions about the meaning of family and same-sex couples. Many older Americans, like this woman in her eighties, drew a line between themselves and the younger generation: "I think that living arrangements is that you are to be married and you are a family. Now I know that the young people don't think this. But, well, that's my opinion." Others implicitly or explicitly frame the difference as one due to cohort, as seen in the following responses by a woman and a man in their late fifties:

> Well, if they have children and they're married. I mean, that's a family. But as far as two men or two women living together, a lotta people said that's a family. But then, I'm from the *old age generation*, you know. So I don't really believe in that stuff.

> I guess I'm from the *old school*. I think that a couple should be married and that the children should be theirs. That's what I think constitutes as a family . . . either their own children or adopted children.

In fact, one of the most common phrases we heard from older, exclusionist interviewees was "old-fashioned"—for example, "I guess I'm just old-fashioned," "It's an old-fashioned reason," "I realize this is year 2000 [*sic*], but I'm an old-fashioned woman and they need to be legally married." These responses signify that older Americans are mindful of the generational schism between their views and those espoused by younger Americans and are thus aware of the ongoing evolution—or revolution—in definitions of family.[13]

Overall, our findings reveal a wide-open split between older and younger Americans' definitions of family. Nevertheless, we are reluctant to proclaim unequivocally that the differences are fully cohort differences. Some youths may alter their views as they move through the different stages of life. Still, the overwhelmingly more positive reaction by younger adults to same-sex and other nontraditional relationships is so great that it is difficult to imagine that this rift will entirely vanish as the younger generation ages. Given the age trends outlined here, the unease expressed by social conservatives about what the future may hold and, correspondingly, the optimism shared by gay advocates who believe that time is on their side are not unfounded.[14]

Educational Differences

While age and cohort are crucial factors in understanding the distinctions that Americans make between families and nonfamilies, other individual characteristics are influential as well. Among the most important of these factors is education. Social scientists have long debated whether—and if so, how—education serves a liberalizing function (Converse 1964; Gilens 1995; Jackman and Muha 1985; Kane 1995). Some scholars assert that with increasing education, individuals are exposed to new networks and new ideas and, in turn, enhance their capacity for abstract reasoning, become less likely to accept authoritarianism, and develop greater open-mindedness (for discussions that summarize this line of reasoning, see Bobo and Licari 1989; Converse 1964; Schuman, Bobo, and Krysan 1992). The political scientist Paul Sniderman and the survey analyst Tom Piazza (1993) go so far as to contend that education is the "single-most important weapon" in the battle against prejudice, most notably racial intolerance.

Correspondingly, education typically is associated with a tendency to espouse, and presumably internalize, more liberal views, especially those regarding gender. Higher education presumably translates into a greater propensity to identify as a feminist, support gender equality, reject gender myths and stereotypes, and, most importantly, take a more liberal stance regarding homosexuality (for illustrations of the liberalizing role that education reportedly plays in attitudes toward gender and sexuality, see Andersen and Fetner 2008; Cassidy and Warren 1996; Davis and Robinson 1991; Herek and Capitanio 1996; McCabe 2005). Others, however, are less convinced and believe that education effects are overstated or artifactual: adults with higher levels of education, they argue, more deftly mask their less tolerant views than do their less educated counterparts. To some critics, then, education may reproduce rather than challenge inequality, albeit in a more subtle form (for illustrations of these positions, see Feagin, Vera, and Imani 1996; Jackman 1981; Jackman and Muha 1985; Kane 1995; Kane and Kyyro 2001).

Our analysis is compatible with the claims that education is a liberalizing force. As seen in the predicted probabilities shown in figure 4.5, over half of Americans with a high school degree or less subscribe to an exclusionist definition of family. In this educational category, exclusionists (52.0 percent) more than double the number of inclusionists (21.8 percent). In contrast, a more expansive—although not wholly expansive—vision of family is adopted by Americans with a college degree or greater, nearly two-thirds of whom assume a moderate (32.9 percent) or inclusionist (32.0 percent) stance.[15]

Figure 4.5   Family Definitions, by Education

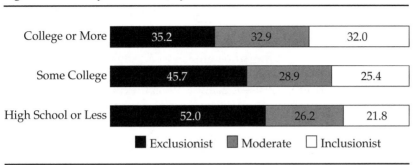

Source: Constructing the Family Survey (Powell 2003, 2006).

We cannot disentangle the underlying causal mechanisms that lead those with greater education to be more inclusive when deciding on the boundaries of family arrangements. One possibility is that Americans with lower levels of education are more likely to interpret the Bible literally—a position that, as described later in this chapter, is implicated in more exclusionist approaches to family.[16] In addition, the open-ended responses suggest that those with higher levels of education have thought more about the issue of same-sex and cohabiting couples than have their contemporaries. They also suggest that college-educated Americans offer more elaborate and lengthier arguments in explaining their definitions of family. Educational differences in the nature of the responses were most notable among inclusionists: those with a college education seemed to borrow from a larger tool kit of frames than those with less education. In explaining her views on what counts as a family, a thirty-two-year-old woman with a college degree offered a nuanced response:

A relationship. I don't think different sexes, living together or not, or opposite sexes or same sexes living together doesn't diminish the fact that people establish relationships with other people. And sometimes maybe you're not, it's not the traditional family. But it doesn't make it any less of a family . . . I mean, there are traditional families that have poor relationships, and they don't even cope or communicate like a family should. And then there are other families where maybe it's a same-sex sex relationship. Where they have a loving relationship, where they're helping each other out. But because it's not made up of the traditional "man, woman, boy, child," it has less value, and I don't think that's true. People can be just as supportive and loving in a same-sex relationship as in a heterosexual one. I think it depends on the nature of the relationship and not so the sex of each individual in the household.[17]

Interestingly, however, the conclusion that higher levels of education produce a more detailed approach to family definitions applies mostly to inclusionists and to a lesser degree to moderates. The pattern does not extend to exclusionists. Educational level affects neither the length nor the complexity of exclusionists' responses. These distinctions are admittedly impressionistic. Less subject to debate, however, are the strong educational differences in definitions of family. The higher Americans' level of education, the greater their acceptance of same-sex and cohabiting heterosexual couples. With each successive generation, the proportion of highly educated citizens has risen, and most scholars do not anticipate any major reversal of this pattern in the foreseeable future. With anticipated increases in the educational level in the United States, the boundaries surrounding what is and what is not a family should become more porous.[18]

Racial Differences

Race is the fourth sociodemographic characteristic that we explore. Racial differences continue to be so pervasive that we fully anticipated substantial racial variation in definitions of family. Consistent differences did not, however, materialize. As seen in appendix 4.A, in only one model are African Americans significantly less likely than whites to be inclusionist (versus exclusionist); however, because this pattern is not consistently sustained in other models, we hesitate to make any firm conclusions here. Interestingly, in supplementary analyses, there is stronger evidence that black respondents are more likely than white respondents to see cohabiting heterosexual couples without children as family, but less likely to grant the same family status to same-sex couples without children.

It is possible that competing forces neutralize racial cleavages. On the one hand, the reported greater reliance on "fictive kin" among the African American community, the higher rates of single parenthood, and the shared experience of prejudice and discrimination should make African Americans responsive to a more all-encompassing conceptualization of family.[19] In fact, moderates and inclusionists often refer to extended or "fictive kin" and the importance of caring. Typical of these responses are the comments of an older black woman who emphasized the role of caring in less traditional living arrangements:

Well, as a member of a family that has a habit of taking in others into our family situations and traditions when we celebrate. And friendships, we take in people who are alone or whose families have died or whose families are a long way away and people who we really just celebrate our life and live our life with and raise our kids with who aren't family genetically but who are family. We call, the kids call us aunt and uncle and that kind of thing. Family is what you call it in your own house—in our family.

A young black man discussed the issue of deference and respect in explaining the inclusion of same-sex couples in the definition of family:

Basically children, 'cause you know, children. You know, they get that idea that that's my uncle even though that's maybe two males. But that's my daddy's friend, so it's my uncle, you know? Everybody, like, give, like that's Uncle Charlie. A lot of people don't have, that's not really an uncle but, due respect as an elder, you pronounce him as uncle.

On the other hand, African Americans in our sample typically had lower levels of education and, more importantly, higher levels of religiosity and religious orthodoxy than other respondents and thus were predisposed to uneasiness about or hostility to certain nontraditional living arrangements, especially same-sex ones. In fact, we noticed that African American exclusionists were more likely than white exclusionists to refer to religious ideology and text in justifying their definitions of family. Because these competing factors (for example, embracing the notion of extended kin versus religious orthodoxy) have divergent effects, they may cancel out each other's expected impact.[20] With the caveat that these weak results also could be a function of the small size of the African American sample, our provisional conclusion is that definitions of family—more accurately, whether one is an exclusionist, moderate, or inclusionist—may represent one of the rare areas where race matters less than expected.[21]

These differences may seem puzzling or unsatisfying, especially given the controversial claims over racial differences in voting in recent initiatives regarding same-sex marriage. For example, some pundits assert that the greater resistance to same-sex marriage among black voters, as compared to white voters, was instrumental in the passage in California of Proposition 8—the anti-same-sex marriage initiative. This assertion has been challenged by some scholars. Still, in our interviews the same racial difference in views explicitly regarding same-sex marriage emerges. Black Americans are more likely than their white counterparts to be opposed to same-sex marriage, and this racial gap increased between 2003 and 2006. These racial differences cannot be explained by racial differences in sociodemographic factors such as education or age. Perhaps even more important, although we demonstrated in chapter 2 that family definitions are a powerful predictor of views regarding same-sex marriage, these racial differences are not attributable to whether the respondents are exclusionist, moderate, or inclusionist.[22] Instead, the key factor explaining the racial gap in these views is the racial difference in religious ideology.[23] Appeals to individual rights—a common tactic used by advocates of same-sex marriage—does not appear to effectively offset the influence that religious conservatism has among many African Americans.[24] Given the comments that African Americans made in our interviews, an alternative strategy that may prove more successful, however, requires more explicitly tying same-sex marriage to issues of caring and of fictive and extended kin—themes that resonate more broadly in the African American community.

Differences by Family Background and Marital Status

We also explore the impact of the family context experienced by our subjects when they were maturing, as well as their current family status. We find strong evidence that individuals who grew up in two-parent families provided significantly more exclusionist responses (44.8 percent) and fewer inclusionist responses (24.3 percent) than their counterparts who were reared by a single parent or grew up in a family of some other form (36.3 percent exclusionist, 35.4 percent inclusionist).[25] These patterns suggest that childhood exposure to living arrangements other than the traditional two-parent family prompts a greater acceptance of nontraditional family arrangements that extends into adulthood.

In addition, compared to those who were currently married or had formerly been married (separated, divorced, or widowed), single and cohabiting individuals were much less likely to hold exclusionist family definitions (36.5 percent versus 47.1 percent) and more likely to hold inclusionist ones (33.3 percent versus 23.0 percent). This pattern may be due mostly to selectivity. That is, people who are less inclined to marry also may be more disposed to broad conceptualizations of family. An equally if not more plausible explanation is that marriage limits whom people consider family members. Perhaps the experience of never having been married oneself makes it easier to believe that definitions of family—and the privileges and obligations given to families—should not necessarily be confined to married couples. Meanwhile, the greater reluctance of married Americans to hold an inclusive definition of family may reflect their group position or their self-interest in distinguishing and privileging the legally married from other statuses (for a discussion of the role of group position and self-interest in shaping heterosexist views, see Bernstein 2004; Bernstein, Kostelac, and Gaarder 2003).[26]

Urban-Rural and Regional Boundaries

The idea that location—or, in more recent parlance, place (Gieryn 2000)—matters is not new. Over a century ago, Émile Durkheim stunned the academic community when he introduced the influence of place—where people live and work—as a sui generis factor motivating how people think and act (Durkheim 1897/1977). Now the very idea that the spheres in which individuals interact with others affects many facets of social life is an important pillar of knowledge in sociology, geography, anthropology, and other social sciences (Gregory 1995; Low 1996).

For decades, social scientists have conveyed the message that there has long been substantial geographical variation in social attitudes in the United States. The variation is so sizable that it would seem as if there are vastly different worlds of public opinion that vary along urban and regional lines. Louis Wirth (1938) was among the first scholars to call attention to the urban-rural gap in life experiences and attitudes such as tolerance toward others from differing social, racial, and cultural backgrounds. He attributed urban dwellers' greater receptivity to people different from themselves to three key elements of urbanism: a larger population, a more dense population, and a more heterogeneous population. He argued that greater contact with a larger and more diverse population pushes urban dwellers toward greater acceptance of difference and more cosmopolitan viewpoints. In contrast, because they live in smaller, less dense, and more homogeneous geographical areas, individuals in rural areas are more sheltered and parochial, and they are rarely challenged to explicitly confront their feelings about diversity. Since Wirth's writings, other social scientists have amassed convincing evidence of the urban-rural divide on social tolerance—most notably with respect to race and gender (Carter and Borch 2005; Carter et al. 2005; Stouffer 1955; Tuch 1987).

Wirth's claims are easily applied to definitions of family and views regarding same-sex couples (for analysis of urban-rural and regional differences in overall attitudes toward homosexuality, see Loftus 2001). The urban-rural gap in the degree of inclusivity (and exclusivity) is wide. The plurality of rural dwellers are exclusionists (46.9 percent), with a much smaller percentage being moderates (28.6 percent) or inclusionists (24.5 percent). In contrast, those who live in urban areas are more evenly distributed among exclusionists (36.3 percent), moderates

(32.4 percent), and inclusionists (31.3 percent). But even these figures, which are based on predicted probabilities from both the 2003 and 2006 surveys, do not tell the full story. By 2006, inclusionists outnumbered exclusionists in urban areas, but the ratio of exclusionists to inclusionists among rural Americans remained almost two-to-one.[27]

Regional differences in definitions of family are even more marked. At least since the writings of the sociologist Howard Odum (Odum 1945; Odum and Moore 1938), social scientists have continued to chronicle—and attempted to explicate—regional differences in a variety of phenomena, most notably racial attitudes and social tolerance (Carter and Borch 2005; Schuman et al. 1997; Stouffer 1955). Some scholars point to the waning influence of region on certain dimensions of racial attitudes through the years (Tuch 1987; Firebaugh and Davis 1988), but still acknowledge distinct attitudinal differences—especially the differences between southern and nonsouthern states.

Even if regional differences in racial tolerance have declined, definitions of family vary remarkably by region.[28] As confirmed in the multivariate analyses (appendix 4.A), southerners show the greatest resistance to inclusive (and moderate) definitions of family, while northeasterners and westerners express the most receptivity to such a broad array of living arrangements.[29] These differences are due in large measure to regional differences in religious beliefs.[30] Midwesterners fall in between: they are more tolerant than southerners, but not as broad-minded as westerners or northeasterners. Of note, just as suburbanites showed the greatest move toward inclusivity between 2003 and 2006, so too did midwesterners. In fact, in 2003 they deviated only slightly from their southern neighbors, but by 2006 the distance between these two regional groups had increased greatly.

We did not ask specifically about the importance of place in our interviews, but regional differences—and to a lesser extent, urban-rural differences—also were apparent to our interviewees, as indicated by the following sampling of responses in which mention of their own geographical location or that of others is frequent and voluntary:

I think any situation where people are coexisting to make a household, that is such [a family]. I live too close to San Francisco to think any other way.

It goes against the laws of God and Man. Now I'll get in trouble with a lot of people who live in 'Frisco.

It's something I've thought a lot about because of my relationship as a teacher with gay students and with gay fellow teachers, and of course, being in California, where, as a Nebraskan once put it, "You live with the fruits and the nuts." Um, I said, yes, they're our sons and daughters.

You know these New Yorkers? You know they're too liberal! Are we too liberal for Indiana standards?

I think that's a problem in Ohio.

There are too many consequences from it [same-sex and heterosexual co-habitation]. It doesn't make them a family, for one thing, in my opinion. . . . I live in a rural area, and I really haven't been too much into things like that.

Although we did not ask how long the interviewees had lived in their current residence, a few brought up this issue. Some claimed that because they came from a different region (or state), their worldview was off-kilter from the predominant views in the place where they currently resided. A man who lived in California in the late 1960s remarked on the schism between his views and those of his neighbors:

I'm very liberal . . . I'm in a minority around where I live. Good God, I'm in southern Indiana!... I spent most of my life in California, so I apologize. So, if you're asking me about family, the family today is a mess. The values should be the same. I don't care if you're two gay people and you got to adopt a kid, you should know the difference between right and wrong. It doesn't matter who—what the hell is this marriage bullshit? I don't give a shit if you marry a telephone pole. That's your business, right?

Within the United States, then, place is important. Urban-rural and regional variation is very strong. It is so strong that it is simultaneously possible for residents from urban areas (and from northeastern and western states) to be genuinely baffled by the resistance to nontraditional family forms and for their rural (and midwestern and southern) counterparts to be equally frustrated by any attempts to loosen the definition of family. These differences suggest that the rate of acceptance of nontraditional living arrangements will be uneven. In fact, during the week that this section was completed, the governor of one state (New Hampshire) agreed to sign a same-sex marriage bill that was approved by the state legislature (Goodnough 2009), while another state legislature (Louisiana) enthusiastically passed a bill aimed at making it even more difficult for same-sex couples to adopt children (Barrow 2009).

Kin or Sin? The Role of Religion

Generational change, educational expansion, and the increased visibility of and contact with gays and lesbians (discussed later in this chapter) lend hope to advocates of more expansive family definitions about what the future may bring. Yet the force that must be reckoned with and that may counteract this apparent shift—or at least slow down its momentum—is religion. Religion has been diametrically portrayed as a source of liberation and a tool of oppression. The history of race relations in the United States, for example, is replete with accounts of religious activism both for and against civil liberties for African Americans and other racial and ethnic groups. In the area of gender relations, however, the general consensus is that religious orthodoxy almost always translates into more conservative views regarding gender and sexuality, at least among the major world religions (Britton 1990; Loftus 2001; McVeigh and Diaz 2009).

Accordingly, it is not surprising to find a strong link between religious views and the exclusivity of family definitions. Still, we remain stunned by the sheer magnitude of this relationship. Our interviews included an array of questions that highlight four dimensions of religion—religious affiliation, self-identified religiosity, religious attendance and participation, and views regarding biblical literalness. The individual and joint effects of these indicators are presented in appendix 4.C.

For illustrative purposes, we spotlight the fourth dimension: whether one views the Bible as fables ("The Bible is an ancient book of fables, legends, history, and moral precepts recorded by men"), inspired text ("The Bible is the inspired word of God but not everything in it should be taken literally, word for word"), or the literal word of God ("The Bible is the actual word of God and it is to be taken literally, word for word").[31] As seen in figure 4.6, among adults who believe in biblical inerrancy, nearly two-thirds (65.0 percent) share exclusionist definitions of family, over one-fifth (22.1 percent) are moderates, and a small number (12.9 percent) are inclusionists. Respondents who interpret the Bible as inspired text or a book of fables, by contrast, see at least some same-sex living arrangements as family. In fact, individuals who consider the Bible to be inspired text are evenly distributed across exclusionists (32.1 percent), moderates (33.9 percent), and inclusionists (34.1 percent). Belief that the Bible is a book of fables, on the other hand, clearly tilts individuals toward inclusiveness (56.5 percent). Interestingly, the percentage in this group who are exclusionists (12.8 percent) is virtually identical to the percentage of biblical literalists who are inclusionists.[32]

Figure 4.6   Family Definitions, by Views on the Bible

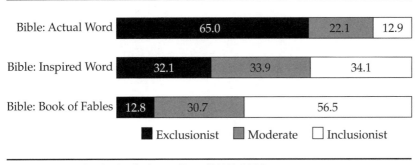

Bible: Actual Word   65.0   22.1   12.9

Bible: Inspired Word   32.1   33.9   34.1

Bible: Book of Fables   12.8   30.7   56.5

■ Exclusionist   ■ Moderate   □ Inclusionist

Source: Constructing the Family Survey (Powell 2003, 2006).

As noted in chapter 2, people commonly rely on religious themes in defending the boundaries they draw between families and nonfamilies. This frame, however, is used infrequently by moderates, and never by inclusionists. But for exclusionists, religion dictates an explicit set of guidelines that disqualify certain living arrangements—in particular, same-sex ones—as family. These are definitive rules, not to be broken; as one respondent declared: "That's against the rules. That's, that's in the Bible!"

Our respondents who relied on religious explanations were among the most steadfast opponents to enlarging the scope of family definitions and extending the rights and privileges of marriage to same-sex couples, frequently invoking "God's will" ("It's not in God's will for it. God created man for woman and woman for man"). Many of these respondents appeared to be so confident in their stance that they apparently felt no need to elaborate on their answers. For example, one man in his thirties responded in two words: "The Bible." Others thought the answer was so obvious that they simply asked the interviewers whether they had ever read the Bible. Others, however, gave more detailed responses; an elderly woman answered the question thus: "Definitely a family consists of a man and a woman, not two people of the same sex. A family is consecrated in marriage. Usually consists of children, but not necessarily because a couple may not be able to have children." She continued:

It usually consists of a marriage ceremony. I believe it's possible, but I just do not believe in same-sex marriages. That is not a family of either sex. They are trying to devirginize something that cannot be devirginized. It goes against nature. It goes against the law of God. Trying to say something's right and it's not. It goes against society, nature, and God. I cannot agree with it. I'm sorry, but I just cannot agree with it.

Still others saw blanket restrictions as a way to protect gays and lesbians—more specifically, to protect their souls from damnation. In one exchange, a black woman in her fifties forcefully argued:

Well, it's a damnation of their souls if you look at the scripture. And I'm just quoting from the scripture. That it is the same sexes, if you lying with those of the same mold, that is a damnation of your soul.

Ironically, a few of the most vociferous responses that invoked religious imagery (for example, Sodom and Gomorrah) were given by self-labeled nonreligious Americans who concomitantly believed that the Bible is a book of fables. We can only speculate on this seeming contradiction. We suspect, however, that these interviewees had a hard time articulating an alternative reason that was consistent with their exclusionist views and, as a result, searched their cultural tool kit and unreflectively selected a religious justification.

Others faced a different contradiction or struggle when they tried to juxtapose their religious ideology with other values and experiences. For example, we were struck by the comments by respondents who perceived a tension between their religious views and their commitment to equality (with comments such as "I am religious, but I want to be fair"). This tension may provide another opening for change in the views of even the most religiously orthodox. In addition, as we discuss in chapter 5, in certain circumstances the invocation of "God's will"— for example, as an explanation for sexual preference—can sometimes be a liberalizing force.

Social Context: Contact with Gays and Lesbians

Over fifty years ago, the psychologist Gordon Allport (1954) proposed the "contact hypothesis," which posits that, under appropriate conditions (such as equal status), intergroup prejudice can be eradicated—or at least reduced—with increased interaction between different groups. Most efforts to apply this hypothesis have focused on interracial and interethnic relationships.[33] Some scholars, such as the psychologist Gregory Herek (1998; Herek and Capitanio 1996), have successfully applied this hypothesis to better understand prejudice and violence against gay men and lesbians.

A reading of our interviews indicates that contact with gays and les-

Figure 4.7   Family Definitions, by Gay-Lesbian Social Networks

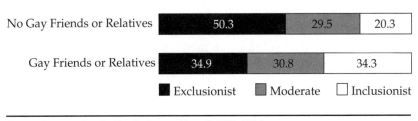

Source: Constructing the Family Survey (Powell 2003, 2006).

bians—especially among relatives and friends—is a potent path to inclusivity. It is so powerful that it can neutralize other less accommodating forces, as illustrated by the words of a self-described devout woman with lesbian friends who is torn in her definition of family:

> I don't know. Like, my faith conflicts with a lot of things simply because I live as far as if I went strictly by my faith. I don't think women together living as a couple constitute a family. But I have close friends that are women that are living together, and they're as much a family as I've ever seen. There's conflicting influences there.

In our interviews, we explicitly asked whether "anybody close to you, that is, a close friend or a relative, identifies themselves as gay or lesbian." Over two-fifths (42.4 percent) of our respondents in 2003 responded affirmatively. Although our question was closed-ended, several respondents offered unsolicited comments with their answers. A disconcerting number of these comments were along the lines of: "No. If I did, I would shoot him."[34]

As demonstrated in figure 4.7, which displays the predicted probabilities derived from the multivariate analyses of the 2003 and 2006 data, having a gay friend or relative is significantly associated with a greater openness to recognizing nonmarried living arrangements as family. Over three-fifths of Americans with gay friends or relatives fell into the inclusionist (34.3 percent) or moderate (30.8 percent) category. In contrast, approximately half (50.3 percent) of Americans who reported having no gay friends or relatives were exclusionists.[35]

It certainly is possible that contact is not the driving force behind inclusivity. Instead, it could be the other way around, at least regarding friends—that is, it could be that inclusivity facilitates friendships with gay and lesbians. A more serious concern is that the percentages regarding gay friendships and relatives are based on our respondents' knowledge of the sexuality of their friends and relatives. We strongly suspect that respondents in 2003 unknowingly may have underreported these figures. In 2006 we asked about gay friends and relatives and noticed a dramatic increase, to almost three-fifths (57.6 percent). Interestingly, the figure is an exact mirror image of the 2003 data, with 57.6 percent in 2003 saying that they had no gay friends and relatives. The increase between 2003 and 2006 is strong—so strong that the statistical significance of this difference cannot be explained away by any of the sociodemographic factors that we explored.[36]

We find it unlikely that all of a sudden people were making friends with gays and lesbians—or, even more implausibly, obtaining gay and lesbian relatives. Instead, we attribute this remarkable increase to the intensified dialogue about homosexuality that transpired between our 2003 and 2006 interviews—resulting from, as articulated earlier in this book, court cases such as *Goodridge v. Massachusetts Department of Public Health* and the heightened visibility of gay men and lesbians in the media (for example, the television show *Queer Eye for the Straight Guy*, which premiered days after the completion of our 2003 interviews). In other words, gays and lesbians may have responded to greater openness in the public arena by becoming more candid with friends and relatives. This also suggests that even bad publicity is not necessarily a bad thing. The virulent responses by social conservatives to "protect" marriage may well have persuaded gays and lesbians to out themselves to friends and relatives in order to counteract these attacks. Of course, this is just a conjecture. But what we do know is that there has been a notable spike in the percentage of Americans who now claim friendships or a familial relation with gay men and lesbians.[37]

Do gay friends matter more than gay family members? Do gay family members matter more than gay friends? Does knowing anyone who is gay matter? In our 2006 survey, we asked an additional set of questions to delineate between Americans with gay friends only, those with gay relatives only, and those with both gay friends and relatives. Of the interviewees who said that they had neither gay friends nor relatives, we also asked if they "personally know anyone who identifies as gay or lesbian." We see a roughly equal distribution across these five categories: 22.5 percent had both gay friends and gay relatives, 19.9 percent had gay friends but no gay relatives, 15.6 percent had gay relatives but no gay friends, 23.3 percent had neither gay friends nor gay relatives but who know someone who is gay, and 18.7 percent reportedly knew no one who is gay.

Although gay friends and gay relatives each appear to have a liberalizing effect, gay friends apparently are more influential. As shown in figure 4.8, nearly three-fourths of respondents with gay friends only

Figure 4.8   Family Definitions, by Gay-Lesbian Social Networks, 2006

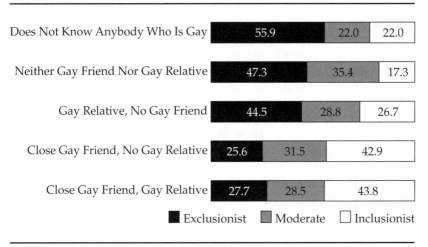

Source: *Constructing the Family Survey* (Powell 2006).

were inclusionist (42.9 percent) or moderate (31.5 percent), while a smaller proportion—over half—of those with gay relatives only were inclusionist (26.7 percent) or moderate (28.8 percent). In fact, having both gay friends and gay relatives offers little change over having gay friends only. These three groups share a more expansive definition of family than the remaining two groups. But even a comparison of the two latter groups highlights the potency of contact. Knowing *anyone* who is gay—even if the person is neither a close friend nor a relative— appears to weaken resistance to same-sex couples. Less than half of the respondents in this group (47.3 percent) were exclusionists, in contrast to those claiming to know no gay people, who were disproportionately located in the exclusionist category (55.9 percent).

Although we have concentrated here on actual contact with gay friends and relatives, scholars in communications studies argue that the contact hypothesis can and should be extended to the virtual realm (Schiappa, Gregg, and Hewes 2005). They contend that "parasocial interaction" with gay men and women (for example, *Queer Eye for the Straight Guy* and *Six Feet Under*) serves a parallel function to actual direct contact with them. Similarly, parasocial interaction with heterosexual people who have gay relatives or friends may prompt some Americans to rethink their exclusionist positions. An elderly woman, for example, discussed how hearing a public figure—in this case, Lynne Cheney, wife of the former vice president—talk about her daughter's sexuality and having a gay cousin of her own had made her more tentative in her views:

> Well, as I saw, I don't know that much about homosexuality, and I hate to make a statement because I don't know. I just, I just saw Lynne Cheney, and she sounded so open about it, and I have this cousin who's in it. But I just can't, I was married for fifty-nine years, loved my husband dearly, I just don't know.

These patterns indicate that Allport's insights from over a half-century ago on intergroup contact can be extrapolated today to understand views regarding same-sex relations and family definitions more broadly. They also suggest that self-disclosure about one's sexuality is on the upswing, as is the impact of such candor on conceptualizations of family.

Conclusion

Taken in their totality, the findings presented in this chapter add weight to predictions of greater openness toward same-sex couples and nontraditional living arrangements more broadly in the not-so-distant future. By examining the links between sociodemographic factors and definitions of family, we find social divisions about what counts as a family—differences between young and old, men and women, the more and the less educated, and the more and less religiously orthodox. Our results also imply that social context matters: increased contact with gays and lesbians is associated with greater receptivity to a broader definition of family. Other factors also have varying, less systematic, or weaker effects on the extent to which Americans are inclusive in whom they accept as family.

Although the effects of sociodemographic characteristics are important in their own right, it is what they foreshadow about how boundaries between families and nonfamilies will be drawn in the future that matters most. The patterns introduced in this chapter—patterns that generally dovetail with the extensive empirical literature on attitudes toward homosexuality—show that there are substantial differences in the United States regarding family definitions, but they also imply a trend toward more tolerance. Although the general patterns for Americans are intriguing and hint at change to come, looking specifically at several of the sociodemographic factors fine-tunes our understanding of how people define family now and how they will define it in the future.

Our results reveal a substantial divide between the "old" United

States and the "young" United States in their worldviews. These differences are linear—each subsequent older group expresses more conservative views—with the aforementioned and pointed exception of baby boomers. This generation is substantially more inclusive than would otherwise be expected for their age. This exception illustrates the importance of political generation—the baby boomers came of age during a period of contentious political and social change and intensified discussion regarding civil rights and gender equality. Their greater openness to different living arrangements suggests that aging itself does not necessarily dilute the powerful effects of cohort. A similar trend can be expected for the youngest generation. It is more than mere speculation to predict that today's young adults will continue the trend toward greater tolerance of different family configurations, even if they themselves become a little more conservative as they age. With the unavoidable generational change that will occur as our younger generations replace the older ones, the ratio of inclusionists and moderates to exclusionists should correspondingly rise. Of course, it is possible that a future cohort—or cohorts—may revert, because of their experiences in their youth or young adulthood, to a more conservative stance.[38] Still, the overall age patterns described in this chapter may be prescient in that they suggest a tendency toward greater acceptance of nontraditional families.

We make similar observations for education. Education clearly assumes an integral role in shaping perceptions of family. Our results can be interpreted as signifying that education fuels social change when it comes to family definitions. If, as projected, the percentage of Americans—especially younger ones—who attend and graduate from college continues to climb, then it is most likely that a climate of acceptance of less traditional living arrangements, such as gay and lesbian couples, will correspondingly rise.

In addition, exposure to nontraditional living arrangements is associated with greater acceptance of varying familial structures. For example, given the high and increasing number of children who live for at least some of their childhood with a single parent, we can expect heightened receptivity to a broadened definition of family in the future. Exposure to gays and lesbians in one's life also expands one's perceptions of what counts as family. Greater exposure should translate into social change. Certainly, there is no current sign that the presence of gays and lesbians in contemporary society and the extent to which they are open about their sexuality will be reversed or will diminish anytime soon. The proportion of people who are thus aware that they have gay and lesbian family members, friends, coworkers, and acquaintances is only likely to increase. Again, if the present shapes the future, this finding presages more tolerance of multiple family forms.

One lesson learned in this chapter is that gender is one of the most important factors in shaping views toward the family. Women show more latitude in their definitions of family than do men. To the extent that women gain leverage in the shaping of public opinion and gain policymaking power, we expect that the support for nontraditional families will grow. Given that there is more room for men to liberalize their views, however, there may be even greater potential for change among them. Exposure to liberalizing factors such as education or gay friends and relatives has as much impact on men as it does on women (who already are more inclusive), if not more. To the extent that future generations of men are more likely to have spent some of their formative years living in a single-parent household, to have attained higher levels of education, and to have increased their network ties with gay men and lesbians, gender differences may narrow as men catch up with women in their more inclusive definitions of family. In the short term, however, gay rights public campaigns would be well served by incorporating themes that especially resonate with men—for example, themes that emphasize instrumentality and especially "responsibility" in the home.

In predicting the direction of social change, social scientists must surely exercise caution. Unanticipated changes can render "guaranteed" predictions incorrect. For example, it was only a few decades ago when men were more likely than women to identify as and vote Democratic. In fact, the sociologist Amitai Etzioni (1968) once used this pattern to make the prediction that "sex control" (the ability to predetermine the sex of one's child) would lead to a greater number of sons relative to daughters and, ultimately, increased dominance by the Democratic Party. And just a few years ago, very few social scientists or pundits would have believed that a biracial man, let alone one with a unique name like Barack Hussein Obama, could be elected president. Thus, while we believe that there is sufficient reason to be optimistic about expanding conceptualizations of family in the future, we are not unequivocal in our predictions.

Another rationale for some guardedness about the future directions of people's views and public policy on the family is the potentially countervailing influence of religion. As elaborated in this chapter, many conservative Christians are staunchly opposed to expanding definitions of families to include nontraditional living arrangements, especially those involving gay and lesbian couples. Religiosity, attendance at religious services, and views regarding the literalness of the Bible powerfully shape what people count or do not count as a family. The unremitting and possibly even increased importance of religion in both people's private lives and the public sphere may provide a substantial counterpunch to the trend toward greater tolerance of nontraditional familial arrangements. Moreover, religious groups currently enjoy a disproportionate influence in American politics—at least given their relative proportion of the population overall—although some believe that this influence is weakening. Accordingly, it is difficult to predict whether an increasingly inclusive "average" position in the population will shape public policy, or whether fundamentalist notions of family will continue to prevail.

It therefore remains to be seen whether conservative religious beliefs based on a literal interpretation of the Bible will be stronger than the overall movement toward more inclusiveness, or whether the trend toward accepting nontraditional living arrangements as family will also reach everyone but the most fundamentalist of Christians. Religious messages do shift over time, as seen in the changing role that religion played in the civil rights movement. If conventional wisdom about biblical messages shifts even slightly (for example, an increased emphasis on "not casting the first stone," which could easily be interpreted as greater tolerance), then the most intransigent exclusionists may become less openly hostile to nontraditional family forms.

An analogous example of the push toward greater inclusiveness regarding same-sex couples is the case of interracial marriage. For much of American history, interracial marriage was not only vigilantly opposed but also illegal in many states. In 1967 the Supreme Court handed down the *Loving v. Virginia* decision that officially prohibited the antimiscegenation laws that still existed in sixteen—mostly southern—states. Still, it took more than three decades for South Carolina (in 1998) and Alabama (in 2000) to officially remove the (by then unenforceable) ban on interracial marriage from their state constitution. The legal changes in these last two states did not come easily and were met with stalwart resistance. In fact, approximately two-fifths of the voters in both states opposed the removal of the ban. Recent surveys (Davis and Smith 2009), however, indicate that support for antimiscegenation laws are at an all-time low (less than 10 percent).[39]

Public figures who oppose same-sex marriage—ironically, some of them African American—have warned against equating interracial relationships with same-sex ones. They argue that any comparison between same-sex and interracial relationships is deceptive. Yet there is a striking similarity between past views regarding interracial couples and current opinions regarding same-sex couples. For example, many of the factors outlined in this chapter that are related to greater acceptance of same-sex couples are precisely the same factors once tied to

Figure 4.9   Attitudes on Interracial Marriage (1972) and Family Definitions (2003, 2006): Effects of Age-Cohort and Education

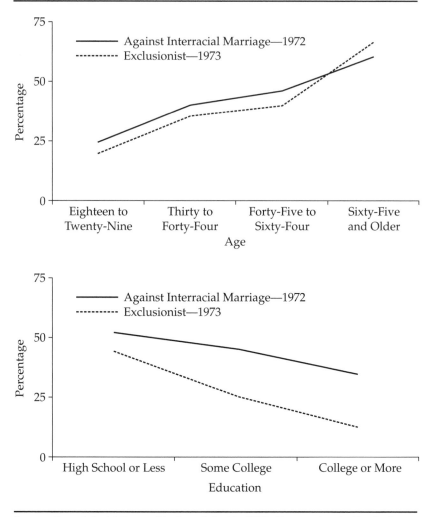

Sources: General Social Survey (Davis and Smith 1972); *Constructing the Family Survey* (Powell 2003, 2006).

greater acceptance of interracial couples. As a simple illustration, we analyzed responses to the question "Do you think there should be laws against marriages between (Negroes/Blacks/African Americans) and whites?" in the inaugural year (1972) of the General Social Survey. By this time, support for antimiscegenation laws was waning, but still not trivial: over one-third (36.8 percent) of those surveyed indicated that they favored these bans. We also explored the influence of various sociodemographic factors on support of these laws. The effect of two of these items—age and education—are displayed in figure 4.9. In this figure, we also juxtapose the effects of age and education on exclusionist views on family—based on the analysis described earlier in this book. One cannot help but notice the uncanny similarity in the patterns: greater resistance to both interracial and gay relations among older and less-educated adults and greater openness among younger and more highly educated adults. We should add that adherence to biblical literalness and living in rural areas and in the South not only are currently linked to an exclusionist family stance but also were associated with resistance to interracial marriage.[40] Even the most recent General Social Survey data on views toward interracial marriage (from 2002) show that the positive effect of education on tolerance of interracial marriage continues, as does the negative effect of age, adherence to biblical literalness, and living in a rural area or in the South.

Despite denials by some of the parallels in reactions to interracial and same-sex unions, it is worth noting that the original justifications for renouncing interracial marriage are very similar to—in some cases, virtually identical with—the objections currently raised against same-sex marriages and against same-sex relations more broadly. Historical arguments against interracial marriage, for example, warned that it would harm children, create social disintegration, violate core religious principles, and produce social discomfort for people who just were not ready for such a radical redefinition of family. These arguments echo those described in chapter 3. Some Americans explicitly make the connection between interracial and same-sex couples.[41] In explaining her resistance to same-sex couples, an elderly woman, for example, discussed the similarities in the problems putatively faced by children from interracial and same-sex couples:

> I don't know that the children should be in that kind of environment. Same thing with black and white. If you want to marry outside their race, that's one thing. But to bring children in and they're all confused, that's another thing. And I've known a few, and their children have had a very, very rough time with it.

Perhaps unwittingly, some comments by our interviewees illustrated the conflation in views regarding interracial and same-sex couples. In describing her definition of a family, a middle-aged southern woman offered an unexpected spin on the meaning of "mixed marriages":

To me it has to be a woman and a man. What I want to say—how to put it to you—is *I don't believe in the mixed marriages, the two women living together as one, you know, a married couple.* I don't believe in none of that, so you take it however you want to take it. I don't believe in that lesbian and gay stuff at all. I'm fifty-two years old, and I just don't believe in it.

To this respondent, then, a marriage between two women (or presumably two men) is the equivalent of a mixed marriage, the term often used to describe an interracial married couple. In another interview, a young southern man, when asked about same-sex marriage, incongruously explained his opposition to same-sex marriage: "I'm opposed to people from different races marrying each other."

Perhaps these were just verbal slips. Or perhaps these statements, along with similar comments, inadvertently reveal the propriety of revisiting the historical record on views toward interracial marriage and considering its implications for same-sex marriage in the future.

= Chapter 5 =

Accounting for Sexuality: God, Genes, and Gays

with Danielle Fettes

U P UNTIL this point we have identified ways in which Americans define family—and in particular, the extent to which same-sex couples are counted in or counted out of these definitions—and have articulated how such definitions are shaped by location in the social structure, among these factors being gender, age, and education.[1] But the boundaries that Americans make between families and nonfamilies tell us even more. As described in the previous chapter, a large segment of the American population is equivocal about or opposed to the inclusion of same-sex couples in the definition of family. This ambivalence or resistance corresponds to a heteronormative vision of family that privileges legal marriage, parenthood, and heterosexuality. The concept of heteronormativity, however, goes beyond the disapproval, discomfort, or antipathy that may be evoked by same-sex relations. It also speaks to other attitudes regarding how families operate, as well as to even broader ideologies regarding gender and sexuality. In the next three chapters, we examine how definitions of family are intertwined with these attitudes and ideologies. We discuss Americans' views on gender, as indicated by their opinions about the unique or overlapping roles of fathers and of mothers in children's lives (chapter 6), and their opinions on the importance of women sharing the same name as their husband (chapter 7). In this chapter, we explore how family definitions tie into beliefs regarding sexuality—more specifically, the genesis of sexual preference.

In our interviews, we listed several traits or behaviors (for example, intelligence, personality, weight, aggressive behavior, mental health, alcohol use, drug use, and sexual preference) and asked Americans whether they believed that these were due mostly to genetic factors, parenting, peer influence, outside environment, or "God's will." Given our interest in family definitions and same-sex relationships, we focus primarily on adults' attributions of sexual preference, although we also briefly touch on their etiological accounts of intelligence and weight. Our mission here is surely not to solve the ongoing and fierce dispute often described as the "nature-versus-nurture" debate, but rather to see whether the views held by the general public about the origins of behavior and traits—especially sexual preference—resemble scientific thinking on this topic and, more importantly, whether these views are implicated in the types of living arrangements they include in their definitions of family. Thus, one of our goals is to identify the extent to which individuals subscribe to particular explanations of sexual preference, as well as the sociodemographic correlates of these views.

More fundamentally, however, we explore how these beliefs—especially those regarding sexual preference—figure into whether people have a more expansive or more restrictive definition of family. We consider whether knowing someone's etiological explanations of human characteristics and behavior affords us greater analytical leverage in understanding, or even predicting, his or her views on what constitutes a family. In exploring these patterns, a final goal of this chapter is to persuade sociologists and other social and behavioral scientists to reconsider some of their own assumptions—in particular, the sociological wisdom regarding the presumed conservative nature of genetic attributions and the meaning of religious frames.

Nature, Nurture, Science, Omniscience

Although it has been described as "simplistic," "old-fashioned," "tired," "old," and "reductionist," the nature-nurture debate thrives. Most college students who take introductory sociology, anthropology, or psychology classes are taught about the putative nature-nurture divide, which would have us consider whether human traits and behaviors (such as intelligence and mental health) can best be understood in the context of biological-genetic or social-environmental inputs. This debate is not confined, however, to classrooms: it signifies the larger chasm separating scholars who privilege social explanations and their counterparts who favor biological ones for a broad array of topics, including child development, poverty, gender differences, and racial inequality.

Such partisanship should come as no surprise given the great implications of determining which factors matter the most. Social scientists who advocate wholly environmental accounts run the risk of criticism from the nature faction for being naive, biophobic, ignorant of scientific advances, overly politicized, and unremittingly insular in their views (Ellis 1996; Lopreato and Crippen 1999; Pinker 2002; Udry 1995). Conversely, advocates of primarily biological or evolutionary (nature) explanations of human behavior often are accused of purposefully or inadvertently advancing an agenda that dismisses, in particular, class, racial, and gender inequality as immutable. They also are portrayed as oblivious to or unconcerned about how scientific practice itself is not free from ideological assumptions, which undercuts the legitimacy of scientific claims regarding objectivity.[2] In turn, they risk being labeled as racist, sexist, or homophobic by their critics. As an illustration, approximately a decade ago, the contention by sociologist Richard Udry (2000) that there are "biological limits of gender construction" and "reconstruction" elicited much criticism from other social scientists who challenged not only his claims but also the appropriateness of the inclusion of his written work on this topic in the *American Sociological Review*. In one critique, the sociologist Barbara Risman (2001) saw the publication of Udry's work and other scholarship in this vein as evidence that the seeming value-neutrality of the academic review process was potentially enabling "weak science" that "is and always has been used to justify the subordination of women and of people of color" (610).

Especially in the past decade there has been a growing, albeit still quite small, movement in sociology and other social sciences toward a more integrative view of the interplay of nature and nurture. In his presidential address to the American Sociological Association in 2001, for example, Douglas Massey (2002) encouraged social scientists to be more receptive to the interconnections between neurological structure, evolutionary changes, emotions, and social behavior. Rather than staking out obdurately held stances, some scholars promote the positions that the nature-nurture debate represents a false dichotomy and that both the social sciences and the natural sciences can profit from efforts to better understand the conditions under which social and biological factors interact (Bearman 2008; Freese 2008; Freese, Li, and Wade 2003).[3] Such efforts have been most prominent in the areas of physical and mental health, where social scientists and geneticists have been increasingly successful in finding common ground to explore the implications of gene-environment interactions (Martin 2008; Schnittker 2008). These efforts have become more visible, as indicated, for example, by the publication of special issues on "Exploring Genetics and Social Structure," "Society and Genetics," and "The Linking of Sociology and Biology" in three major sociological journals (*American Journal of Sociology, Sociological Methods and Research*, and *Social Forces*, respectively).

Despite the influx of social-scientific analyses that underscore the reciprocal relationship between nature and nurture, many—arguably most—sociologists view these developments with caution, disdain, or even horror. Four years after Douglas Massey implored sociologists to be more amenable to nature-based arguments, Troy Duster (2006), in his presidential address to the American Sociological Association, cautioned about the challenges and dangers of such open-mindedness. Especially in the areas of intelligence, race, gender, and sexuality, many scholars continue to be suspicious of the consequences of this line of inquiry, as well as the motives and conservative political agenda of scholars who promote an integration of the natural and social sciences (Nelkin and Lindee 1995/2004; Omi and Winant 1994; Reardon 2004).[4]

Regardless of the relationship (or absence of a relationship) between academicians' views regarding the etiology of human behavior and their political and social attitudes, we have even less information about how the public views the nature-nurture debate and whether their attributions of the causes of behavior correspond to scientific argument and have further consequences for attitudes on social issues (for some exceptions, see Ernulf and Innala 1989; Hunt 1996; Jayaratne et al. 2006; Kluegel and Smith 1987; Schnittker, Freese, and Powell 2000; Wood and Bartkowski 2004).

Ironically, as "science"—or at least genetic and other physiological or evolutionary explanations that typically derive from the natural sciences—has gone under critique by some social scientists for its putatively conservative or even reactionary tone, it also has been censured by certain religious groups for its ostensible incompatibility with religious principles. Tension between religion and science appears to have accelerated, as evidenced, for example, in recent clashes over creationism—or intelligent design—and evolutionary theory. This disagreement now takes center stage in public discourse and prompts fundamental questions about the causes of human qualities and behavior. Predestination, a prominent doctrine in some Christian denominations, subscribes to the position that humans simply fulfill a God-given destiny—or "God's will." Although religions and denominations vary in the extent to which they embrace predestination, many interpret earthly events as under the control of the deity or some extra-individual or extra-environmental source. Biologists and other natural scientists, however, often reject the idea of preordained destiny and see behavior and human development as a result of an ongoing evolutionary process. In many ways, then, the science-religion debate is a mirror image of the nature-nurture debate. And as in the latter debate, we do not know whether public views correspond to those of the pundits, the religiously orthodox, or the scientists, nor do we know whether these views extend to attitudes regarding other social issues.

Entering the Fray: Intelligence and Sexuality

At their core, both debates—especially the nature-nurture debate—have been particularly heated when attached to the origins of intelligence and sexuality. Questions about whether parents influence children through their genetic or socialization legacies and whether factors such as peers or "God's will" are even more influential in children's development segue into contentious debate over the extent to which the behaviors of children—and ultimately adults—are alterable.

The controversy over the causes of intelligence is a case in point. In 1969 the educational psychologist Arthur Jensen (1969) angered many members of the academic community with his views that racial differences in intelligence were attributable to genetic variation. Twenty-five years later, the psychologist Richard Herrnstein and the political scientist Charles Murray (1994) rekindled this debate with *The Bell Curve: Intelligence and Class Structure in American Life*, which elicited a great deal of attention in the public media and a commensurate—but mostly unsympathetic—response from academicians. The evolutionary biologist Stephen Jay Gould (1996) expanded and reissued *The Mismeasure of Man*, a powerful rebuke of the intelligence testing industry and a critical rejoinder to Herrnstein and Murray. Meanwhile, a team of sociologists from the University of California at Berkeley reanalyzed the data used in *The Bell Curve* and concluded that Herrnstein and Murray had overestimated the influence of genetic factors on intelligence and in turn underestimated the role of family background (Fischer et al. 1997). One can easily see how critics might react so forcefully to biological and genetic explanations in light of their social policy implications. To the extent that intelligence—and class or racial differences in intelligence—are mostly due to genetic factors, then environmental interventions to compensate disadvantaged children could be seen as essentially futile. For critics, then, the focus on seemingly immutable genetic factors provides a dangerously legitimate means to justify discrimination and inequality.

Arguably, the contemporary debate over the causes of sexuality is even more controversial and impassioned. In 1991, *Science* published the results of the neuroscientist Simon LeVay's (1991) research that suggested core differences in a component of the brain structure of heterosexual and gay men. Subsequent publications by LeVay and other scientists also suggested that physiological and genetic factors distinguish heterosexuals from homosexuals (Byne et al. 2001; LeVay 1996; McFadden 2002; Rahman, Kumari, and Wilson 2003; Savic, Berglund, and Lindström 2005; Savic and Lindström 2008).

Reactions to this line of inquiry within the gay and scientific communities were and continue to be divided. The idea that sexuality is genetically based and therefore immutable could be seen as an effective rationale for the extension of rights and benefits to gay men and lesbians. But to some commentators this justification does not come without its costs (Epstein 2003, 2007). Some gay activists counter that genetic or essentialist accounts of homosexuality dangerously reify the idea of fixed identity and ignore the real possibility that sexuality is neither preset nor binary (Gamson 1995). Other critics contend that explanations that focus on differences between heterosexuals and homosexuals further ghettoize gay men and lesbians. Still others are worried that the possibility of a genetic cause, if identified, could lead to selective abortion of fetuses believed to carry the "gay gene." This possibility is the subject of Jonathan Tolins's play *Twilight of the Golds*, a fictional account of expectant parents discovering that their future son has a genetic predisposition to homosexuality. Even more controversial, however, have been statements by the psychologists Aaron Greenberg and J. Michael Bailey (2001) that parental decisions to genetically select for the heterosexuality of their children would be "morally acceptable."

Ironically, however, the critique of scientific explanations for sexuality comes mostly—although not entirely—from those who see presumably immutable genetic factors as providing a dangerously legitimate means to justify the *expansion* of rights to gay men and women. To some of these critics, many of whom are affiliated with the religious right, efforts to present sexuality as genetically based are part and parcel of the "homosexual agenda" (also described as the "gay agenda" or the "hidden gay agenda"). In *The Agenda: The Homosexual Plan to Change America*, the Reverend Louis Sheldon (2005), founder of the Traditional Values Coalition, warns of the dangerous strategies that the homosexuals are employing, with the assistance of the media, schools, and other forces, to "normalize" homosexuality. Echoing his comments, others also challenge this agenda.[5]

Perhaps most ominous, in the view of these critics, is the agenda's putative "ultimate goal" of "the enlistment of our children. Because they can't reproduce, homosexuals have to recruit" (McPhee 2005). Implicit in this quote by Indiana state senator John Waterman is the standpoint that homosexuality is contagious and easily spread through indoctrination. This indoctrination can take many forms—from television shows (for example, *Sponge Bob Square Pants*, *The Ellen DeGeneres Show*, and *Will and Grace*) to children's books (*Heather Has Two Mommies*), to music (Katy Perry's "I Kissed A Girl"), to school programs (including gay-straight clubs and anti-bully programs, which, in the view of some critics, valorize gay youths).

The proposition that sexuality is so easily alterable is central to anti-gay advocates' refutation of the parallelism between interracial and same-sex couples. To them, race is fixed, but sexuality is not. Correspondingly, this proposition is also fundamental to their opposition to the extension of marital and familial rights to gays and lesbians. In promoting a bill to prohibit gay foster parents, Texas state representative Robert Talton contended that "there's a risk that more of the children will go into homosexuality because it's a cultivated and learned behavior" (Donaldson 2005). Similarly, the Reverend Andy Hunt, in advocating for an Indiana bill to prohibit same-sex marriage, referred to same-sex relations as a "learned human perversion" (*Indianapolis Star* 2005).

According to this view, not only is homosexuality learned, but it also can be unlearned. A variety of "pro-family" and religious organizations therefore offer reparative therapies to facilitate the return of gays and lesbians to heterosexuality. Thus, the idea that sexuality is predetermined—owing to factors such as genetics that are beyond the control of the individual or his or her family and community—is antithetical to the core assumption of reparative therapies that homosexuality is a choice or a "lifestyle" that runs contrary to God's will or God's design. Some religious zealots go so far as to say that this "voluntary" lifestyle, along with increasing tolerance of this lifestyle, has prompted God's wrath, resulting in the deaths of American soldiers in the Iraq War, the devastation of Hurricane Katrina, and the terrorist attack of 9/11.[6] Admittedly, these views were voiced by the staunchest or most extreme opponents to same-sex rights. Still, we do not know whether these claims have gained any traction with the American public.

Public Views Regarding the Etiology of Sexual Preference

Do Americans subscribe to a more decisively biological and genetic (nature) argument or a more forceful environmental (nurture) argument when explaining sexuality? Or do they invoke a religious—or seemingly religious—explanation? And do these attributions map onto their definitions of family?

As noted earlier, in the Constructing the Family Survey, we asked respondents a series of questions that solicited their position on the causes of particular childhood characteristics. Specifically, we identified several traits and behaviors and asked if each is influenced mostly by "parenting practices, genes or genetic inheritance, the child's friends, the outside environment such as school, media, and so forth, or God's will." The traits and qualities covered in the 2003 survey included aggressive behavior, weight, mental health, alcohol abuse, drug use, intelligence, and, most importantly, sexual preference.[7] Because we recognize that Americans might believe that several of these causal factors are influential, we also asked, "Which is the second most important factor?"[8] We replicated some of these questions in 2006 (although we did not ask respondents to select the second most important factor). We report here on the combined responses from the 2003 and 2006 surveys. The patterns in 2003 and 2006 are similar, with a few striking exceptions that we discuss later in this chapter.

Overall Patterns

We begin by simply looking at the distribution of responses about the attribution of sexual preference.[9] As seen in figure 5.1, the plurality of Americans (39.0 percent) saw genes or genetic inheritance as the most important factor in determining sexual preference. As noted elsewhere in this chapter, "sexual preference" might imply more of a choice than the term "sexual orientation," which may connote immutability. So this figure, although already quite high, may underestimate the extent to which Americans invoke genetics in their explanation of sexuality. In other words, nearly two-fifths of our sample believed that sexual preference is rooted in genetic differences and therefore is fixed, not a choice.

How do the remaining three-fifths of Americans explain sexual preference? A sizable, but still notably smaller, percentage of respondents (21.0 percent) attributed sexual preference to parenting practices. Even fewer believed that sexual preference is due mostly to friends (6.4 percent) or to outside environment (14.8 percent). For the remainder of this chapter, we usually pool the responses of these two groups together and refer to the single category as "other". Perhaps unexpectedly, almost one-fifth of the sample (18.7 percent) believed that sexual preference is predicated primarily on "God's will." Interestingly, this percentage is greater with respect to sexuality than it is for any of the other qualities and traits asked about in the survey. That is, more people believe that "God's will" is implicated in sexuality than in intelligence, mental health, drug usage, alcohol usage, aggressive behavior, and personality.

At first glance, "God's will" might be seen as an inherently conservative explanation, or at least as antithetical to genetic explanations and closer to familial and environmental ones. But in certain ways this attribution may have more in common with genetic ones. Just like ge-

Figure 5.1   Perceived Cause of Sexual Preference

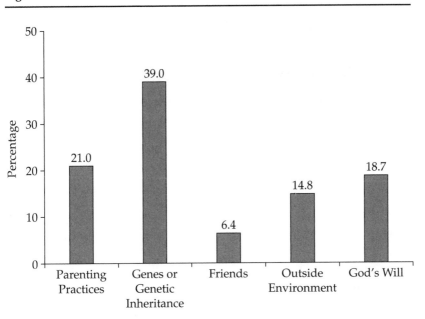

Source: *Constructing the Family Survey* (Powell 2003, 2006).

netic explanations, "God's will" minimizes environmental factors. By suggesting that sexual preference is supra-individual (that is, it comes from beyond the individual) and supra-environmental (it comes from beyond the environment), "God's will" implies that sexual preference is not avoidable or controllable and, consequently, not a choice. It is not clear whether "God's will" reflects a religious ideology or the attempts of both religious and nonreligious Americans to find an explanation that goes beyond biological and environmental ones—a point that we return to later in this chapter. But it is clear that if we add those who use genetic explanations to those who use "God's will," over half of respondents (57.7 percent) believed that the primary cause of sexual preference is beyond the control of individuals or the influence of environment.

Group Differences in Attributions of Sexual Preference

In chapter 4, we observed social cleavages—some pronounced, some less so—in the boundaries that people draw between families and non-families. We saw that women, the young, the more highly educated,

Figure 5.2   Perceived Cause of Sexual Preference, by Gender

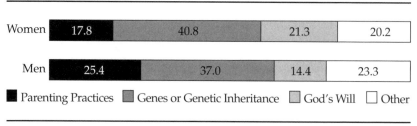

Source: Constructing the Family Survey (Powell 2003, 2006).

and the less religious are more inclusive in their definitions than men, the elderly, the less educated, and the more religious (especially those who advocate a literalist interpretation of the Bible). Meanwhile, sociologists who have explored individuals' etiological explanations of a wide array of phenomena, from mental illness to financial success to homelessness, have noted similar sociodemographic divisions.[10] Do these divisions extend to explanations of sexual preference?

Figure 5.2 displays women's and men's attributions of sexual preference. As in chapter 4, we illustrate statistically significant group differences by presenting predicted probabilities derived from multivariate models. These predictions illustrate the group differences that exist net of other central sociodemographic characteristics.[11] As can be seen in the figure, approximately one-quarter (25.4 percent) of men saw parenting as the primary cause of sexual preference, while one-fifth (17.8 percent) of women used this explanation. Interestingly, women were more than twice as likely to use genetic explanations as they were to use parenting ones (40.8 percent). While women were somewhat more likely to invoke "God's will" (21.3 percent) than parenting explanations, the reverse was true for men, 14.4 percent of whom invoked "God's will."

At first blush, it may seem counterintuitive that women were less likely than men to attribute sexual preference (as well as most other traits included in the survey) to parenting. After all, women by and large have shouldered the primary responsibility in child care. And the salience of the maternal role—both to the mother and via social expectations—may lend itself to greater scrutiny through the eyes of both the public and the mother. But women may be disinclined to use a parenting explanation and more disposed to use genetics or "God's will" precisely because of their typically more extensive involvement in the lives of their children. Unlike many if not most men, women may be positioned to appreciate the limits of parenting and, concurrently, the error

Figure 5.3   Perceived Cause of Sexual Preference, by Age-Cohort

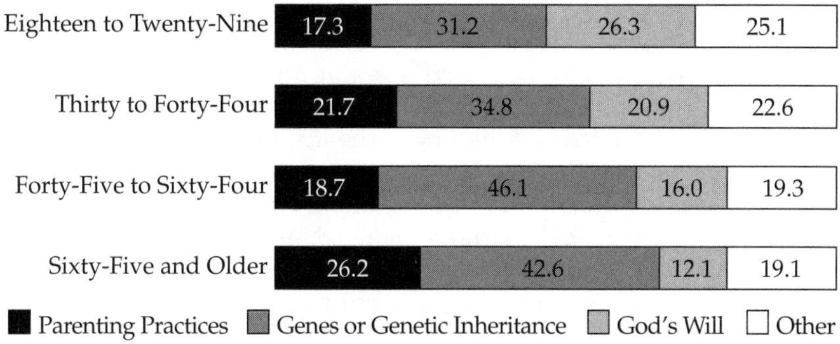

Eighteen to Twenty-Nine	17.3	31.2	26.3	25.1
Thirty to Forty-Four	21.7	34.8	20.9	22.6
Forty-Five to Sixty-Four	18.7	46.1	16.0	19.3
Sixty-Five and Older	26.2	42.6	12.1	19.1

■ Parenting Practices   ▨ Genes or Genetic Inheritance   ▢ God's Will   ☐ Other

Source: Constructing the Family Survey (Powell 2003, 2006).

of holding parents—especially mothers—accountable for their children's actions. From observing their own children and those of others,
they also may better appreciate the influence of other factors that are
inherent to the child (genes) or beyond rational explanation (God's
will). Given their life experiences, women may hesitate to place onto
parents the credit or, especially, the blame for a child's destiny, whether
it involves the child's sexuality, intelligence, or, in the following case of
a mother in her fifties, drug use.[12]

> (*nervous laugh*) You've got me there. I've got one son who's a druggie.
> And it's got *nothing* to do with parenting!

Differences by age are even more surprising. These patterns appear
in figure 5.3. There were distinct and significant differences in the reasons offered by adults from different age cohorts for the causes of sexual preference. As we anticipated, parenting explanations were most
likely to be offered by the elderly (26.2 percent among adults at least
sixty-five years old) and least likely to be given by the young (17.3 percent among adults age eighteen to twenty-nine).[13] Perhaps unexpectedly, adults between the ages of forty-five and sixty-four were the most
likely to endorse genetic explanations (46.1 percent), while their
younger counterparts under the age of thirty were the least likely (31.2
percent).[14]

To us, however, the most unforeseen age differences emerged in the
incorporation of "God's will." Younger adults were more likely than
any other age group to link sexual preference to "God's will." It is well

documented that age is positively associated with religiosity.[15] But here age was negatively—and strongly—associated with belief in "God's will." Endorsement of this explanation steadily decreased with age: 26.3 percent for adults under the age of thirty, 20.9 percent for adults between thirty and forty-four, 16.0 percent for adults between forty-five and sixty-four, and only 12.1 percent for those age sixty-five or older. It is striking that adults under the age of thirty constitute the only group that selected "God's will" more frequently than parenting practices, while the elderly were more than twice as likely to advocate parenting explanations than they were to choose "God's will."

At first, it might seem difficult to reconcile young adults' greater emphasis on "God's will." Some observers might be tempted to see this as evidence of a religious revival—or at least greater spiritualism—among the young. But younger adults in our interviews did not describe themselves as religious more frequently than did older adults. To the contrary, young adults were less likely than their older counterparts to describe themselves as very, or even moderately, religious. A more plausible explanation for this seeming anomaly is that for some respondents in our interviews—especially the youngest ones—the meaning of "God's will" may have had little to do with religion or, for that matter, God. As a young man in his twenties volunteered:

> Are these my only choices? I guess I choose God, God's will. It's not that I'm religious. I'm not even sure that I believe in God. I believe that other forces determine it [sexual preference], forces that have nothing to do with parents or friends or genes.

As suggested by this quote, "God's will" can be interpreted as a potential source of randomness in the universe. The respondent expressed an agnostic view about religion, but ironically, his use of "God's will" to explain what cannot be explained otherwise fits precisely what often has been seen as one of the primary—and most comforting—functions of religion.

Regardless of the interpretation of "God's will," the patterns demonstrate that younger adults were more likely to attribute sexual preference to an external factor, to something beyond the individual's control. Still, their reluctance—at least compared to the older groups—to use the external factor of genetic explanations may be puzzling. It could suggest an interesting type of postmodern faith in something intangible. Or it could signify a belief that sexual preference is beyond the control of the individual or environment but is still fluid over the life course, as determined by some outside force.[16] Alternatively, as science is increasingly critiqued by media pundits and scholars—from

Figure 5.4   Perceived Cause of Sexual Preference, by Education

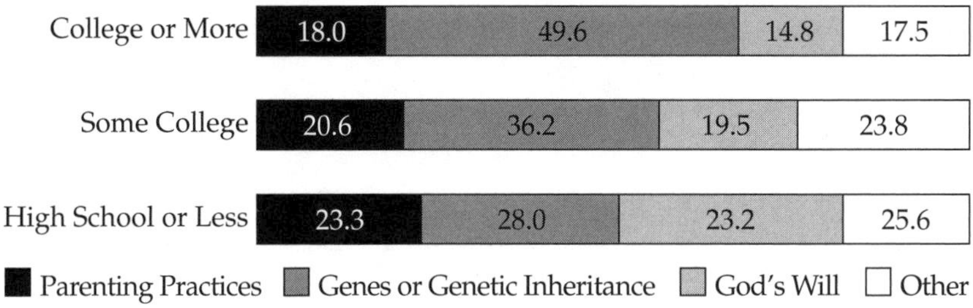

College or More	18.0	49.6	14.8	17.5
Some College	20.6	36.2	19.5	23.8
High School or Less	23.3	28.0	23.2	25.6

■ Parenting Practices   ■ Genes or Genetic Inheritance   ■ God's Will   □ Other

Source: Constructing the Family Survey (Powell 2003, 2006).

both the left and the right—it may not be surprising that younger people are less likely to utilize genetic explanations. At the same time, however, they are also unlikely to endorse parenting explanations. For this group, the debate is not about nature (genes) versus nurture (parents). Instead, their answer is neither nature nor nurture.

Like age differences, educational differences are very strong. But unlike age differences, educational differences are more predictable. Figure 5.4 illustrates the marked variance in attributions of causes for sexual preference for individuals at various educational levels. Almost one half (49.6 percent) of adults with at least a college degree believed that genes or genetic inheritance is the primary cause of sexual preference. This group was over twice as likely to emphasize genes as it was to draw on parenting explanations (18.0 percent). In contrast, the responses of adults with a high school diploma or less were spread more evenly across the categories. In other words, we see that, with increasing education, there is a slight decrease in the number of adults who attribute the roots of sexuality to parenting and "God's will," but a substantial increase in the number who trace sexual preference to genetics.

In chapter 4, we noted that racial differences in definitions of family were mixed or weak. In contrast, as seen in figure 5.5, black and white respondents offered very different accounts of the causes of sexual preference. The plurality of white Americans (42.5 percent) endorsed a genetic explanation. In fact, they were approximately twice as likely as African Americans (21.7 percent) to see genes as the source of sexual preference. In fact, "genes" was the least likely response for African Americans.[17] Interestingly, this black-white cleavage in responses parallels the young-old schism. Similar to younger respondents, black respondents also were more likely to select "God's will" as the basis of sexual preference.

Figure 5.5   Perceived Cause of Sexual Preference, by Race

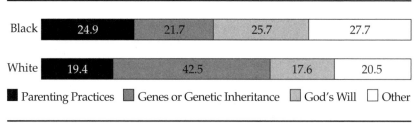

| Black | 24.9 | 21.7 | 25.7 | 27.7 |
| White | 19.4 | 42.5 | 17.6 | 20.5 |

■ Parenting Practices   ▦ Genes or Genetic Inheritance   ▨ God's Will   ☐ Other

Source: Constructing the Family Survey (Powell 2003, 2006).

African Americans' disinclination to use genetic explanations may seem anomalous at first. But we suspect that they are more skeptical of genetic accounts because of the historical usage of such an explanation to pathologize blacks and to justify racial inequality. Hereditarian positions historically have been used to explicate racial differences in intelligence, morality, and criminality. Blacks' generalized resistance to these explanations and receptiveness to alternative ones, such as "God's will," make sense—even when such explanations are used to account for qualities that are not necessarily racialized. For example, in examining public explanations for mental illness, the sociologists Jason Schnittker and Jeremy Freese—along with one of the authors of this book, Brian Powell (2000)—found that African Americans were more opposed than their white counterparts to genetic accounts. They also detected some limited evidence of African Americans' endorsement of "God's will" explanations.

Religious Views and Attributions of Sexual Preference

Returning to the question on sexual preference, African Americans' greater use of "God's will" compared to whites could speak to their greater religiosity and religious orthodoxy.[18] If so, the rationale behind their use of "God's will" runs counter to the reasoning of the youths who also selected "God's will" as the primary cause of sexual preference. Meanwhile, our small subsample of self-identified gay and bisexual adults also endorsed "God's will" explanations (and genetic explanations) with much greater frequency than they used parental ones.[19]

Given that such divergent groups find "God's will" an attractive account for sexual preference, we set out to better understand the role of religious ideology, self-described religiosity, and religious participation

Figure 5.6   Perceived Cause of Sexual Preference, by Views on the Bible

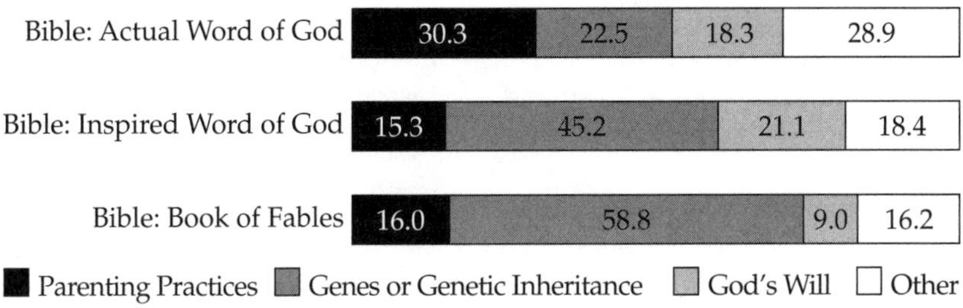

Bible: Actual Word of God | 30.3 | 22.5 | 18.3 | 28.9 |

Bible: Inspired Word of God | 15.3 | 45.2 | 21.1 | 18.4 |

Bible: Book of Fables | 16.0 | 58.8 | 9.0 | 16.2 |

■ Parenting Practices   ■ Genes or Genetic Inheritance   ■ God's Will   □ Other

Source: Constructing the Family Survey (Powell 2003, 2006).

in Americans' etiological accounts for sexual preference. Although ideology, religiosity, and religious participation constitute different elements of religion, their linkage to the various explanations of sexual preference is conspicuously similar. So, as in chapter 4, we report on only one: adherence to biblical literalness. As shown in figure 5.6, Americans who believed that the Bible is the "actual word of God [that] is to be taken literally, word for word," placed the responsibility for sexual preference more frequently on parents (30.3 percent) than on any other factor such as friends and environment (28.9 percent), genes (22.5 percent), or, most tellingly, "God's will" (18.3 percent). In other words, despite their emphasis on the "actual word" of God, they were reluctant to use "God's will" as the key force that drives sexual preference. Instead, they mostly (59.2 percent) endorsed parental or other environment explanations that assert that sexual preference can be controlled.

At the other side of the spectrum, the majority of respondents who regarded the Bible as an "ancient book of fables, legends, history, and moral teachings recorded by man" believed that sexual preference is influenced primarily by genetics (58.8 percent). "God's will" was the least popular choice for this group (9.0 percent)—mirroring the pattern for biblical literalists. In fact, the respondents who were the most likely to consider "God's will" a pivotal factor were those who saw the Bible as "the inspired word of God, but not everything should be taken literally, word for word." Still, the plurality of this group (45.2 percent) invoked genetic accounts. Despite some differences, these two groups shared the belief that sexual preference is not environmentally induced but instead is shaped by factors outside of the control of youths, as well as of their family and environment.

Attributions of Sexual Preference and Definitions of Family

To summarize what we have seen so far in this chapter, Americans diverge in their beliefs regarding the cause of sexual preference. Some emphasize "controllable" factors, such as parenting, that insinuate that sexual preference involves a choice. Others highlight factors that are not controllable and that in turn stress the apparent immutability of one's sexuality. But these latter factors are rooted in ostensibly diametric positions: genetic attributions that privilege scientific principles, on the one hand, and "God's will" explanations that would seem to favor religious values, on the other. Yet these religious claims are met with resistance by the religiously orthodox, who also question genetic explanations. Meanwhile, those who question the Bible also see little merit in "God's will" explanations but favor genetic accounts. And to confuse the matter even more, young adults and African Americans are more predisposed than their older and white counterparts to support "God's will" explanations and to challenge genetic ones. Given these diverse patterns, it is unclear whether beliefs about the origins of sexual preference map onto American's definitions of family. Does endorsement of certain etiological assumptions imply a more inclusive vision of family, while support of other attributions indicates a more exclusive view?

General Patterns

As is strikingly apparent from figure 5.7, Americans' stances regarding the origins of sexual preference are indeed implicated in their acceptance or rejection of atypical family forms. Of those who drew on a genetic explanation, approximately three-fourths (75.9 percent) agreed that a lesbian couple with children counts as family. In a near-reversal, this hypothetical couple is seen as a family by roughly one-third (34.8 percent) of those who attributed sexual preference to parenting practices. Perhaps not so incongruously at this point, adults who invoked "God's will" in their discussion of sexual preference were inclusive: over three-fifths (61.2 percent) recognized a lesbian couple with children as a family.

Further support for these patterns is evident in figure 5.8. The plurality of Americans who took a genetic position regarding the roots of sexual preference were inclusionists (40.7 percent). Although exclusionists were the largest group among those who attributed sexual preference to "God's will" (39.4 percent), this is a much smaller propor-

**Figure 5.7   Do Lesbian Couples with Children Count as Family?
Differences by Perceived Cause of Sexual Preference**

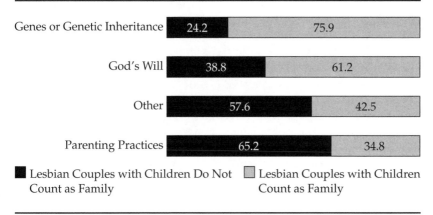

Genes or Genetic Inheritance   24.2   75.9

God's Will   38.8   61.2

Other   57.6   42.5

Parenting Practices   65.2   34.8

■ Lesbian Couples with Children Do Not   □ Lesbian Couples with Children
   Count as Family   Count as Family

Source: Constructing the Family Survey (Powell 2003, 2006).

tion than for those who adopted parenting (64.9 percent) or other environmental (57.2 percent) explanations. These patterns echo the idea that people who believe that sexual preference—notably, same-sex attraction—is neither "treatable" nor mutable tend toward a more expansive view regarding same-sex relationships.[20]

**Figure 5.8   Differences in Family Definitions, by Perceived Cause of Sexual
Preference**

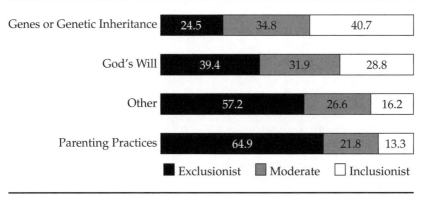

Genes or Genetic Inheritance   24.5   34.8   40.7

God's Will   39.4   31.9   28.8

Other   57.2   26.6   16.2

Parenting Practices   64.9   21.8   13.3

■ Exclusionist   ■ Moderate   □ Inclusionist

Source: Constructing the Family Survey (Powell 2003, 2006).

First Choice, Second Choice

Most Americans may not believe that there is a single factor that entirely accounts for sexual preference. So, in our interviews in 2003, we also asked our respondents to identify the "second most important factor." A fairly small number indicated that they did not believe that there was a plausible second choice. Interestingly, this type of response disproportionately came from advocates of "God's will" and, especially, genetic explanations. Among those who offered a second choice, every combination emerged. Still, advocates of genetic explanations were more than 50 percent more likely to choose "God's will" than parenting as a second factor. Similarly, Americans who gave "God's will" as their first choice were also more than 50 percent more likely to select genetics than parenting as a second choice. Meanwhile, supporters of parenting explanations were resistant to placing much responsibility on genetics or "God's will." Instead, they were over twice as likely to identify other environmental factors as the second most influential cause.

Still, for Americans who chose parenting as the primary cause of sexual preference, definitions of family were minimally affected by their second choice. That is, their reluctance to see lesbian couples as family was consistently high regardless of their second choice. In contrast, as seen in figure 5.9, Americans who believed that genetics or "God's will" is the *only* explanation for sexual preference concomitantly endorsed the most liberal position in our sample: 88.6 percent and 83.4 percent, respectively, saw a lesbian couple with children as a family.[21] Those who paired genetic explanations and "God's will" explanations followed (78.0 percent for those who chose genetics first and "God's will" second, and 70.2 percent for those who chose "God's will" first and genetics second). Choosing parenting as a second choice considerably lowered the support for lesbian couples with children: 61.8 percent for those who saw genetics as the most influential factors and only 37.6 percent for those who rooted sexual preferences primarily in "God's will." The finding that the tandem of genetics and religious beliefs creates a more liberal acceptance of same-sex parents is compelling. It offers a formidable challenge to those who pitch science against religion. It also calls into question the view—often found in the social sciences—that reflexively portrays any biological or religious argument as inherently conservative.

Causes of Intelligence and Definitions of Family

Of course, it is possible that the apparent liberalizing influence of genetic and "God's will" accounts is idiosyncratic and applicable only to

Figure 5.9   Do Lesbian Couples with Children Count as Family?
Differences by Genes/God's Will as Most Important Cause and
Additional Factors as Second Most Important Cause of Sexual
Preference

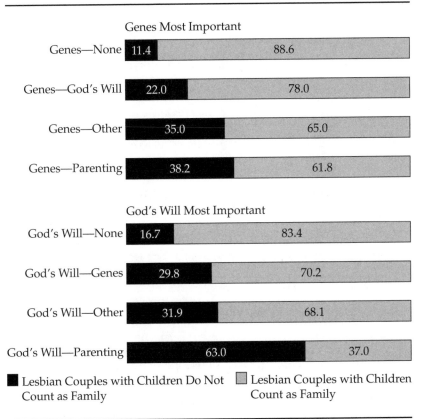

Genes Most Important

Genes—None   11.4   88.6

Genes—God's Will   22.0   78.0

Genes—Other   35.0   65.0

Genes—Parenting   38.2   61.8

God's Will Most Important

God's Will—None   16.7   83.4

God's Will—Genes   29.8   70.2

God's Will—Other   31.9   68.1

God's Will—Parenting   63.0   37.0

■ Lesbian Couples with Children Do Not   □ Lesbian Couples with Children
Count as Family   Count as Family

Source: Constructing the Family Survey (Powell 2003).

explanations of sexual preference. In other words, adherence to a more
encompassing genetic perspective—or belief in "God's will"—may not
necessarily yield a more encompassing familial perspective. Wondering about this issue, we analyzed Americans' causal explanations of a
variety of childhood traits and behavior—for example, intelligence.
Certainly, discussion regarding the primary cause of intelligence has
been highly contentious and perhaps the most pivotal issue in the
nature-nurture debate. The nature side appears to have been more successful. As seen in figure 5.10, the majority of Americans attributed intelligence to genetic inheritance (53.8 percent), while approximately
one-third offered some type of nurture explanation: 30.3 percent said

Figure 5.10   Perceived Cause of Intelligence

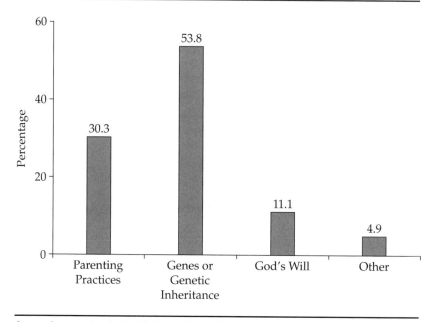

Source: Constructing the Family Survey (Powell 2003, 2006).

intelligence stems from parenting, and 4.9 percent attributed it to friends or outside environment. Over one-tenth (11.1 percent) of our respondents implicated "God's will" here.

Although intelligence and sexual preference are very different phenomena, the patterns of responses to questions about their origins are quite similar. For both, the most common etiological explanation is genetic. In fact, genetics was used more frequently for intelligence and sexual preference than for all the other traits and behaviors that we asked about in the interviews, except for weight. Similarly, "God's will" was more often invoked to explain sexual preference and intelligence than to account for most other traits and behaviors. In fact, the overlap in choices—especially for genetics—is strong. Or to put it another way, if we know Americans' explanation of sexual preference, then we have a fairly good idea of where they stand on the causes of intelligence (and vice versa). For example, nearly three-fourths (72.3 percent) of the respondents who believed that sexual preference is due primarily to genes also believed that intelligence is rooted in genetics. And upon closer inspection of sociodemographic predictors of Americans' beliefs about the causes of intelligence, we find that the patterns very closely follow those outlined earlier in this chapter: for example, women were less likely than men to attribute intelligence to parenting, more highly educated respondents were more likely than their less-educated peers to rely on genetic explanations, and African Americans were more likely than their white counterparts to turn to "God's will."

But does having a similar belief structure about the causes of intelligence and sexual preference mean that using genetics—or "God's will"—to explain intelligence translates into a more inclusive view of family? For genetics, the answer is unequivocal. Americans who use genetic explanations for intelligence are more inclusive in their definitions of family than are those who offer alternative explanations.[22] In other words, genetic attributions even for some items that have nothing to do with sexual preference can be coupled with liberal views, at least in regard to definitions of family. The same, however, cannot be said about the attribution of intelligence and sexual preference to "God's will," which is not significantly linked to definitions of family.

Continuity and Change: 2003 to 2006

In the 2004 presidential debates, CBS anchor Bob Schieffer broached the topic of the immutability of sexual preference by asking the candidates, President George Bush and Senator John Kerry, whether they believed that homosexuality is a choice. Bush's response was equivocal, although he implied that there is an element of choice: "I don't know. I just don't know . . . I also know in a free society people, consenting adults, can live *the way they want to live* [emphasis ours]." Kerry's response challenged the notion that choice is involved. Instead, he invoked "God's will" as a possible causal force:

> We're all God's children, Bob, and I think if you were to talk to Dick Cheney's daughter, who is a lesbian, she would tell you that she's being who she was. She's being who she was born as. I think if you talk to anybody, it's not choice. I've met people who struggled with this for years. . . . I've met wives supportive of their husband or vice versa when they finally sort of broke out and allowed themselves to live who they were, *who they felt God had made them* [emphasis ours].

This was among the most publicized exchanges in the presidential debates. Kerry's statement prompted an outcry from certain political camps because of what was perceived as its overly personalized nature and Kerry's ostensible outing of Mary Cheney, even though she already had been public about her sexuality. As noted in chapter 4, even

Figure 5.11   Changes Between 2003 and 2006 in Perceived Cause of Sexual Preference

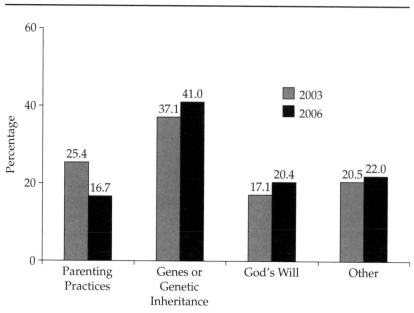

Source: *Constructing the Family Survey* (Powell 2003, 2006).

this public discussion about Mary Cheney—accompanied by comments from and interviews with her parents—may well have, purposefully or not, led some Americans to reevaluate and even loosen their views about sexuality. But to us the exchange between Kerry and Bush was even more telling because it distinguished two opposing views of the causes of homosexuality to a large portion of the American public. This dialogue regarding the causes of homosexuality was one of many, however, that occurred between 2003, when our first interviews were conducted, and 2006, when our second round of interviews was completed.

Bush won the election, but if the change in responses in our surveys between 2003 and 2006 is any indication, Kerry won the argument. As we can see in figure 5.11, Americans have come increasingly to believe that sexual preference is not a choice but instead is due to genetics (from 37.1 percent in 2003 to 41.0 percent in 2006) or "God's will" (from 17.1 percent to 20.4 percent). At the same time, support for parenting explanations has plummeted (from 25.4 percent to 16.7 percent). In fact, by 2006 more Americans attributed sexual preference to "God's will" than to parenting practices. These changes are strong and remain statistically significant when factors such as education are taken into account.[23]

We believe that the discourse that privileges genetics, and to a lesser degree "God's will," over familial and environmental explanations seems to have taken hold. Although it is true that the causes of sexual preference were debated long before 2003, most of this discussion was geared to an academic audience or a much smaller number of gay rights and anti-gay rights activists. The average American rarely talked about the causes of homosexuality—or even brought up the general topic of homosexuality—in conversation. With the remarkable changes that have occurred since 2003—some mentioned in chapter 2 (including court cases such as *Lawrence et al. v. Texas*, which overturned the anti-sodomy statute in Texas, *Goodridge v. Massachusetts Department of Public Health*, which enabled same-sex couples to marry, and the corresponding legislative efforts to mostly restrict marital rights to same-sex couples)—these topics were covered much more extensively in the media and, according to our interviewees, became more common topics of daily conversation as well. The more people heard about or participated in discussions of sexuality, the more they felt comfortable with the topic and, given the patterns identified here, the more receptive they became to seeing sexual preference less as a choice and more as a fixed phenomenon.

Of course, it is possible that Americans have moved away from parenting explanations and toward genetic ones across the board. This shift would imply that public discourse about sexuality has not been as influential as we believe it to have been. To evaluate this possibility, we also examined the changes in Americans' views of the causes of intelligence, aggressive behavior, and weight. Since there was no noticeable flurry of media discussion regarding aggressive behavior and intelligence between 2003 and 2006, we anticipated little change in Americans' etiological accounts of these two qualities. As predicted, we witnessed very little change in their views on these topics during that period of time.

At the same time, however, there was a heightened—some critics have described it as frenzied—focus on childhood obesity and the role that both parents and schools have played in exacerbating this problem. Correspondingly, Americans apparently changed their views regarding the causes of children's weight. Figure 5.12 displays these changes. In 2003, genes were most commonly considered the explanation for childhood obesity (49.2 percent), but in 2006 support for this explanation had shrunk to 41.3 percent. Accompanying this decline was a significant rise in the percentage of Americans who attributed

Figure 5.12   Changes Between 2003 and 2006 in Perceived Causes of Children's Weight

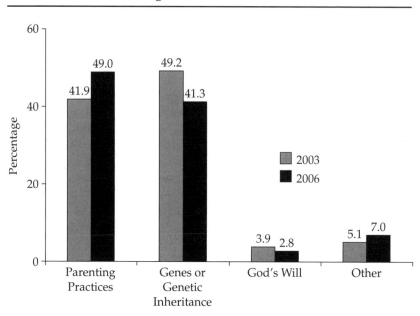

Source: Constructing the Family Survey (Powell 2003, 2006).

children's weight to parenting (from 41.9 percent in 2003 to 49.0 percent in 2006).[24] In other words, in 2003 more people thought genes were the primary determinant of children's weight, but in 2006 more people thought that parenting was the principal factor. So at the same time that Americans were retreating from the view that sexual preference is malleable, they also were drawing closer to the position that obesity is controllable. These divergent patterns suggest that Americans' views are sufficiently fluid that they are responsive to various accounts of human behavior.

Clearly, the numbers suggest genuine changes in how Americans think about the causes of sexual preference. More revealing, however, are the words they use, especially when discussing such matters as same-sex marriage. As much as the quantitative data suggest that Americans are reevaluating their attributions of sexuality, even more striking evidence comes from the qualitative, open-ended responses in our interviews. As detailed earlier in this book, in the interviews respondents were given multiple opportunities to discuss their views about the meaning of family. The key themes underlying the ways in which exclusionists, moderates, and inclusionists distinguish families from nonfamilies were outlined in chapter 3, where we noted that there were few changes in the overall themes between 2003 and 2006. But our interviews also offered opportunities to speak out on other issues regarding family—some of which we discuss in the next two chapters. In listening to the interviews and reading the transcripts, we found it impossible *not* to notice a shift in emphasis between 2003 and 2006—specifically, the mention by many interviewees of the genetic or fixed nature of sexual preference when discussing same-sex marriage. In 2003 this concept was virtually absent in the open-ended responses—even though earlier in the interviews we explicitly asked closed-ended questions about the causes of sexual preference and other traits and behaviors that provide the empirical foundation of this chapter. By 2006, Americans who were supportive of same-sex marital rights were bringing up this issue as a rationale behind their position, as illustrated in the comments of a woman in her thirties:

> Because I don't feel like, I don't feel like that's a personal choice of theirs that they are like that, and I feel like that they should have the same rights as straight people. And that's basically it. I don't think they choose that. They can choose to hide it, but I don't think that's fair. So I think that if that's who you are, you should have a right to other perks, so to speak, that other people in the society enjoy. Like being married and having your union recognized under the law and having all the benefits of that.

Like many others, this woman contended that the absence of choice in one's sexuality should not translate into an absence of choice regarding marital relations. "Choice" was frequently invoked in both of these senses in the 2006 interviews:

> Someone cannot *choose* their sexuality, and if they are in love, they are in love.

> Because they should have the same rights to mess up their lives like everyone else. I think if two people love each other, they can't help who they are sexually attracted to. And they should, if they love someone and are sexually attracted to them and *choose* to build a life with them, then they should be able to.

> Oh, I don't know. We can get into a long discussion on this. I just feel there are some people who don't have a *choice* in the matter. And if they love someone else, you know, and they commit to a relationship like

other people, they should be allowed to have the same benefits as married couples have.

In these quotes, the respondents do not identify why gays and lesbians have no choice in their sexuality. But others did. Some emphasize that a person's sexuality is controlled not by the individual but instead by God, as seen in these responses by two men:

> Because of God's will. They are the way they are because of God, and I think it's God's will that they love each other and they want to get married.

> Well, if it is the path God chose them to go in and they find the right partner, they should not be held back from society's term of marriage.

Interestingly, men were more likely than women to bring up "God's will"—and, as we will shortly see, genetic explanations—when defending their support for extending rights to same-sex couples. This pattern does not mean, however, that they were unequivocally supportive of homosexuality or same-sex relations, as exemplified by the comments of a man in his fifties:

> If they want to marry, then just let them marry just as long as they don't push it on other people. If that's God's will for them to be that way, then it's God's will. And there's nothing you can do about that.

Admittedly, the number of people in the interviews in 2006 who specifically brought up "God's will" as the reason to favor the extension of marital rights to same-sex couples was fairly small. They remained outnumbered by opponents of same-sex marriage—and same-sex relations in general—who relied on their religious views or interpretation of religious text to justify their position. But the important point here is that "God's will" emerged in the framing of the discourse to defend same-sex relations—a type of discourse that was virtually absent in the interviews in 2003.

The increased presence of genetic explanations of sexuality as the basis of their advocacy of same-sex relations is even more noteworthy. As noted earlier in this chapter, in 2003 the plurality of Americans responded in the closed-ended questions that they believed sexual preference is due mostly to genes or genetic inheritance. And yet this issue was not part of the discourse used in their open-ended responses regarding the rights and benefits of same-sex couples. By 2006, however, this explanation had become a common theme in the open-ended responses. Typical of this response are the comments of a mother in her forties:

> I believe that your sexual orientation is genetically made up, that you have the same rights as anyone else no matter what your sexual orientation is. I should say you should have the same rights and therefore that you should be able to marry, whether you're two girls, two boys, or a girl and a boy. Sorry, men and women.

As also seen in the closed-ended responses regarding the causes of sexual preference, some Americans fused genetic and "God's will" accounts in defending their views about same-sex couples. A woman in her fifties, for example, explained:

> I believe that God made them the way they are made. This was a matter of birth, genetics, and what they were born that way. And they should have every bit of equal rights as I who happen to be born straight have. In a country that is so intent on giving other people rights, it just blows my mind that we can look at a group of people that's one out of ten and decide that they aren't as good as the rest of us. It's just ridiculous. So I just think that all things being as they are, they should have as many equal rights as I get to enjoy.

Genetic explanations also were used in conjunction with discussions of discrimination; respondents often saw direct parallels between the treatment of gays and lesbians and the historical (or contemporary) treatment of racial minorities, as seen in the following comments by a man in his fifties:

> Well, if you believe that sexual orientation is basically genetics, then it would be very discriminatory to think otherwise. But you know our system. You know, most societies likes [sic] to have scapegoats. So I suppose since we can't scapegoat the minorities anymore, or different racial types, we gotta do somebody. (laughs) So they're fair game.

Underlying this man's reasoning is the premise that sexual orientation, like race, is an ascribed status or trait—something that one is born with and that is therefore beyond one's control. He did not explicitly tie antimiscegenation laws of the past to the current prohibition of same-sex marriage. But it is evident that he saw the resistance to same-sex couples as part of a legacy of societal discrimination that he believed should not be sustained because a person's sexuality is no different than his or her race—something that is not a choice, but rather preordained.

Employing genetic attributions—or more broadly, mentioning the fixed nature of sexuality—did not necessarily translate into a more favorable view of homosexuality per se. Importantly, several Americans seemed to respond to homosexuality with ambivalence, discomfort, or even strong disapproval, but still supported the extension of marital rights to same-sex couples because of their belief in the genetic basis of sexual preference. This uneasiness sometimes is implied, as in the case of a man in his fifties who noted that it is "not their *fault* that they have this preference." Others more explicitly expressed their disapproval but used genetic explanations of sexuality to distinguish their uneasiness regarding homosexuality from their support for equal rights. For instance, another man in his fifties explained:

> Although I don't agree [with] it, they, I believe, have a genetic code that puts them in that circumstance. And I believe they have the right to life, liberty, just as much as any other person does.

Still others expressed an even stronger aversion to homosexuality—often stated in notably graphic terms—but decoupled this view from their position on same-sex rights. In nearly all cases, this type of response was given by men, especially middle-aged ones:

> You have to give me these hard questions! Well, I surely don't want to suck a cock. I'm sorry. That wasn't nice of me. I just don't think it's right. But if they want to do that, then they can do it, not me.

> I think most of them are screwed up in the first place. You want my honest opinion: I think genetics are a huge part of the choice they've made, and I don't think that people should judge them and tell them they can't be married. That's what they should be able to do.

We should emphasize that in the closed-ended questions in 2006 (as well as in 2003), men were not more likely than women to select genetics as the primary cause of sexual preference. Instead, among Americans in 2006 who supported the provision of same-sex rights, men were more likely than women to bring up these factors as the reason behind their support. The genetic explanation may especially resonate with these men precisely because it enabled them to distance their personal views regarding homosexuality from their views about the rights and obligations of same-sex couples. It allowed them to volunteer that they were dismayed or even disgusted by homosexuality, thus clearly signaling that they were not gay. But since they saw homosexuality as genetic—and therefore not communicable, or contaminating—they could more safely avoid guilt by association and, perhaps most importantly, challenges to their masculinity.[25] That is, they could endorse same-sex rights without fearing that others would see them as gay or a candidate for conversion.

These responses suggest that the increased discourse over the past few years promoting genetic claims about sexual preference has been successful not only in increasing Americans' support for same-sex couples but also in giving Americans a framework that they can comfortably use to justify their support. Appealing to the fixed nature of sexuality may be especially effective in reaching men who otherwise are uncomfortable with the idea of homosexuality. Importantly, this appeal seems to be most influential when directed at a particular age group— middle-aged men and, to a lesser extent, women. It is telling that so many respondents who interjected the issue of genetics in their open-ended responses were in their forties and fifties. This age cohort appeared to be more prone to spontaneously mention the fixed nature of sexuality than either their younger or older counterparts—even those who endorsed an inclusive view of family and endorsed same-sex familial rights. We suspect that younger adults who are supportive of gay rights do not see the need to mention the fixed nature of sexuality (even if they agree with it) when explaining why they endorse same-sex rights. They may see less need to differentiate between their views on homosexuality per se and their views on same-sex rights. At the other end of the spectrum, older adults may feel so disquieted about or uncomfortable with the issue of homosexuality that they are unable to employ a framework, such as genetics, that disentangles their views about homosexuality and their position about same-sex rights.

Conclusion

In this chapter, we have engaged the nature-nurture debate to identify the views held by the general public about the origins of traits and behaviors—especially sexuality—and importantly, to explore how these views are linked to the types of living arrangements that Americans include in their definitions of family. Collaterally, we consider the commonalities and distinctions in what is often labeled an adversarial schism between scientific and religious explanations and their implications for definitions of family. Overall, the patterns described in this chapter are evocative.

Our primary focus is on public understandings of the causes of sexual preference. We find that more Americans attribute sexual preference to genetics than to parenting and that a nontrivial number of Americans turn to "God's will" for their answer. These attributions are interesting in and of themselves. Given the current cultural climate in which parents are counseled to always know where their children are, to talk to their children about drugs, smoking, and sexual behavior, and to be proactive in their children's school and extracurricular activities, it may seem surprising that Americans are over twice as likely to rely on genetic or "God's will" explanations as they are to endorse parental ones.

We also see important social cleavages in the endorsement of various explanations of sexuality. Women are more cautious than men in believing that parents are responsible for their progeny's sexual preference. This gender difference may stem from women's more frequent participation in child care, which, in turn, facilitates women's recognition—and perhaps acceptance—of the limits of parenting. Younger adults also are less likely than their older counterparts to attribute sexuality to parenting, although they also are less persuaded by genetic explanations but less resistant to "God's will" explanations. Still, their usage of "God's will" does not necessarily imply an endorsement of religious ideology per se, but rather an attempt to find a supra-individual and supra-environmental explanation that privileges the immutability of sexuality. Individuals with higher educational levels are more likely than others to trace sexual preference (as well as intelligence) to genetics, even though this group probably has been more exposed than their counterparts with lower levels of education to the nature-nurture debate and the social-scientific critiques of genetic explanations. It may seem counterintuitive that as the objectivity of science is increasingly scrutinized, the more educated are increasingly inclined to perceive the causes of sexual preference as rooted in biology. Yet, by using genetic explanations, more highly educated Americans are selecting causes that are outside the purview of the families and the environment and, in turn, are fixed.

To better understand the relationship between these beliefs, we dig more deeply into the main focus of this chapter—how respondents utilized their accounts of the root causes of sexual preference to accept or reject specific living arrangements as families. Overall, we see that acceptance of nontraditional family forms is significantly related to one's beliefs regarding the etiology of sexual preference. That is, adults who perceive sexual preference as rooted in genetics are more accepting of same-sex couples as family. Perhaps unpredictably, adults whose beliefs are predicated on "God's will" are also more inclusive in their definitions of family. Certainly, we may not have anticipated that science and religion would come together in such a fashion. In contrast, parenting arguments lend themselves to markedly greater resistance to nontraditional family forms. We see a unique pattern in which belief in causes that are stable—genetics and "God's will"—and consequently are not controllable by parents, the environment, or individuals themselves is related to more inclusive positions regarding same-sex relationships. Still, the pairing of genetic and "God's will" explanations is a fragile one that does not extend beyond views on sexual preference. That is, endorsement of genetic explanations for intelligence and other factors also is linked to greater inclusivity, but the endorsement of "God's will" for these items is implicated in a more restrictive vision of family.

As noted earlier in this book, critics of same-sex unions often discount the claim that the opposition to same-sex couples today is analogous to the hostility to interracial couples from several decades ago. In chapter 4, we noted the similarity in the sociodemographic predictors of attitudes toward interracial couples several decades ago and predictors of attitudes toward same-sex couples today (such as age and education); moreover, we cited some respondents who inadvertently and explicitly linked their opposition to both same-sex and interracial marriage. Some critics, however, may not be persuaded by these patterns and may still believe that the equation of interracial couples and same-sex couples is misguided—in part because, in their view, race is fixed while sexual preference is a choice. This distinction does not appear, however, to be shared by most Americans: over half (54.2 percent) in 2003 saw sexual preference as being beyond the control of the individual. That this figure increased in just three years to 61.4 percent suggests an increasing convergence in a core factor linked to the support of same-sex and interracial couples.

Perhaps even more indicative of a real change in Americans' views is the notable increase in the number of respondents who in their open-ended responses explicitly discussed how their support of same-sex rights was due in part to their belief that sexual preference is not a choice. Discussions regarding the fixed or fluid nature of sexual preference were highly publicized—and vigorously contested—between the two waves of the Constructing the Family Surveys. And it certainly appears that public opinion is tilting more decisively toward the position that sexual preference is unchangeable. The apparent success of this frame in reaching the public can be juxtaposed with another highly publicized—but less successful—claim regarding the potential dangers of same-sex unions for heterosexual ones. Indeed, when asked to discuss their views about same-sex couples, our interviewees rarely if ever talked about gay and lesbian unions harming heterosexual marriages, despite the ubiquitous use of this frame in the media by pundits and politicians alike. In other words, although the idea that heterosexual marriage would be irreparably damaged by same-sex marriage may have been a good sound bite, it apparently did not resonate with the populace—or at least did not do so to the point that individuals echoed this view in our interviews. In contrast, the idea that, like race, sexual preference is due to factors beyond the control of individuals appears to have gained ground.

Taken together, our findings both square well with and stand in opposition to what we have come to know and expect as social scientists. The social-psychological literature on attribution suggests that individuals often are more sympathetic toward those who cannot "control" their circumstances. This holds in a variety of situations—from beliefs about poverty to beliefs about mental illness. As such, we might have anticipated that a leaning among our respondents toward genetic explanations would translate into a more liberal and inclusive position about gays and lesbians. But at the same time, social scientists often have shown a skeptical if not hostile reaction to biological (and especially genetic) explanations across the board. Their skepticism is understandable given the historical and, in some arenas (such as race and ethnic relations), contemporary use of these etiological accounts to justify inequality (Hunt 1996; Jayaratne et al. 2006). Still, the responses from our interviews may surprise and even reassure scholars who dedicate themselves to the notion that biological arguments are inherently conservative. To date, genetic accounts have not been seen as a potentially liberalizing force. Yet, in this case, they apparently have such potential.

Whether this potential is short-lived or long-lasting is unclear. The success of genetic explanations may lead those opposed to the extension of gay rights to co-opt the explanation and turn it on its head. For example, in his commentary, "Is Your Baby Gay? What If You Could Know? What If You Could Do Something About It?" Albert Mohler (2007), the president of the Southern Baptist Theological Seminary (the flagship seminary of the Southern Baptist Convention), warns other advocates of "traditional" families that the growing evidence of the biological basis of sexual preference may compel a reevaluation of the stance that homosexuality is a choice. But rather than suggesting that this reassessment should result in greater acceptance of gays and lesbians, he contends that the evidence of a genetic cause does not excuse the "sin" of homosexuality. Instead, he welcomes future scientific advances that would enable parents to identify whether their unborn children are gay and would offer treatments that could successfully reverse the sexual orientation of these children.

Such statements are among the reasons there is disagreement in the gay community over what some see as the overreliance on genetic explanations to justify same-sex rights. Others express ambivalence about the use of genetic or other scientific explanations because, on the one hand, they may ultimately increase tolerance, but on the other hand, these explanations may also increase the notion of "difference" between gays and heterosexuals.[26] Thus, there may be risks in revealing or endorsing the genetic roots of sexual preference in the future.

Despite these cautionary notes, we believe that at this particular juncture in American history the overall endorsement of genetic explanations—as well as of other accounts that see sexual preference as fixed instead of changeable—promotes the rights of gays and lesbians. These patterns should give pause to those who portray genetic and other scientific arguments as unremittingly reactionary. Such a portrayal does a disservice not only to those arguments but also to the social sciences. Categorical refusal to concede any merit in such arguments and to explore the intersection of biological and social factors may ultimately marginalize the social sciences and forgo an opportunity to further both social-scientific understanding and social awareness.[27]

Additionally, new scholarship needs to question the *meaning* of "God's will" more explicitly. Throughout the centuries, "God's will" has been used to justify sexism, racism, class inequality, ethnocentrism, violence, terrorism, and even foreign policy. Even today, we continue to see conservative religious figures using religion—and, in particular, "God's will"—to justify the disenfranchisement of particular groups of people. Yet, in listening to our interviewees, we find that Americans are using "God's will" to justify *equality*, even if they do not always view that as an explicit religious explanation. Perhaps, however, this use of the concept should be expected: we need to remember that "God's will" has been invoked elsewhere to justify participation in the civil rights movement, activism in the various peace movements, and care for the disadvantaged (see, for example, Davis and Robinson 1996). Moreover, some religious denominations—for example, the United Church of Christ—have been "open and affirming" to same-sex couples. This contemporary use of what seems to be a religious explanation as a means of liberation suggests a greater complexity to these explanations that may compel many of us to reconsider our reflexively dismissive views about religious frames.

Many social scientists also will need to reassess their views regarding the role of biology in human behavior. All too often sociologists and other social scientists have had viscerally negative reactions to biological and genetic explanations, characterizing them as a means to maintain sexist and racist ideologies and institutions. Yet, in our interviews, we find that individuals who support genetic explanations (especially regarding sexual preference) are significantly more likely to take an inclusive view of family than are those who subscribe to more social-based explanations (such as environment, peers, or parents). At this point in time, it appears that genetic explanations, at least when used to challenge the idea that homosexuality is a "choice" or a "learned human perversion," can sometimes be used as a tool not to perpetuate the status quo but rather to promote social equality.

= Chapter 6 =

Discounting Sex:
Gender, Parenting, and
Definitions of Family

IN THE previous chapter, we saw that Americans' views about the etiology of sexual preference are intertwined with their definitions of family. When respondents attributed sexual preference to external factors beyond individual control, including genetics and "God's will," they were more likely to express a wide-ranging view of family that included same-sex couples. By contrast, those who endorsed the idea that sexuality is "controllable" and sexual preference is due to parenting or environmental factors were much more restrictive in whom they counted as family. Among the most conservative members of our study, parents matter because it is their duty to shield their children from engaging in intimate unions that, for many Americans, carry social disapproval. What, then, are their views regarding *how* parents matter?

In this chapter, we build on what we previously observed about parenting, but here we move on to the question of gender. More specifically, we address whether views regarding gender and parenting are linked to Americans' definitions of family by examining the perceived relative importance of fathers and mothers and whether these perceptions vary by the sex of the child. In 2003, respondents were asked whether in a single-parent household girls are better off living with their mother or father and whether boys are better off living with their mother or father. These questions tap into the importance of gender by assessing not only which gender is considered a better custodial parent but also whether a gender match between parent and child matters. Interviewees were then asked to elaborate on the reasons behind their preferences.

Some social scientists contend that single-parent families, not unlike

137

same-sex families, challenge heteronormative assumptions that exalt the heterosexual, gendered nuclear family (Bernstein and Reimann 2001b). But our main interest is not in Americans' views about single-parent families per se. Rather, by focusing on single-parent homes, we can assess how respondents evaluated the well-being of children in structurally equivalent families that differ on two simple dimensions: the residential parent's gender and the child's gender. In effect, we asked our respondents to arbitrate who should be awarded custody or what should be the presumptive standard in custody decisions.

Custody decisions pose a quintessential Solomonic dilemma that often requires turning a child over to one parent and not the other. Resolutions to this dilemma of choosing between parents can reveal a great deal about gender norms regarding both parents and children. The link between gender attitudes and homosexism (or homophobia, or sexual prejudice) has been theorized and documented in a number of articles (Britton 1990; Herek 1988; Pharr 1988; Polimeni, Hardie, and Buzwell 2000). Determining which living arrangements Americans prefer, and understanding why they favor them, allows us a glimpse into how individuals think and talk about gender—and, at least indirectly, about sexuality. Americans' responses capture various child-rearing philosophies regarding how boys and girls should be socialized and how mothers and fathers should behave in their roles as parents. Equally if not more importantly, we contend that the distinctions that Americans make between fathers and mothers and between sons and daughters are also implicated in their views on homosexuality and, in turn, the boundaries they draw between families and nonfamilies. For that reason, we return at the end of the chapter to our main theme—who is counted as family and who is counted out?—to see whether family definitions are associated with gendered views about child custody.

Child Custody: What Is Best for the Child?

The debate over what is best for children is hardly new. This issue not only is one of the most disputed matters in scholarship today but also is a highly contentious point of debate in the public arena. Certainly, much debate regarding same-sex couples—and, in particular, the extension of marital and parental rights to same-sex couples—centers on the question of whether children are better off living with a mother and father and, by extension, whether gay men and lesbians make "bad" parents.

Recent court cases that favor or oppose prohibitions of same-sex marriage at the state level are telling. For example, in *Andersen v. King County*, which upheld a Washington state law banning same-sex marriage, Justice Barbara A. Madsen of the Washington Supreme Court wrote that it is reasonable to conclude that "limiting marriage to opposite-sex couples furthers the procreation essential to the survival of the human race, and furthers the well-being of children by encouraging families where children are reared in homes headed by the children's biological parents." This conclusion privileges both biological parenthood and father-mother-child households—the Standard North American Family (Smith 1993). The implication is that "blood" families are preferable—a theme that echoes the comments of some exclusionists (see chapter 3)—and, by extension, that children need both a father and a mother.

Ironically, however, courts typically have been reluctant to explain why opposite-sex parents are needed, although the implicit assumption is that mothers and fathers are different—that they serve unique but complementary and necessary roles in the upbringing of children.[1] Others are more frank: they maintain that fathers are critical for boys' healthy development into manhood (and, presumably, heterosexuality) or, conversely, that mothers who are too motherly may effeminize their sons. Such assertions underscore the presumed correspondence between gender, sex, and sexuality—an association that is enormously difficult to challenge.

Contemporary discourse on the optimal way to rear children, then, is certainly not limited to motherhood but also encompasses a strengthened role of fathers, especially with respect to sons. These discussions often parallel views regarding fathers and mothers—and sons and daughters—dating back at least to the 1800s. Thus, we begin with a brief historical overview of the changes in the standards governing the norms and laws about which parent—the father or the mother—should be awarded custody of a child, and the gendered assumptions behind these standards.

Historical Changes in Custody Determination

The historical records of the last two centuries chronicle a dramatic shift in public perceptions about how children should be reared and who is best suited to do so.[2] In the early 1800s, custody decisions typically were governed by the presumption that fathers made better custodians than mothers. After a marital disruption, the father, as the patriarchal head of household, was customarily awarded custody. During this period, women were thought to lack sufficient authority to govern children, regardless of the child's gender. Parenthetically, grown women were themselves seen as being in need of firm guidance from a husband in most if not all aspects of life and, not unexpectedly, often were treated like children themselves. Indeed, both mothers and children were subject to paternal oversight and were considered men's chattel. Even upon a man's death, his imprint lived on because his will could designate someone other than the mother of his children as their guardian.[3]

By the mid- to late 1800s, economic, social, and legal changes had precipitated a transformation in views about paternal authority. As the family unit moved into private quarters and away from other relatives, lodgers, and servants, motherhood evolved into a calling. A "special" bond that presumably only mothers could share with their children, because mothers bore and nursed them, offered the rationale behind the "tender years" principle. Parenting paradigms underwent a complete reversal. Women emerged as better candidates to care for children despite—or perhaps causing—concerns about whether too much mothering might feminize boys. Although the lone maternal figure was not considered a threat to femininity for daughters, the mother-son relationship still troubled many. As we discuss later, this concern continues today and may influence how custody decisions are rendered and how "good parenting" is envisioned.

In his analysis of public writings regarding gender in the late 1800s and early 1900s, the sociologist Michael Kimmel (1987) underscores how social changes filtered down to families. Economic changes, shifts in American geography, and the settling of the American West influenced what was taking place in families—namely, the increased segregation of socially desirable maternal and paternal roles. With women's increased prominence in parenting—and in teaching—came serious concerns that boys would be reared in overly feminized ways. Male-exclusive organizations such as the Boy Scouts sprang up to shield boys from this threat of overfeminization and to reinforce traditional masculinity. Boys were admonished to avoid activities thought to foster femininity—for example, sleeping on soft featherbeds or reading. Homosociality, not to be confused with homosexuality, encouraged men to engage in activities that did not include women, such as hunting, to reassert and defend their masculinity.[4]

For more than the first half of the twentieth century, discussion about proper parenting centered on mothering, as mothers, by default, were the primary caretakers of children within and outside of coupled families. By the second half of the twentieth century, the "tender years" principle, which officially favored mothers in custodial disputes, was supplanted by the seemingly sex-neutral "best interests of the child" standard. According to this standard, the judge determines which parent would be better for a child, regardless of the parent's sex. Pointing to the high rate of decisions in which mothers are awarded custody, however, many scholars observe that compliance with this standard is sex-neutral in theory but not in practice. Indeed, critics of the "best interests of the child" standard contend that fathers are routinely advised by their lawyers to avoid legal challenges for child custody as futile, since most judges favor mothers. Others discount this claim. In her writings, the feminist legal scholar Martha Fineman (1991, 1995) asserts that men unfairly benefit while women and children suffer from the "best interests" standard, as judges interpret it.[5]

To explore judicial views regarding custody and, in particular, the "best interests of the child" principle, the sociologist Julie Artis (2004) interviewed family court judges in a midwestern state about the reasons behind their custody rulings. In these interviews, most judges, especially older male judges, subscribed to sex stereotypes that worked in favor of women in contested child custody cases.[6] Many judges, including those who explicitly rejected the "tender years" doctrine, confessed that they had a hard time imagining men nurturing children, especially the very young. Yet some judges identified instances in which they might have been inclined to favor the father. These exceptions focused less on the father's qualities and more on a serious problem (or "high negative") of the mother—such as drug use or "sexual misconduct" (which, in one judge's assessment, included working as a stripper), justifications that are heavily gender-stereotyped. Our interviews can assess whether the public, like judges, is prone to gendered assumptions about parenting and whether these assumptions carry over in their distinctions between families and nonfamilies.

The Same-Sex Argument

Throughout this book we have used the term "same-sex" interchangeably with "gay and lesbian." But when it comes to custody, there also is a second meaning of "same-sex": a household in which both the parent and the child are of the same sex. This second meaning has become increasingly important as the father's role in child rearing has been transformed over the past few decades. One sign of this change is the increase in the number of single-father households. Although the proportion of single fathers has been and continues to be small—less than one-fifth of all single parents—the single-father household actually ranks among the fastest-growing family forms.

Whether in single-parent or two-parent homes, modern fathers are encouraged to participate more fully in child rearing. Such engagement is considered important for their children in general, and for boys in particular. Consequently, some legal and family scholars, along with several men's organizations, advocate the position that even if mothers might (still) be the parent best suited to rear girls, boys might benefit more from living with their fathers when parents separate or divorce.

Bolstering the same-sex argument is the idea that boys require male role models and girls female ones. Psychoanalytical theories of childhood development often depict exposure to and interaction with a same-sex parent as essential to a child's well-being (for more details regarding the same-sex argument, see Santrock and Warshak 1979). Same-sex parenting also is seen as important from a social learning perspective, which is based on the view that children model their interpretations of masculinity and femininity from observation and identification with the same-sex parent. This reasoning assumes that parents identify more readily with their same-sex offspring—and vice versa—resulting in more effective parenting and close bonding. This line of reasoning further implies that boys cannot be masculine—and will have difficulty "becoming a man"—without their father's presence. Often unsaid—but still strongly accepted—in this line of reasoning is the putative link between not being masculine and not being heterosexual. Interestingly, this same-sex argument is more often used in scholarly and legal discussions of why boys need their father than in discussions of why girls need their mother. An additional argument often trumpets the different needs of boys and girls for authority. Fathers, rather than mothers, are seen—perhaps unrealistically—as more capable of exercising authority, a practice often judged as more essential in the rearing of boys, who presumably are generally more noncompliant than girls are.

Despite the obvious implications of this claim for custody decisions and for a keener understanding of gender, the alleged benefit of boys living with their fathers and girls living with their mothers has rarely been empirically tested. Among the exceptions is the work of the sociologists Douglas Downey and Brian Powell (one of the authors of this book) (1993; Powell and Downey 1997), who examine the implications of living with same-sex versus opposite-sex single parents. Using multiple national data sets that covered more than forty developmental outcomes, they found no support for the same-sex hypothesis, or even for the idea that either parent provides a clear-cut advantage over the other. These null findings challenge the idea that gender distinctions between men and women—and between boys and girls—are so forceful that it is next to impossible to transcend them. Similarly, in a recent overview of the extant scholarship on parenting, the sociologists Timothy Biblarz and Judith Stacey (2010) caution against reflexively assuming that the gender of parents is consequential for children's personal and social development. Instead, being a good parent matters more than being a good father or a good mother (see also Risman 1987).

Public Views Regarding Child Custody

Each custody standard discussed here is based on clear, sometimes rigid assumptions about gender. In the absence of convincing evidence that children are better off living with their same-sex parent or that, in fact, there is any unequivocal benefit of either custodial arrangement, what do Americans believe is best for children? Do they make die-hard distinctions between fathers and mothers—and between sons and daughters? Or do they minimize or entirely discount such gender distinctions? More importantly, do these different viewpoints have implications for how Americans view family and, in particular, whether they hold more inclusive or exclusive definitions of family?

As noted earlier, we asked respondents their views about the optimal living situation for girls and for boys in single-parent households. We asked whether girls and boys are better off with their mothers or their fathers or whether the gender of the parent (or the gender of the child) matters less than other factors. They then were asked to elaborate on their rationale.

As observed in figure 6.1, there was a great deal of agreement among respondents with respect to girls. Over three-fourths (78.5 percent) agreed that a girl would be better off living with her mother, while fewer than 5 percent responded that a girl would be better off with her father. The remaining respondents shared either the view that the better living arrangement depends on the specific circumstances or the belief that either parent could manage the job. In other words, Americans hold an exceptionally strong maternal preference when it comes to daughters.

In contrast, the preferred living arrangement for boys in single-parent households elicited more divided reactions. Approximately the same percentage chose the father (35.9 percent) or the mother (38.8 percent) as the preferred custodial parent. These numbers reveal a split between those who apparently believed that mothers are universally better suited to raise children, regardless of the child's gender, and those who endorsed a same-sex parenting perspective. The remaining one-fourth of the sample (25.4 percent) believed that the best living arrangement depends on the specific circumstances or that either parent is suitable. Note that this figure is higher than that given when determining the best living arrangement for girls (17.1 percent). Apparently, the child's gender qualitatively alters the prism through which appropriate parental roles are interpreted.

Figure 6.1   Custody Preferences for Boys and Girls

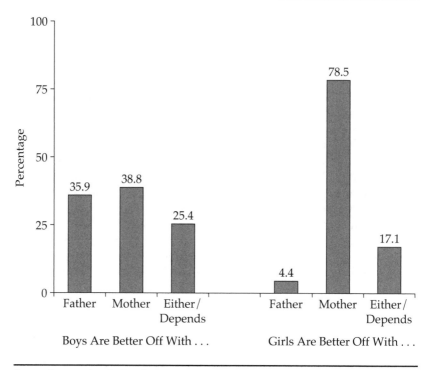

Source: *Constructing the Family Survey* (Powell 2003).

Group Differences in Views on Custody

Are there deep social cleavages in Americans' assessments of the best living arrangement for girls and especially for boys? Among the most striking findings are the disparate responses by men and women, as illustrated in figure 6.2.[7] The plurality of men (41.6 percent) believed that boys are better off living with their father, while the plurality of women (39.8 percent) believed that mothers are the superior option. Perhaps more importantly, women also were more likely than men (29.2 versus 19.1 percent) to respond that there is no clear-cut gender choice: that either parent could be better, especially when taking into consideration the specific circumstances. Interestingly, both men and women backed a maternal presumption for daughters (82.3 percent and 78.0 percent, respectively). That women also were more likely than men to suggest that what is best for boys—and for girls—depends on the situation sug-

Figure 6.2   Custody Preferences for Boys and Girls, by Gender

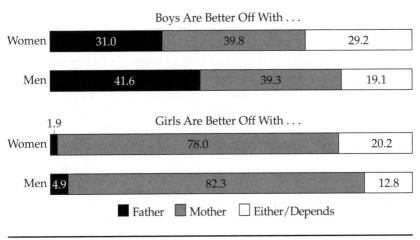

Source: Constructing the Family Survey (Powell 2003).

gests that their judgments of what is best for a child are more wavering (or accommodating) and less monolithic.

Perhaps surprisingly, our analysis indicates few differences by age and inconsistent racial patterns.[8] In contrast, education is strongly tied to gender preferences in child custody. As shown in figure 6.3, respondents who had earned up to a high school degree were significantly

Figure 6.3   Custody Preferences for Boys, by Education

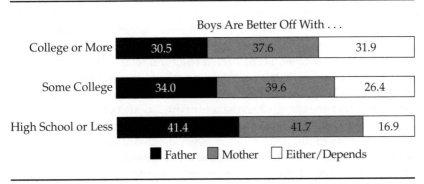

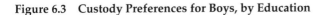

Source: Constructing the Family Survey (Powell 2003).

more likely than respondents with some college education or with a college degree to subscribe to the same-sex standard for boys (41.4, 34.0, and 30.5 percent, respectively) and less likely to indicate that child custody should depend on the situation (16.9, 26.4, and 31.9 percent, respectively).[9] These differences suggest that increasing education may heighten appreciation of the complexity inherent in family situations, increase endorsement of relativist worldviews in which there are no clear or "true" answers, and, as discussed in chapter 4, minimize adherence to traditional views on gender.

Religion and Views on Custody

As discussed in chapter 4, the boundaries drawn between family and nonfamily vary dramatically by people's religious views. In linking religion to views on custody, we once again return to views about the inerrancy of the Bible, taken often as a proxy for evangelical Christian beliefs.[10] As seen in figure 6.4, Americans who interpret the Bible literally also expressed greater certitude—or what some might label greater intransigence—regarding the right thing to do: they were more likely than others to say that boys should be with their father (40.2 percent) and were also more likely to stipulate that boys should be with their mother (41.5 percent). Correspondingly, they were less likely (18.4 percent) to indicate that either parent is good or that the decision rests on the particular situation. Interpreting the Bible in absolutist terms is strongly linked to seeing parenthood in more absolutist terms. Respondents who interpret the Bible literally were more doctrinaire about what is best for boys or girls. Some felt strongly that the father represents the best caretaker for a boy, while others preferred the mother. It also is apparent that those who believe that the Bible is the literal word of God were more likely to avoid the ambiguous territory of "it depends." In other words, they were more likely than their less religiously orthodox counterparts to think that the parent's gender matters.

In comparison, Americans who see the Bible as the inspired word of God were more likely to believe that sons are best off living with their mother (41.2 percent) than with their father (34.6 percent) and more likely than biblical literalists to note that the best choice depends on the particular circumstances (24.3 percent). The likeliest group to decouple gender from good parenting comprised those who believe that the Bible is an "ancient book of fables, legends, history, and moral teachings." The plurality within this group (40.4 percent) believed that the best choice for boys is contingent on the situation (or that either parent is a reasonable choice). For them, gender appears to play a less pivotal role when adjudicating where the best interests of children lie.

Figure 6.4   Custody Preferences for Boys, by Views on the Bible

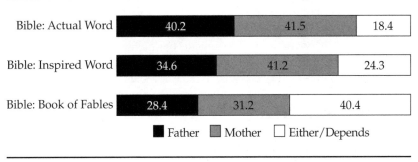

Source: *Constructing the Family Survey* (Powell 2003).

Etiological Explanations of Sexual Preference and Views on Custody

Much public interchange about child custody centers on achieving the normative goals of socialization and ensuring that girls grow up to be "real" women and boys develop into "real" men. This stance goes to the heart of the argument about same-sex parenting. Underlying these arguments about gender—and more broadly, about gender conformity and nonconformity—are related perspectives regarding sexual orientation (Kane 2006; Martin 2009; Stein 2005). Many Americans—especially men—see being a "real" man as the opposite of being gay. In chapter 5, we demonstrated that people's views regarding the causes of sexual preferences are inextricably linked to their definitions of family. Those who subscribe to genetic or "God's will" explanations of sexual preference are more expansive in their definitions of family, while those who believe that parents are mostly responsible for their progeny's sexual preference set firmer limits in their definition of family. We turn now to an examination of how these explanations are related to gendered views on custody issues.

Consistent with the themes that emerged from the previous chapter, figure 6.5 shows that more than one-fourth of those who endorse genetic explanations for sexual preference believed that what is optimal for a boy depends on the family's situation. Admittedly, this percentage is not high, but it is higher than that of any other group. At the same time, this group was less likely than others to favor father-son custody arrangements. Belief in genetic explanations of homosexuality apparently minimizes the perceived threat that absent fathers or overly present mothers play in their children's sexual preference. Custody preferences for Americans who use the "God's will" explanation were

Figure 6.5   Custody Preferences for Boys, by Perceived Cause of Sexual Preference

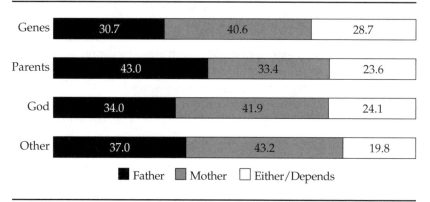

	Father	Mother	Either/Depends
Genes	30.7	40.6	28.7
Parents	43.0	33.4	23.6
God	34.0	41.9	24.1
Other	37.0	43.2	19.8

■ Father ▨ Mother ☐ Either/Depends

Source: Constructing the Family Survey (Powell 2003).

mostly similar to the preferences of those who attribute sexuality to genetic causes.

In contrast, the belief that sexual preference—and presumably gender identity[11]—can actively be shaped by parents corresponds to responses that boys are better off with their fathers. Indeed, individuals who attributed sexual preference primarily to parenting practices were also those who clearly favored paternal living arrangements for boys (43.0 percent). One may suspect that their choices reflect a desire for boys to be properly socialized into masculine gender roles, which, for many in this group, explicitly or implicitly is affixed to heterosexuality.

In summary, views about custody are linked to gender and education but are not easily predicted by some other traditional demographic characteristics, such as age. Similarly, views regarding the Bible and the causes of sexual preference are important in understanding respondents' opinions on custody issues. These patterns suggest that Americans' views regarding a boy's or girl's optimal living arrangement not only speak to the specific question at hand but also mirror their worldviews regarding gender, masculinity, femininity, and parenthood.

In Their Own Words: The Case for Paternal Versus Maternal Custody

Rather than just inferring the underlying rationale for people's preferences, we asked respondents *why* they thought a girl/boy was better off living with her/his mother/father.[12] Answers to this question varied widely, from those Americans who gave seemingly equivocal or self-contradictory responses to those who offered unambiguous and apparently intransigently held positions. Here we discuss the most common themes used in three categories of response: those in our sample who preferred a same-sex custodial arrangement, those who endorsed a maternal presumption, and those who believed that there is no clear-cut preference.[13]

Themes Used by Advocates of Same-Sex Custodial Arrangements

More than any other theme, gender is at the core of the explanations used by Americans who believe that boys should live with their fathers and girls should live with their mothers. In fact, over three-fourths of the Americans who invoked the same-sex presumption talked about the fundamental differences between fathers and mothers *and* those between sons and daughters.

The focus on gender, however, can assume several forms. Among the most common emphases is the importance in the lives of boys of a same-sex figure as a role model, which was seen as much less important in the lives of girls. Indeed, the term "role model" was explicitly used with great frequency (over 20 percent), as indicated in the following examples: "they need a role model"; "to have a role model"; "the boy can assimilate to the other male—a role model."

Many of these responses were very brief, despite attempts by our interviewers to elicit more detailed comments. From our interviews, it is apparent that the brevity of the responses signifies that these interviewees saw the term "role model" as so palpably obvious that a comprehensive explanation seemed to them unnecessary. Some, however, did elaborate on the pivotal and purportedly inimitable role that fathers play, as seen in the following comments by a middle-aged woman:

> He has more direction as to how the boy should lead his life and having a male role model. To be both, the man is supposed to be the strongest. People are supposed to lean on the man to teach the boy things like that.

When asked to identify the "things" a father would teach a boy, she replied: "Other than, what, everything? Honesty and working hard and being the strong role model in a relationship, that's all I can think of."

Another older woman was clear and firm in her preference for same-sex custodial living arrangements for boys in single-parent homes:

> Because the father would be able to be a better role model for that gender than the mother would. I think that there are still different expectations for men than women. And the child watching his father cope with those expectations would at least, would come to realize what they were, where a mother may not be able to convey those expectations because she may not have—she would not have experienced them.

After being asked to offer some examples of these expectations, she responded:

> Let's see. Although not as much now as it used to be, but athletics—the expectation that this is what boys do, and participate in, and do an awful lot of. Like my stepmother who can't throw a football for nothing. I would not be able to guide my child in how to do that.

A man in his sixties relied on "expert" opinion in explaining the importance of a male role model: "Because Dr. Phil says same sex is most important. Because it's a role model to him, to converse on the same level." When pressed to offer some examples of what fathers and sons would "converse" about, he noted: "Well, I think maybe the idea of sex. That would certainly be one, and sports would be another, and competition would be another."

These references to role modeling underscore the importance that these respondents attached to sons maintaining a special relationship with their father, imitating their father, and learning "gender-appropriate" tasks and traits. Fathers presumably are essential because of their unique ability to guide a boy to "become a man." Indeed, the phrases "be a man" and "become a man" are mentioned with approximately the same frequency as the term "role model." These phrases transcend age, although they were more commonly used by men. In the words of a young man: "Because as a father, a father can teach a boy to be a man. That's all I have to say." This sentiment was echoed by a man over four decades older: "He [the son] would mimic after his father, he would learn from his father, he would learn to be a man through his father, in acting with his father."

In the views of most respondents who used a same-sex presumption, mothers are less capable or even incapable of teaching boys their appropriate societal role. As one woman briefly noted: "So they can do manly things together, things that women don't know too much about." She chose not to specify what counts as manly, but another interviewee, who also privileged "manly things," did:

> There's a lot of things that, oh, a mother can't show a boy how to do, or not as well as father. I don't know. More manly things. I just—we grew up without my dad—and I don't know. My brother—my younger brother—he liked to play baseball, and was really more sporty than my other one was. And my mom really wasn't the sporty type of a person. And he needed, I guess, a male figure there for him to be shown, you know—somebody that would like football, baseball, basketball, you know, whatever. Sometimes mothers aren't really into sports.

These examples show that views about gender preferences, in particular regarding boys' custody, are often couched in terms of proper "masculine" socialization as the implicit antithesis to femininity. The concerns sometimes extend to boys feeling insecure in their masculinity or even behaving "like girls," as seen in the following response: "It's just the father-son bond. I've noticed that boys who are raised strictly with their mother and no male figure do not feel as secure." An older male respondent drew on his own parenting experiences and used a term—"whiny"—as a code for femininity: "I raised a boy that was raised by his mother. He was just a little *whiny* and so forth, and we took him and raised him for ten years, and he turned out to be a fine man." A middle-aged man also expressed concerns about the feminizing influence of mothers on sons, but used a different code word:

> Because you're given the opportunities to be more of a—I don't know. I think it's important that they're brought up by or at least have that father influence. I've seen too many cases where a child is brought up with a mother and they're not at all quite—what's the word to use?—but they're not nearly as strong. I mean, I hate to put it this way, but they're kind of *wimpy*.

Some interviewees were even less guarded in their phrasing, like this middle-aged woman who was resolutely opposed to boys living with their mother:

> His mother is subject to make a little *sissy* out of the boy. She'll baby him too much, and she won't let him go outside and play—afraid that he might fall and skin his knee. The father just makes him tougher, just makes him be a man and not a sissy-baby.

The terms "sissy" and "sissified" were used in several other interviews. Although no one explicitly linked maternal living arrangements to homosexuality, the tone implied that this possibility was an unspoken concern of at least a few of the interviewees. Interestingly, however, almost no one volunteered that girls need their fathers to learn about men or that mothers are best suited to guard against "masculine" behavior in their daughters. Still, there was widespread consensus among men and women that girls need to be taught specific domestic tasks and exposed by their mothers to other "feminine" topics.

In fact, over half of our sample who believed that boys should live with their father and girls should live with their mother explicitly discussed gender-specific knowledge that mothers convey to their daughters. Since women perform the majority of household tasks, it is not surprising that respondents believed that mothers are ordinarily better counselors in this arena. A middle-aged woman, for example, stressed that boys and, in particular, girls need to learn specific skills. Here she itemized the feminine skills a girl needs:

> How to do general daily living type of things, how to cook and how to clean, how to do chores, structure, and how to keep a checkbook, all things. Those types of things [you need] when you're getting older. Curfews, and everything. (laugh) Just general overall living. And how to communicate and disagree with people, and get along with others.

We continue to be struck by the starkly diametric and traditional views of what girls need to learn and what boys need to learn and what fathers are (in)capable of teaching and what mothers are (in)capable of teaching. To this group, "girls are different, man," and "when she is with her father, she isn't going to learn nothing." The responses by a middle-aged father exemplify this gender distinction:

> A young boy needs to know how to grow up and become a man and so he would learn from his father. I think boys need to know how to go camping, and go fishing and ride motorcycles and surf. And I don't know if moms would be able to do that for him and to teach him respect and things of this nature.

Still, he saw mothers as the preferred choice for a girl:

> She needs to learn how to become a woman and have the examples set by her mom. I have a daughter, and I've never taught her how to sew, I've never taught her how to cook. She knows how to surf. She knows

how to ride a motorcycle. (*laughs*) But you know, all of those things, I just, I don't know about, and I think a young girl needs her mother.

In addition to teaching daughters "feminine" tasks as well as how to be and look feminine (for example, "beauty secrets," "clothes and dates"), mothers also were seen as having a distinct biological advantage in teaching daughters about puberty. Maternal competency to understand what daughters are going through during puberty and to advise them through this milestone was one of the most frequently mentioned justifications by advocates of a same-sex living arrangement. More often than not, our respondents appeared uncomfortable mentioning this issue, using such vague (but still understandable) phrases as "when it's time," "natural aspects," "female problems," "that time when she needs more care, you know, when she grows things," "the change," "personal hygiene things, just knowing the workings of women," "that baggage that comes with being female," "well, you know, you get to a certain age when she's going to, you know, (*pause, heavy breath*) . . . growing up things."

Among those who were less circumspect in their phrasing, a young woman used her own personal experiences in explaining why she believed that it is better for a girl to live with her mother: "Maybe I would have had inhibitions like talking to my father about my period or something, but I, of course, I didn't feel that way with my mom."

Men typically appeared even less comfortable or willing to explicitly mention menstruation or puberty, with a few exceptions, such as a middle-aged man who listed topics that mothers can more easily talk to their daughters about: "Her period and about boys in general, and the mother's experiences, and, I guess, home economics."

In contrast, very few references were made to boys' sexual maturation or, for that matter, physiology. One man briefly mentioned that fathers and sons have the "same equipment," while another man saw core biological differences in what mothers and fathers can provide:

Because a woman can't make a man, she can make a baby, but she can't make a man. I mean, a man knows just what's going on with another man's body. You know, if he comes along and tells me something is wrong with his groin or something, I could relate better to that than with a girl, a woman, with his mama there.

But these two quotes are more telling in that they were so atypical. More common were responses that emphasized fathers' ability to teach boys physical tasks (from carpentry to surfing to sports to auto mechanics) and fathers' advantage (in part physically derived) over sons (mentioned by over 10 percent in this group) that enables fathers to discipline sons more effectively. Mothers were portrayed as less adept at maintaining control ("mothers are too easy," "the mother couldn't control them by herself") than fathers ("they listen to the father but don't listen to the mother," "he has more authority than the mother"). Boys were seen to be in special need of paternal discipline. Ironically, boys were seen as needing their father so that they will not be too feminine *and* so that they will not be "too aggressive" or "too wild." In contrast, girls apparently were seen to be in less need of discipline. In fact, rarely were girls described as disobedient or unmanageable. In the few interviews that included such a depiction, girls typically then were seen as better off living with their father, who presumably would be better than the mother at preventing unruly and reckless behavior in their daughter. Although this view was clearly in the minority, it also was firmly held, as demonstrated in the following comments by a middle-aged father:[14]

> I'd say the father. Because in a single family household, the girl's mother probably ain't the best girl in town. Let's not push that girl into that situation. You know what I'm saying, though . . . I mean, I've picked up my son and some of his girlfriends—you know, they're twelve, thirteen years old—and these girls look like they're ready to hit the strip. You know what I mean? That's what I'm saying.

Thus, advocates of same-sex custodial arrangements see clear gender divisions between fathers and mothers and between sons and daughters. To this group, boys need their father to "become a man," while girls need their mother to make the physiological transition from girl to woman. Boys need to learn about sports, hunting, and other "manly things," while girls need to learn about cooking, cleaning, dating, and other ostensibly feminine skills. Boys need to avoid being too feminine and being too wild or aggressive, but there is less concern over girls being too masculine (indeed, there was no explicit mention of this issue) or being too wild. Fathers know "nothing" about girls, while mothers know little about the tasks that boys must learn. Fathers can discipline, while mothers cannot. To this group, children have explicit gendered rules and worlds, and parents do as well. These separate spheres are seen as so distant from each other that it is unimaginable for either sex to transcend them. Of course, there were some exceptions among advocates of same-sex custodial arrangements, but these were based more on personal and idiosyncratic experiences than on an overall worldview regarding gender. The prevailing vision of

this group is one of firm boundaries between boys and girls and between mothers and fathers that cannot be broken.

Themes Used by Advocates of Maternal
Custodial Arrangements

Like those who prefer a same-sex custodial living arrangement, Americans who believe that both sons and daughters are better off living with
their mother are not immune to gendered assumptions. The difference,
however, is that those who endorse a maternal presumption differentiate primarily—and often only—between mothers and fathers and
mostly see few differences in the needs of sons and daughters. In other
words, the perceived gender boundaries between mothers and fathers
are strong (although perhaps not as strong as the lines drawn by those
who believe in a same-sex principle), while the gender boundaries between sons and daughters are more blurred.

Whereas an overriding theme of same-sex custodial advocates is
that "boys need their father to become a man," a recurring theme
among maternal custodial supporters is that "every child needs their
mother" ("all children need their mother," "every child needs his
mother more than his father"). To this group, fathers do not—or cannot—equal mothers in their ability to love ("I think all children need
their mother's love," "I don't know. I think the mother's more loving or
something") and to nurture ("because a mother is more nurturing in
general. . . . This is a big generalization, but mothers are, in general,
more nurturing and more prepared to take care of the child"). Approximately two-fifths of the respondents in this group explicitly mentioned
nurturance, compassion, or love. This group privileged care and emotional needs and saw promoting the emotional well-being of sons and
daughters as a key ingredient in successful parenting. A middle-aged
woman explained:

> Well, I just think that the emotional attachment that is important for a
> child is the one that he has with his mother originally. And without that
> foundation built on, you have basic problems.

When asked to identify these problems, she listed the following: "Well,
attachment problems, security problems, abandonment problems, self-
esteem, that's just off the cuff. I just think they would have a feeling of
not being loved."

Maternal love and nurturance purportedly are manifested in several
ways. Perhaps foremost is mothers' presumed greater availability ("his
mother is more available"). Mothers are, in the words of a woman in

her twenties, "there for you emotionally and physically and for every situation."

The portrayal of fathers is more mixed: some were depicted as hard workers who meet the expectations of a breadwinner role, and others were described as derelict in their duties. To some respondents, men's unavailability at home is attributed to their work responsibilities, as noted by an elderly woman:

> Because a mother is more nurturing in general and will probably pay more attention to the child. The father most often is out working, building a career, and doesn't have enough time to give to the child, and is not as nurturing. You know, this is a big generalization, but mothers are in general more nurturing and more prepared to take care of a child.

But others took a decidedly more critical view of fathers. They did not believe that responsibilities outside the home account for fathers' inattention to their children. Instead, they simply saw men as irresponsible. As a woman in her early thirties succinctly observed: "Well, most men lack responsibility, (*laughing*) and women don't."

In fact, we were surprised by the frequency with which respondents alluded to the inattentive father who chooses to ignore his children. Both men and women discussed the "deadbeat dad" and the "father who wanders around," although it was women, especially younger ones, who were much more likely to characterize fathers this way. A young woman in her twenties, for example, showed her frustration with what she saw as the typical father:

> Mothers show him [son] more attention. Moms teach him what's right and wrong. But fathers don't. They just go off whenever. They love doing what they want to do.

Another young woman offered a similar judgment: "Men can be insensitive and selfish at times. I mean, they can't help it. They just are."

Beyond their presumed greater availability and levels of responsibility, women were seen as more capable of doing the various tasks of parenting, whether the tasks are to "cook and clean the house" and "keep a little girl's clothes washed and ironed" or to "teach the son a little better than the father would." Several men even professed their own ignorance about parenting. A middle-aged man was candid about his limitations and speculated that he would fail at single parenting:

> I think that, how can I put this? You are not going to get a hold of my wife, are you? (*laughs*) I think she just does a better job than I would.

She'd take care of him more and make sure his clothes were clean and all that other stuff. I just can't do that. I don't even know how to use the washing machine.

Advocates of a same-sex principle see fathers as uniquely qualified to handle certain parenting tasks—especially pertaining to sons—but Americans who believe that children are better off living with their mother see mothers as uniquely qualified to handle *both* maternal and paternal roles ("If there's no father around, she makes sure that, for the most part, she has what it takes to be a father"). In other words, mothers can mother *and* father children, but fathers cannot mother, and some of them cannot even father. In offering evidence to support this idea, a young woman relied on her own family background:

> My mother had to be a mother and father. My brother knows everything a boy's supposed to know. My mother played both the role of the father and mother. So I think that if he would have lived with my father, my father doesn't really know how to be a mother. So I don't think my brother would be as nurturing as he is.

Most respondents did not speculate on why mothers and fathers differ, but when they did offer an explanation, it usually was framed in terms of "mother nature." Similar to the rationale behind the "tender years" principle, women's ostensibly inimitable bond with children and their maternal instinct are believed to stem naturally from the uniquely female ability to give birth: "That's what/where he came from. Tough question, yeah. Why is he better with his mother? It's just, it's biological."

Whether or not the cause is seen as biological, the conclusion is the same to advocates of maternal custody: mothers make better parents than fathers. They are more capable, more responsible, more caring, and more loving than fathers. But as unambiguous as this distinction may appear, the overall tone here is much less gendered and absolute than that conveyed by Americans who believe that boys should live with their father and girls should live with their mother. More qualifiers are used by advocates of a maternal presumption ("in general," "not all fathers but …," "I guess fathers would be okay," "I hate to say, this is sounding like a generality," "though I don't strongly agree with what I said," "I don't know if I'm right, but I think that …"). In addition, those who prefer maternal custody tend not to see much difference in the needs or behaviors of sons and daughters. Indeed, the most common responses regarding the optimal arrangement for girls (which followed the question about boys[15]) suggest that what is seen as good for sons is also seen as good for daughters (for example, "pretty much the same reason I state for the sons," "same," "probably the same reason").

When members of this group, however, discussed special needs, they typically focused on sons. Interestingly, the most common concern was not that "boys need to become men," but rather that boys need to avoid rigid expectations about masculinity. Whereas advocates of the same-sex principle worried about the feminizing ("sissifying") influence of mothers on sons, supporters of the maternal presumption saw the very same feminizing influence as a real advantage for boys. This implicit—or explicit—critique of masculinity was invariably mentioned by women and, with just one exception, not by men. A woman in her thirties noted: "Because he will get nurturing values, learn to be a better man, grow up with morals and values, and be in touch with their feelings and not bottle them up." Another middle-aged woman pointed to the "softer side" that mothers can provide their sons: "Because there is too much 'men rule,' 'shape up' there in the world, and boys need the softer side of a mother." The only man who warned of the dangers for sons living with fathers was a high school principal who explained:

> I think moms tend to be more, to give better guidance to their sons and protect them from becoming risk-takers, whereas dads are sometimes either too restrictive or they just let the kid become involved in too many high-risk activities, and they get totally out of control.

Advocates of the same-sex principle believe in role modeling, with sons emulating their fathers. Americans who believe that the optimal living situation for boys is with their mother also believe in role modeling, but they privilege a qualitatively different set of lessons:

> I think if a boy is raised with his mother, he not only gets the nurturing care, he learns to be—I don't know—more tender-hearted. That's not the right word I want. He learns to be more comforting.

To this group, then, traditional masculinity—the very core of which is promoted by advocates of the same-sex principle—is to be avoided. This group may see core differences between mothers and fathers, but they do not want to see these differences in their sons and daughters and believe that it is important to move beyond an unbendingly enforced binary view of gender.

Themes Used by Advocates of Alternative Custodial Arrangements: Gender-Neutral or Ambivalent?

As noted earlier, a smaller proportion of our interviewees were unwilling or unable to choose either the father or the mother as the preferred custodian for boys (and for girls). For many of these respondents, good parenting is not attached to gender. Indeed, among the most common responses were that gender "doesn't matter" and "it depends." In fact, some expressed frustration with this question (more so than with other questions in our interview), as seen in the following comments from a middle-aged woman:

> I mean, it depends. This is going to go out nationwide, isn't it? This Indiana University did this survey, correct? You know, I think it's such an unfair questionnaire, because it depends on every situation. I just think it depends on each situation. I mean, honey, some would be better off with the father.

Interestingly, this respondent apparently believed that younger adults have a more absolutist view regarding gender and that, with age, they come to a greater appreciation of the situational nature of custodial arrangements. In responding to our question regarding the optimal custodial arrangement for a girl, she explained:

> You're way, way younger than I am—but you know, some of these things just depend on the situation. I don't think there's a right or wrong answer to any of them [the questions]. I think they're very suggestive. But I know you didn't make them up. You're just asking them.

For this respondent, other parental—and in some cases, child—qualities and traits trump gender as the decisive factors in determining custodial arrangements. These qualities and traits include:

> The type of person that each person is; the type of parent that they are; their ability to provide for that child; the child's relationship with that parent. There're so many more factors involved in that . . . I wouldn't be able to say it would be better for him to live with a mother or father just because it's their mother or father.
>   I think it depends, on the whole, on who the parent is, who the child is, and the relationship with their parents. Because I believe any parent can raise a child as long as they are dedicated and love that child and

make their child their first priority. A good mom could raise a son or a good dad could raise a son.

This group privileged the "good parent" over the "good mother" or "good father" and refrained from setting fixed boundaries between fathers and mothers. While some saw gender as secondary to being a "good parent," others emphasized the "bad parent"—or as a middle-aged man somewhat facetiously answered: "It depends on which one is the ax murderer." The succinct response of a middle-aged male respondent may best exemplify this viewpoint: "It depends on the individual. There can be bad moms and there can be bad dads."

In fact, we were taken aback by the frequent references to "bad parents," "bad fathers," and "bad mothers," who often are characterized as "deadbeat," "alcoholic" or "drunkard," "violent," and "druggies" or "crack addicts." For some respondents, the question was not "who makes the better parent?" but rather "who is the lesser of two evils?" Our respondents' focus on unfit parenting mirrors the emphasis that judges put on "high negatives" in their interviews with Julie Artis, mentioned earlier in this chapter. Some of the "high negatives" were gender-neutral, as illustrated by the comments of a middle-aged woman who was concerned about the importance of children living with the "sober parent":

> It depends on who's the alcoholic or the drug person. I feel they have to live with someone who's sober. It really doesn't matter who it is, as long as they're a sober person. . . . It doesn't matter what their sex is. If it's the father or the mother, they need to be with the one that's straight.

More often than not, however, gender was implicated in the use of "high negatives." Only fathers are "deadbeats" who "couldn't make any money to support him [son]," as well as "abusive" and "into trouble and [in] jail all the time." Similarly, fathers are more likely than mothers to be "alcoholics" or "drunks." Although drugs were mentioned in connection with both fathers and mothers, fathers were called "druggies" while mothers were "crack addicts." "High negatives" linked to sexuality or sexual morals were applied to mothers only. Interestingly, several comments juxtaposed a "masculine" negative with a "feminine" negative:

> If the father's a scumbag or if the mom's a, you know, promiscuous person, then it's probably better for them to live with the other parent.

I don't know how to answer that. It totally depends on the parent. The father could be a drunk and the mother could be a whore. I don't know.

Others offered an array of gender-specific indicators of bad parenting that paralleled the concerns expressed by advocates of same-sex custody. For example, when asked about the optimal living arrangement for a boy in a single-parent home, a middle-aged woman reflected:

Again, that's kind of tricky, because you would need to know what type of mother and what type of father. Because you can get a situation [in which] I know you just need a mother or father. But I have to say this. Because if you've got the right type of mother who has a level that is God-fearing—and the reason why I say God-fearing, meaning that she will fear God and not the child—then a mother can do fine with the child. But if you got a father who's wimpy or got some problems, then the mother would be better off. But if you've got a mother who's running around and is a Jezebel, then the father would be better with the son. So whoever poses the greatest ability, I think, would be the best for the child, whichever one.[16]

Ironically, this group of respondents chose a seemingly nongendered response regarding the preferred custodial arrangement for boys and girls ("it depends") but did so only because their focus on the "bad parent" was often filtered through a gendered lens. A smaller number also selected what at face value appears to be a gender-free choice, but did so precisely because they believed that fathers and mothers are different. That is, their notions of parents were so strongly gendered that they struggled with the question's lack of specificity, as illustrated in the response by a middle-aged women who hesitated when asked who should have custody of a boy:

Ewww ... (laughs) ... that depends on the age. [In] younger years, he would definitely need the nurturing of a mother. But in the teenage years, he needs the (pause) more of the manly, you know, influence, boundaries. A father can keep the healthy boundaries better than a mother can. So it just depends on the age.

As seen in this response—and in several others—a small number of respondents took into consideration the child's age as a pivotal factor in determining which parent would be a better guardian. To these respondents, mothers typically are better candidates to rear younger children, while fathers were often thought to be better at handling adolescents—especially boys.

In sum, Americans who are unwilling or unable to choose between the mother and the father as the preferred custodian are a diverse group. Some focus on the "bad parents," relying on a sex-specific interpretation of the "bad mother" and the "bad father." Others view the maternal role as more critical in children's earlier years and the paternal role as more central during adolescence. Despite these variable responses, however, the most common reaction was that gender is secondary to other characteristics and fathers and mothers are equivalently competent. Overall, this group saw many fewer gender differences than did those who espoused a same-sex custody standard or a maternal presumption. For this group, the boundaries between fathers and mothers and between sons and daughters are much less rigidly delineated and can more easily be crossed.

Views Regarding Single-Parent Homes and Definitions of Family

So far we have explored how individuals vary in their views regarding same-sex versus "opposite-sex" parenting in single-parent households. Are these views on parenting, which often reflect fundamental beliefs about gender, implicated in the central concern of this book—what Americans count and do not count as family? Indeed, custody preferences are a powerful predictor of whether or not gay and lesbian couples are included within familial boundaries. This pattern is evident in figure 6.6. Americans who believe that a boy is best off living with his father were less likely than their peers to consider lesbian couples with children a family (43.1 percent). In contrast, individuals who believe that what is best for a boy is situational were also the most likely to see lesbian couples with children as family (65.2 percent).

This pattern is even more visible in figure 6.7, which differentiates between exclusionists, moderates, and inclusionists. Nearly three-fifths of Americans (56.8 percent) who adhere to a same-sex stance regarding boys' custody adopt an exclusionist definition of family. In fact, they are over three times more likely to be exclusionists than inclusionists (16.6 percent). A plurality of those who express a maternal preference are exclusionists (42.2 percent), but the majority fall into the categories of moderate (33.4 percent) or inclusionist (24.4 percent). And those who believe that the best living condition for boys is situational are more likely than others to hold an expansive definition of family (34.5 percent). In other words, views regarding gender—at least as measured by views regarding parenting and gender—are inextrica-

Figure 6.6   Do Lesbian Couples with Children Count as Family? Differences by Custody Preferences for Boys

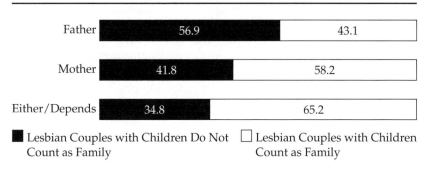

Father   56.9   43.1

Mother   41.8   58.2

Either/Depends   34.8   65.2

■ Lesbian Couples with Children Do Not   ☐ Lesbian Couples with Children
Count as Family   Count as Family

Source: Constructing the Family Survey (Powell 2003).

Figure 6.7   Differences in Family Definitions, by Custody Preferences for Boys

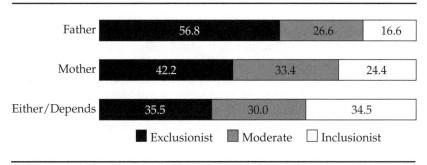

Father   56.8   26.6   16.6

Mother   42.2   33.4   24.4

Either/Depends   35.5   30.0   34.5

■ Exclusionist   ■ Moderate   ☐ Inclusionist

Source: Constructing the Family Survey (Powell 2003).

bly tied to the boundaries that Americans draw between families and nonfamilies.[17]

Gender in Two-Parent Homes and Definitions of Family

In this chapter, we have considered whether and how individuals differentiate between maternal and paternal roles in single-parent homes and the extent to which these differences translate into various family definitions. It remains unclear, however, whether beliefs regarding gendered spheres in two-parent households are associated with definitions of family. Fortunately, the 2003 Constructing the Family Survey also included a limited set of items that asked about the appropriate or preferred division of parental labor in a heterosexual two-parent household. More specifically, these items asked:

Who do you think should have the main responsibility for taking care of a child's physical needs, such as making meals, giving baths, or dressing them?

Who should have the main responsibility for disciplining the child?

Who should have the main responsibility for listening to the child's problems; for example, trouble with friends, worries about school, and so forth?

Americans were split in where they assigned responsibilities. Some saw separate but complementary gendered spheres of responsibilities in which women attend to both the physical and emotional (that is, listening) needs of children, while fathers address disciplinary issues. Others saw much greater overlap, with both parents equally sharing in each of these tasks. More specifically, fathers were rarely seen as "always" or "usually" responsible for tending to children's physical needs (fewer than 1 percent) or listening to their problems (fewer than 4 percent). These responsibilities were more often seen as the province of mothers: nearly two-thirds (66.3 percent) believed that mothers should always or usually be responsible for taking care of a child's physical needs, and over two-fifths (44.5 percent) indicated that mothers should be responsible for listening to a child's problems. Fathers were slightly more likely than mothers to be seen as the disciplinarian (31.0 percent versus 23.0 percent), although some unsolicited comments indicate that respondents were much more likely to see fathers in the disciplinary role when dealing with adolescents.

Notably, a large percentage of Americans did not make these gender distinctions. Roughly one-third (32.6 percent) believed that mothers and fathers should equally share in taking care of a child's physical needs. A higher percentage endorsed gender egalitarianism in disciplining the child (46.1 percent) and talking with the child (51.7 percent).[18]

Consistent with the patterns regarding paternal and maternal custody, we find that knowing people's views about the gender division in child care can help us better understand their views on what counts as a family. As seen in figure 6.8, traditional sex-specific views regarding the division of labor are closely tied to a more traditional definition of

Figure 6.8   Differences in Family Definitions, by Views Regarding Preferred Parental Responsibilities

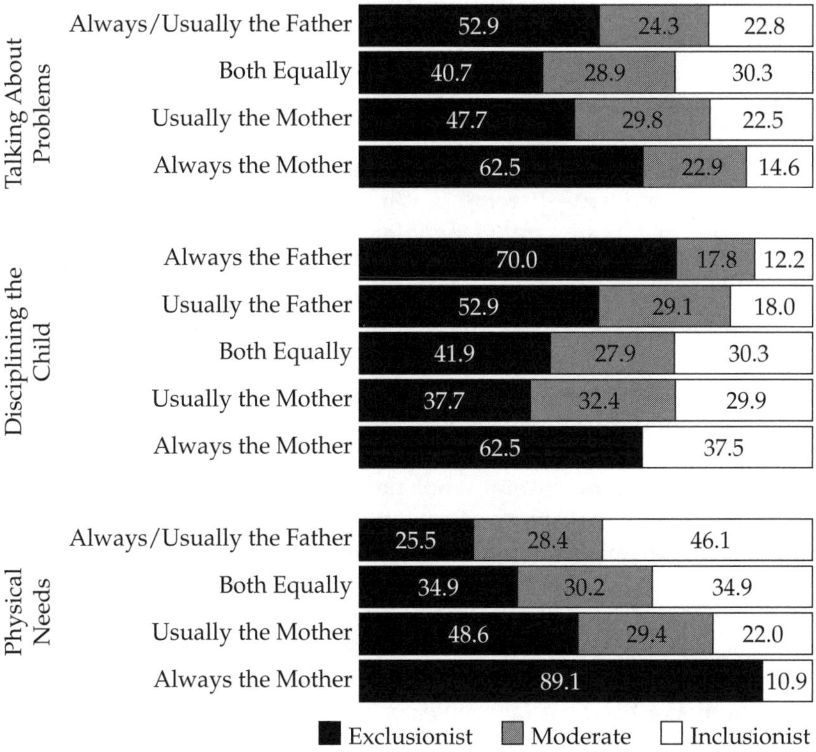

		Exclusionist	Moderate	Inclusionist
Talking About Problems	Always/Usually the Father	52.9	24.3	22.8
	Both Equally	40.7	28.9	30.3
	Usually the Mother	47.7	29.8	22.5
	Always the Mother	62.5	22.9	14.6
Disciplining the Child	Always the Father	70.0	17.8	12.2
	Usually the Father	52.9	29.1	18.0
	Both Equally	41.9	27.9	30.3
	Usually the Mother	37.7	32.4	29.9
	Always the Mother	62.5		37.5
Physical Needs	Always/Usually the Father	25.5	28.4	46.1
	Both Equally	34.9	30.2	34.9
	Usually the Mother	48.6	29.4	22.0
	Always the Mother	89.1		10.9

■ Exclusionist   ▨ Moderate   ☐ Inclusionist

Source: Constructing the Family Survey (Powell 2003).

family. For example, the plurality of Americans who believed that the mother should always or usually be responsible for a child's physical needs also agreed with an exclusionist definition of families (89.1 percent and 48.6 percent, respectively). In contrast, approximately two-thirds of Americans who believed that fathers and mothers should equally tend to a child's physical needs fell into the inclusionist (34.9 percent) or moderate (30.2 percent) category.

Paralleling these patterns, Americans who believed that mothers and fathers should share equally in disciplining and listening to their child were more inclusive in their definitions of family than were their peers. Regarding discipline, over half of those who believed that fathers should always or usually be in control were exclusionists (70 percent and 52.9 percent, respectively). Interestingly, however, the majority of the very few Americans who believed that mothers should always be the disciplinarian also were exclusionist (62.5 percent). In other words, adhering to either a traditionally gendered view or an absolutist view ("always") regarding discipline is linked to greater rigidity in the definitions of family.[19]

Conclusion

For most of this chapter, we have discussed how Americans conceptualize good—and bad—parenting. What they emphasize when discussing the optimal living arrangement for children in single-parent homes tells us a great deal about the extent to which gender permeates assessments of parenting. It tells us whether Americans see patent gender differences in parenthood, thereby distinguishing mothers from fathers, or whether instead they see gender as secondary to other core qualities of parenthood. Their responses also tell us whether they differentiate children along gender lines and distinguish between the needs of sons and daughters, or whether they believe that the needs of sons and daughters closely, if not perfectly, overlap. Their responses therefore tell us whether Americans see gendered boundaries—or separate gendered spheres—for parents and for children.

But how they talk about the optimal living arrangement for children in single-parent families tells us even more. The boundaries they draw in these discussions are closely connected to—and perhaps, judging from some of the interview comments, inseverable from—the boundaries they make between families and nonfamilies. Views of parenting fall onto a continuum: (1) those with the *most gendered* views said that boys should be placed with fathers and girls should be placed with mothers; (2) those whose views were *moderately gendered* deemed mothers more capable of child care, owing to the presumed gender differences in nurturance or just their knowledge of how to do the things that children require; and (3) respondents with the *least gendered* views saw gender as less central to the concerns of parenting. As we move across this continuum, we also see that Americans start to loosen where they demarcate familial boundaries. In fact, Americans who have the most relaxed view of gender are correspondingly the most likely to endorse an expansive definition of family that includes gay and lesbian couples.

Our most conservative respondents tended to make the same-sex parenting argument that boys are better off with fathers and girls with mothers. From their standpoint, boys require a strong male role model who instills both aggressiveness and self-discipline in sons, traits that this group of respondents believe mothers cannot cultivate. With respect to daughters, the focus pivots to female-specific roles (often in the domestic arena), puberty, and sexuality. The emphasis often is on female maturation and how to handle this transformation, which is seen as something that grown women are knowledgeable about and men are incapable of attending to. Apparently gender beliefs about fathers and mothers, as well as sons and daughters, are so profound that many Americans reflexively turn to them when explaining their views about custody. For this group, it seems almost unimaginable that men or women are capable of transcending gender roles—and unspeakable if boys, and to a lesser extent girls, actually cross gendered boundaries.

The reasoning expressed by this group—especially regarding the importance of fathers for boys—is not new. Comments from our interviews easily could have been given by members of men's organizations over a century ago who, as described by Michael Kimmel (1987), worried about the contaminating effects of an escalating influence of women at home and at school and a correspondingly increasing feminization of American boys. Their remarks also bear an uncanny resemblance to the rhetoric of conservative family activists of today who decry the "crisis in masculinity" and attribute this crisis in part to the waning influence of fathers in sons' lives. In his book *Bringing Up Boys: Practical Advice and Encouragement for Those Shaping the Next Generation of Men*, James Dobson (2001), founder of Focus on the Family, explicitly warns that the absence of men in boys' lives and, perhaps as a result, the absence of gender-appropriate roles for boys are key causal agents in the development of homosexuality. In advocating this position, he relies on the claims of Joseph Nicolosi, cofounder of the National Association for Research and Therapy of Homosexuality, an organization that promotes reparative therapy for gays, lesbians, and bisexuals. Nicolosi contends that: "The truth is, Dad is more important than Mom. Mothers make boys. Fathers make men" (Nicolosi and Nicolosi 2002, 23). Nicolosi's characterization of the paternal role dovetails closely with those offered by many of our respondents:

> Meanwhile, the boy's father has to do his part. He needs to mirror and affirm his son's maleness. He can play rough-and-tumble games with his son, in ways that are decidedly different from the games he would play with a little girl. He can help his son learn to throw and catch a ball. He can teach him to pound a square wooden peg into a square hole in a pegboard. . . . (2002, 24).
>
> In fifteen years I have spoken with hundreds of homosexual men. Perhaps there are exceptions, but I have never met one who said he had a loving respectful relationship with his father. . . . When boys relate well with their fathers, beginning to understand what is exciting, fun, and

energizing about them, the relationship will evoke the boy's own masculine nature. Through his dad, he will find a sense of freedom and power in being different from his mother, outgrowing her and moving on into a man's world, and finally maturing into heterosexual manhood (2002, 103–104).

This view of fatherhood apparently is shared by the Vatican. It has been reported that recent rules regarding the priesthood include explicit prohibitions of gay seminarians—even celibate ones—from entering the priesthood. The Vatican released a litany of ways to identify gay seminarians, including "trouble relating to their fathers." According to this viewpoint, the presence of a strong father-son tie is fundamentally tied to the development of healthy masculinity and, implicitly or explicitly, heterosexuality. In other words, masculinity, sexuality, and a strong father presence form a trinity that cannot—and should not—be dismantled.

Of course, not everyone in our sample who advocates a same-sex custodial arrangement so firmly believes in the conflation of masculinity, sexuality, and strong fatherhood. In fact, the unremitting emphasis on masculinity among this group could indicate that masculinity is the litmus test for males, regardless of sexuality. Correspondingly, some sociologists speculate that views regarding masculinity could be—and in some settings already are—severed from views regarding homosexuality. The sociologist C. J. Pascoe, for example, describes how male adolescents label each other with the slur "fag" but use the term to mean unmasculine rather than homosexual—implicitly suggesting that being gay might be acceptable, or at least less objectionable, if a young man retains his masculinity (Pascoe 2007). Although this decoupling of masculinity and heterosexuality may be occurring in some areas, our interviews suggest that it remains far from the norm. Instead, Americans who believe that boys are better off living with their fathers strongly tilt toward rigidity in their conception of what a family is. They are strikingly more likely than others to voice an exclusionist definition of family and less likely to embrace an inclusionist one. In other words, it is difficult to imagine how those who offer such heavily gendered, binary views of parents and children will readily shift to a broader position regarding who counts as family and who is counted out.

Nonetheless, there is greater room for movement toward inclusiveness among the other respondents. Those who adhere to the "tender years" principle that women make better parents regardless of the child's sex are a case in point. To this group, mothers are just better than fathers at nurturance and at meeting the emotional—and many of the instrumental—needs of children. The ability to do emotion work is visualized as a female stronghold. Under such reasoning, daughters and sons generally would be better off in the custody of their mothers than their fathers. Again, the general thought that females are superior caretakers is stereotypic, but not as firmly so as the same-sex presumption. In fact, a recurring theme among this group (more accurately, the women in this group) is the need to prevent boys from becoming stereotypically masculine and instead to socialize them so that they too can become more "tender-hearted." This group may not be free of gendered notions of parents, but they see the need to move beyond the rigidly imposed boundaries of masculinity and femininity. Given their willingness to see the possibility of crossing these boundaries and their focus on love and nurturance regardless of gender, they tend to be moderately inclusive in their definitions of family and may become even more expansive in the future.

Our final set of respondents, many of whose answers imply that gender is not relevant, represents a wide berth. Of course, it would be misleading to think that the most liberal group of respondents encompasses a gender-neutral zone, as revealed by comments that invoke such gender stereotypes as the inebriated husband and the wayward wife. Still, the overriding theme expressed within this group is that alternatives to traditional gendered roles might be the best solution for the rearing of a child. To these respondents, a good parent is a good parent, regardless of the parent's sex. And the needs of a child are the needs of a child, regardless of the child's sex. Just as they see the value in loosening the entrenched boundaries of gender, they also see the virtue in widening the definitions of family. After all, a good family is a good family, regardless of the sex of its members.

= Chapter 7 =

Family Names Count: Marital Name Change and Definitions of Family

with Laura Hamilton

I N THE last chapter, we explored how gendered views of the ideal parent in single-parent living arrangements are related to the boundaries that Americans draw in defining family.[1] Respondents who had the most gendered approach to parenting had the most restrictive view of who counts as a family. From this perspective, a same-sex arrangement—boys with fathers and girls with mothers—is ideal because fathers and mothers have fundamentally different parenting capabilities that are best suited to meet the gendered needs of sons and daughters, respectively. Those with a more moderately gendered view—they see mothers as the ideal parent regardless of the child's gender—were more inclusive of different family types than those who prefer same-sex custodial arrangements. Finally, although a mixed group, respondents with the least gendered perspective—those who advocate for the best or least unfit parent, regardless of parental or child gender—were most likely to endorse the most expansive definition of family. These results indicate that beliefs about gender and the identity of both parents and children are inextricably linked to people's views of family.

In this chapter, we look at a different aspect of family identity—family names. Specifically, we explore respondents' views regarding women's and men's last-name change upon marriage and, as in the last two chapters, highlight social cleavages in terms of these beliefs. Most importantly, we examine the extent to which views regarding this practice map onto the boundaries that Americans draw between families and nonfamilies. In the 2006 interviews, respondents were asked a series of questions on marital name change—including whether it is generally better for women to change their names, whether women should be legally required to so, and whether it is okay for men to change their names. Respondents were also asked to explain *why* they held certain beliefs about name change. Their responses reveal the cultural frameworks that people use to make sense of marital name change.

At first glance, it may seem surprising to find a chapter on marital name change in a book examining Americans' attitudes toward same-sex relations and family life. However, as we have illustrated and others have argued, heteronormativity is displayed and enacted through more than just attitudes toward homosexuality. In fact, the belief that men and women are polar opposites with complementary and natural family roles is critical to the boundaries that Americans draw when defining who counts as a family. Marital name change is a traditionally gendered practice that reflects this notion of family life. Thus, the topic of marital name change offers an ideal opportunity to investigate respondents' understandings of gender in family life and an important avenue into the central goals of this book.

Marital name change is often taken for granted in the United States, where most families share a common family name—generally the husband's last name. The very familiarity of this naming practice and its long-standing roots in this country make it an ideal topic for research on gender attitudes. People generally see names as no more than labels, uncomplicated by issues of social rights and equality. Yet names reflect the categories, like gender, that we use to classify and understand our social world. We argue that these orientations to gender speak to understandings of family identity—what family means, how it should be created, and the differing roles of men and women in creating family. Most importantly, attitudes toward name change also may speak to Americans' willingness to move beyond a definition of family that places a diametric masculine-feminine or even man-woman pairing at its center. Consequently, we return to the central concern of this book—whether same-sex families are counted in Americans' definitions of family—and consider the extent to which broadness (or narrowness) in these definitions is related to Americans' views about the traditional gendered practice of marital name change.

Gendered Language and Marital Name Change

Marital name change represents only one example of gendered language—although it is perhaps one of the most ubiquitous and persistent examples in American history. Here we provide an overview of gendered language, describing what it is and how it affects our lives. We then describe the history of women's name change in the United States and examine marital naming practices in other countries. Finally, we turn to the study of names and gender, looking at how beliefs about family names clue us in to how individuals perceive and understand gender and family.

Gendered Language

Upon opening a dictionary in virtually any language, it is apparent that gender infuses much of how humans think, write, and communicate with each other. In the English language, one of the most obvious examples is the privileging of a male standard, seen in words like *mailman*, *spokesman*, and *mankind*. In cases where gender is not specified, the use of the gender-specific pronouns *he*, *his*, and *himself* to refer to all individuals also reflects a masculine generic. In addition, gender is visible in the use of male and female identifiers. Occupational terms such as "judge" and "doctor" may seem gender-neutral, but the attachment of feminine modifiers—such as "*lady* doctor" or "*woman* doctor"—reveals that prestigious jobs are often male-identified, whereas jobs like nurse or flight attendant are automatically assumed to be occupied by females.

The connotations of various words are also gendered. For instance, the words *pretty* and *nice* are most commonly applied to women, while *strong* and *brave* are more frequently associated with men. Words associated with women are also more likely to acquire a negative meaning; thus, the word *master* still carries a meaning of control and stateliness, while its feminine corollary, *mistress*, is also a sexual referent. Masculine terms tend to refer to much weightier matters, such as the term "*mastermind*," and feminine terms are used for more delicate and trivial matters, such as "*lady*fingers" (small sponge cakes). Finally, there are gender differences in the number of words with a particular meaning. As the linguist Julia Stanley argues, women are much more defined by their sexuality than men are, as is apparent in the prolific number of terms of sexual insult for women and the relative rarity of such terms for men (for these and other examples of gendered language, see Lakoff 1973, 1975; Bodine 1975; Stanley 1977, 1978; Nilsen 1977).

Not only the content of language but its usage may be gendered. As the sociolinguist Robin Lakoff famously explains, speech styles and patterns may vary dramatically by gender. Specifically, she argues, women learn to speak in ways that are non-imposing, that minimize their own status, and that make others feel good. For example, Lakoff notes, women are more likely to be extremely polite, beginning requests with phrases like, "If it's not too much to ask …," apologizing even when unnecessary, and avoiding harsh languages or expletives (Lakoff 1973, 1975). Women may also speak less frequently than men, phrase their requests indirectly, hedge when they speak (using phrases such as "kind of" and "it seems like" to soften their statements), and insert tag questions at the end of statements (for example, "This book is the best, don't you think?").

During the 1970s and 1980s, gendered language was a hotly debated topic. Feminists argued that gendered language hurts women in three different ways: first, by defining women as second-class citizens who are of less importance than men; second, by deprecating the feminine as unimportant, trivial, or even debased; and finally, by excluding women as topics of discourse and limiting their power as speakers (Henley 1987; Miller and Swift 1976). Many activists indicated that gendered language is largely deterministic of a male-dominated culture—that is, it plays a critical role in the creation of gender inequality. While others were more sanguine about the effectiveness of this approach (Lakoff 1973, 1975), a number of feminists argued that changes in gendered language would ultimately reduce levels of gender inequality overall (Kramarae and Treichler 1985). They were met with considerable resistance, and some of their critics claimed that language is simply too deeply ingrained or cumbersome to change. This appeal to practicality is one that we will see later in our respondents' explanations of their views on marital name change.

Ultimately, the efforts of activists and researchers to transform gendered language have been realized, at least in part. We now have established guidelines for "nonsexist," "gender-neutral," or "gender-sensitive" language that are used by professional groups, organizations, and publications (for example, the American Psychological Association, the Associated Press, and the *New York Times*). Gender-neutral language in textbooks, in other printed material, and in everyday speech has increased (Pauwels 1998). Nevertheless, as the sociolinguist Deborah Cameron (1995) highlights, scholars have more recently recognized that, as much as things have changed, gendered language is also a reflection of gender inequality—that is, changes to language cannot completely alleviate gender differences in practice and culture. Certainly, at least one aspect of gendered language—marital name change—has long survived in the United States.

Marital Name Change

The traditional naming practice in the United States is for a woman to relinquish the last name she was given at birth for her husband's last name at the time of marriage. This practice has roots in the patriarchal family system in which women were considered the property of their husbands (Weitzman 1981). Upon marriage, they were expected to leave behind their previous identities and take up the roles of wife and mother connected to their marriage and family (Morgenstern Leissner 1997). Feminists have argued that this practice is a prime example of gendered language, as it reflects a male standard (women and their children are marked by the husband's name) and delegates women to a secondary position relative to their husbands.

The concept of women's marital name change originates in English common law, under coverture, as explained in William Blackstone's *Commentaries on the Laws of England* (1765, 442–43):

> By marriage, the husband and wife are one person in law: that is, the very being or legal existence of the woman is suspended during the marriage, or at least is incorporated and consolidated into that of the husband; under whose wing, protection, and *cover*, she performs every thing;… and her condition during her marriage is called her *coverture*.

Coverture was understood to mean that a woman had to use her husband's name for all legal purposes, although she could maintain her own name for private and personal uses. In practice, however, women's name change upon marriage became customary in both the United States and England (Stannard 1973). It also became incorporated into aspects of American law. Up until the early 1980s, many states forbade women to use their own surnames after marriage, while others denied women rights, such as the ability to vote, unless they adopted their husband's name (Goldin and Shim 2004; Penfield 1987).

Today the legal aspects of coverture have gradually been removed from law, yet its legacy remains. The vast majority of American women (estimates range from 90 to 95 percent) still take their husband's name, despite not being required to do so. The rate of name change is even higher among some groups of women: those with lower levels of education, older women, those who are not employed full-time, and women who live in the South (Brightman 1994; Johnson and Scheuble 1995). In addition, laws surrounding name change upon marriage still bear a gendered legacy. Although women may now find it easy to either change or keep their name upon marriage, some men have found it cumbersome and expensive when they choose to adopt the last name of their wife. A few years ago, the American Civil Liberties Union, for example, filed a gender discrimination lawsuit against California and Los Angeles County on behalf of a man who struggled to do so. His experience is not unique: few states currently allow men to change their name at the time of marriage as easily as women do.

The practice of women's name change is common in many English-speaking countries (including the United States, Canada, and the United Kingdom), yet it is far from universal. Other countries have their own gendered practices that are equally entrenched in patriarchy—often it is fathers' names that are passed down rather than husbands'. For example, in many Muslim Middle Eastern countries, such as Iran, Jordan, Syria, and Yemen, women retain their birth name (derived from their father's name) after marriage (Friess 2007). Similarly, in several European countries, such as France, women have to petition to adopt their husband's name upon marriage. These countries use last names for national identification (instead of a number, as in the American social security system), and changing them creates confusion (Glendon 1989). Women in Spanish-speaking countries also retain their birth name, even passing it down to their children. However, children generally pass only their paternal name on to their offspring. For Icelanders, there is no equivalent to the family name: last names are derived from the father's first name, with the suffix of -*son* or -*dottir* (daughter) to indicate the child's sex (Friess 2007).

Names, Gender, and Family Life

Names may seem like an odd topic on which to focus in a study of Americans' views regarding gender. After all, most people assume that names are just labels chosen by individuals who have idiosyncratic tastes and encounter variable circumstances. Yet recent research suggests that names reflect larger social processes. For example, the sociologist Stanley Lieberson and his colleagues Susan Dumais and Shyon Baumann (2000) have traced the use of gender-androgynous first names over time and found a pattern of "symbolic contamination." That is, as more parents use specific gender-androgynous names for their daughters, these names are less frequently used for boys. The authors argue that the pattern we see in names reflects a more general gendered trend: because men are still a more advantaged group in society, when women begin to occupy the same social space, the prestige of that social space is lowered. One can see this same process in occupations like teaching that were once male-dominated but are now seen as lower-status occupations typically held by women.

Most of the past research on names, like the work of Lieberson and his colleagues, relies on the *usage* of names to understand gender. However, *attitudes* about names can also convey the meanings that people assign to gender. Names are one way to classify and organize people into social categories, and they carry messages about particular social identities and locations. Therefore, assessing people's attitudes about names, including appropriate and desirable naming options, allows us to understand their underlying orientations toward the gendered, raced, and classed images that names evoke (for more on the sociological importance of names see Lieberson 1984; Lieberson and Bell 1992; Lieberson and Mikelson 1995; Miller 1927; Rossi 1965; Sue and Telles 2007; Watkins and London 1994). Naming practices also have the added benefit of not being heavily politicized public issues—people are less concerned about providing the "right" or "politically correct" response than they are when asked about social rights or discrimination.

Despite the promise of using names to understand gender attitudes, very little has been done on the topic. One important exception is scholarship on the once-controversial title of "Ms." While the title of "Mr." does not indicate marital status, women were traditionally addressed as "Miss" (unmarried) or "Mrs." (married). The use of "Ms." was an attempt to make terms of address more gender-egalitarian by removing the focus on women's marital status. In the late 1980s and early 1990s, psychologists found that "Ms." evoked stereotypes of being more successful, business-oriented, and assertive, while women who did not adopt this title were seen as warmer and more expressive (qualities traditionally associated with women) (Dion 1987; Dion and Cota 1991; Dion and Schuller 1990). Although "Ms." is now widely used (Pauwels 1998), this research suggests that people do associate gendered meanings with names and labels.

Married names, or family names, provide a unique opportunity to assess attitudes toward gender *within the context of family*. The persistence of marital name change practices reflects the fact that family is an institution in which gender is deeply rooted. As the sociologists Candace West and Don Zimmerman (1987) argue in their well-known work on "doing gender," women and men end up enacting gender and behaving in traditionally gendered ways, particularly when there are social and interactional expectations that they will do so. Family life is strongly shaped by these expectations, as seen in the persistence of a traditional division of labor; on the whole, women continue to do more household work despite the fact that many now share the breadwinner role with their husbands (Bianchi et al. 2000; Blair and Lichter 1991). Even the notion of marriage as exclusively heterosexual, or between two "opposite" sexes, reflects the gendered basis of family life. By tapping into respondents' beliefs about how families should be named, we also access their understanding of how gender should be enacted in families, whether gender polarity is seen as a necessary component of family life, and what families should look like.

Public Views Regarding Marital Name Change

We currently know very little about what Americans believe about name change.[2] What do they see as the best practice? Do they endorse a more traditional approach to name change, in which women adopt their husband's names upon marriage? Or do they take a more liberal approach and see other practices as acceptable—such as husbands taking their wife's name or individuals retaining their own name? Most centrally, are different beliefs about name change linked to different understandings of what groups count as families?

As we discussed earlier, we asked respondents to strongly agree, somewhat agree, somewhat disagree, or strongly disagree with a series of issues regarding women's name change. Of central focus in this chapter is the question about whether it is generally better if a woman changes her last name to her husband's name when she marries. We also asked respondents if it is a good idea for states to legally require a woman to change her name to her husband's last name, and if it is okay for a man to take his wife's name when he marries. Respondents were then asked to elaborate on their rationale.

As illustrated in figure 7.1, there was a considerable amount of support for traditional name change practices: 71.5 percent of respondents agreed, either strongly or somewhat, that it is generally better for a woman to adopt her husband's name upon marriage. Only a small percentage (12.2 percent) strongly disagreed with this statement—suggesting that very few respondents take the most liberal approach to women's name change.[3]

The views regarding legal requirements and male name change were more evenly split. For instance, 50.2 percent of respondents agreed strongly or somewhat that women should be legally required to change their names. The slightly lower levels of agreement are likely due to the stricter standard implied by the question—that is, some people who think traditional practices are generally better may be uncomfortable with legal or state intervention in family life.

Similarly, about half of respondents (46.9 percent) disagreed either strongly or somewhat with the idea that it is okay for a man to take his wife's name. At first glance, this finding may seem surprising—given how many respondents felt it was better for *women* to change their names. However, our interview recordings allowed us to consider how respondents were interpreting this question. It quickly became apparent that for many respondents male name change was such an implausible proposition or even a joke that they offhandedly agreed it would be okay. For example, as one middle-aged man responded: "Sure, why

Figure 7.1   Views Regarding Name Change

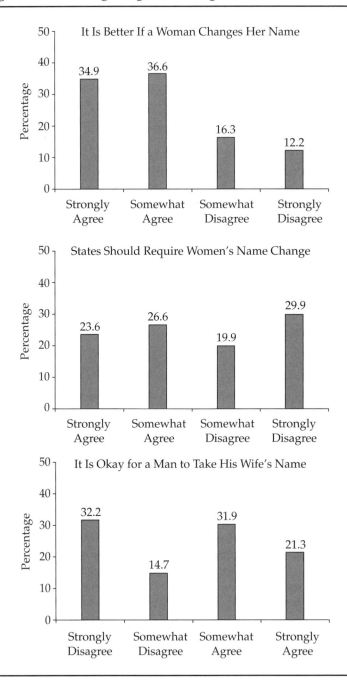

Source: Constructing the Family Survey (Powell 2006).

Figure 7.2   Views Regarding Name Change, by Gender

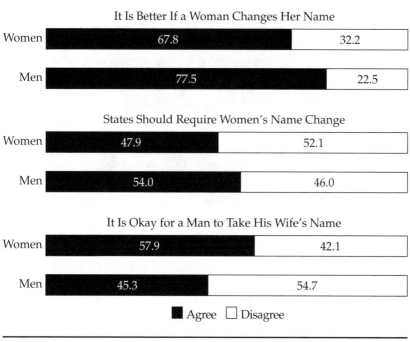

It Is Better If a Woman Changes Her Name

	Agree	Disagree
Women	67.8	32.2
Men	77.5	22.5

States Should Require Women's Name Change

	Agree	Disagree
Women	47.9	52.1
Men	54.0	46.0

It Is Okay for a Man to Take His Wife's Name

	Agree	Disagree
Women	57.9	42.1
Men	45.3	54.7

■ Agree   ☐ Disagree

Source: Constructing the Family Survey (Powell 2006).

not. (*chuckle*) Hey, in America, anything goes. It's a free country." Or as another noted: "Oh, I've never heard of that, I don't have a problem with that. Somewhat agree, I guess. (*laughs*) If he wants to change his name, okay." Both of these respondents had previously agreed that it was better for women to change their names.

Group Differences in Views on Name Change

Are there significant group differences in how Americans assess marital name change practices? Responses on this issue are patterned along the lines of key sociodemographic characteristics.[4] As in the previous chapter, one difference occurs by gender. Figure 7.2 demonstrates that more men (77.5 percent) than women (67.8 percent) agreed that it is better for women to change their names upon marriage. Similarly, more men than women believed that there should be legal requirements for name change (54.0 percent versus 47.9 percent)—although the most

Figure 7.3   Views Regarding Name Change, by Education

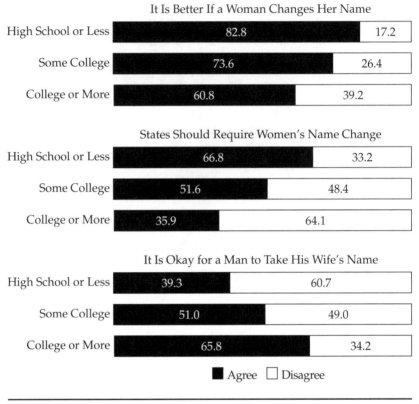

Source: *Constructing the Family Survey* (Powell 2006).

striking gender difference is in beliefs about male name change. Men were more likely than women to disagree with the statement that it is okay for men to change their names (54.7 percent versus 42.1 percent). In other words, men tended to hold the most traditional views regarding name change.

Education is also strongly linked to views on marital name change. As shown in figure 7.3, Americans who had earned up to a high school degree were most likely (82.8 percent) to agree that women's name change is better. As education increases, the percentage of respondents who agree with this practice decreases. Thus, 73.6 percent of those with some college background believed that it is better for women to change their names, and only 60.8 percent of those with a college degree did so. The same pattern characterizes responses to the other two questions. Two-thirds of those with up to a high school degree (66.8 percent), one-half of those with some college (51.6 percent), and only one-third of those with a college degree (35.9 percent) agree that there should be a legal requirement for women's name change. Similarly, we see that disagreement with the statement that it is okay for men to change their names decreases as education increases (60.7, 49.0, and 34.2 percent, respectively). These patterns are consistent with the educational differences in name change practices noted earlier. As discussed in earlier chapters, they also indicate that increasing education makes it more likely that respondents will adopt a relativist perspective in which there is no single "right" approach to family life.

There are also clear patterns by age. Figure 7.4 reveals that there are considerable differences between those who were sixty-five or older and the youngest respondents who were under the age of thirty. The oldest were more likely than the youngest to agree that women's name change is better, to support a legal requirement, and to disagree with men's name change (80.7 percent versus 67.0 percent, 68.0 percent versus 47.7 percent, and 68.8 percent versus 37.8 percent, respectively). Thus, as age increases, we see that respondents are increasingly more likely to support traditional practices.

Figure 7.5 illustrates racial-ethnic differences in views toward name change. Blacks were the most likely to espouse traditional views toward name change. While nearly two-thirds of blacks (63.6 percent) believed that there should be a legal requirement for name change, fewer than half of whites (48.9 percent) did. We see a similar pattern in responses to the question of whether it is okay for men to change their names: 63 percent of blacks disagreed with this idea, in comparison to 45.5 percent of whites. (Although the question about whether it is better for women to change their names was consistent with the previous items, it did not approach significance at the bivariate level.)[5]

Parental status and marital status also matter for views toward name change. Parents were more likely to believe women's name change is better (74.1 percent versus 63.1 percent), to support a legal requirement (52.6 percent versus 41.9 percent), and to disagree that it is okay for a man to adopt his wife's name (49.0 percent versus 39.2 percent). Responses to the question regarding whether it is better for women to change their names also show significant differences (at the bivariate level) by marital status. Three-fourths of married respondents agreed (74.5 percent), but only two-thirds of the nonmarried did so (67.5 percent). These findings indicate that, in general, those who are part of a

Figure 7.4   Views Regarding Name Change, by Age-Cohort

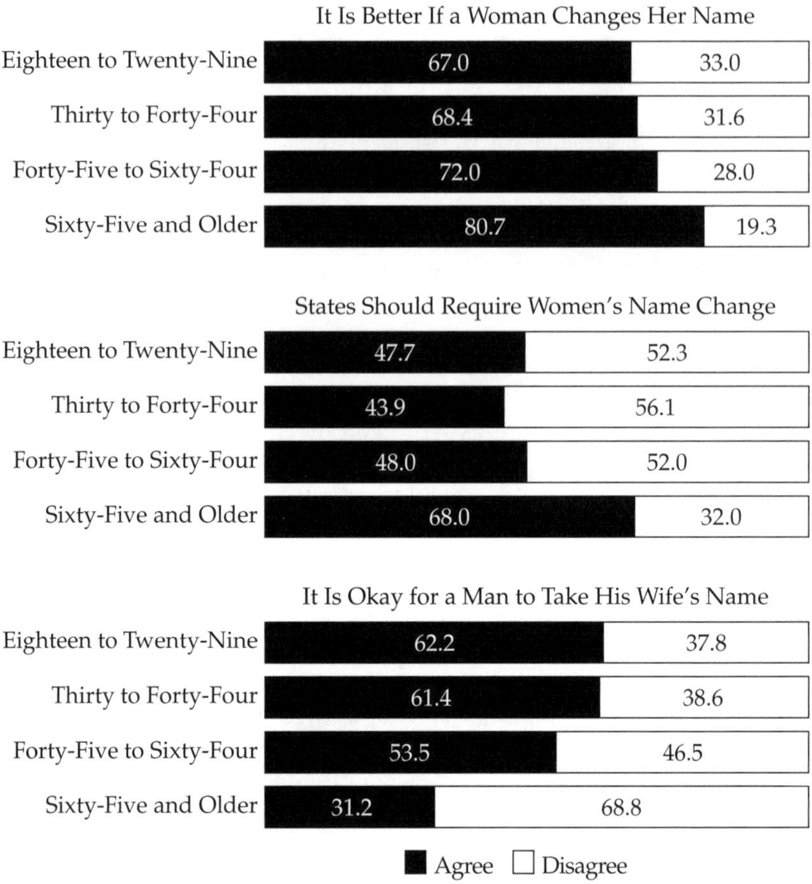

It Is Better If a Woman Changes Her Name

Eighteen to Twenty-Nine	67.0	33.0
Thirty to Forty-Four	68.4	31.6
Forty-Five to Sixty-Four	72.0	28.0
Sixty-Five and Older	80.7	19.3

States Should Require Women's Name Change

Eighteen to Twenty-Nine	47.7	52.3
Thirty to Forty-Four	43.9	56.1
Forty-Five to Sixty-Four	48.0	52.0
Sixty-Five and Older	68.0	32.0

It Is Okay for a Man to Take His Wife's Name

Eighteen to Twenty-Nine	62.2	37.8
Thirty to Forty-Four	61.4	38.6
Forty-Five to Sixty-Four	53.5	46.5
Sixty-Five and Older	31.2	68.8

■ Agree   ☐ Disagree

Source: Constructing the Family Survey (Powell 2006).

family with these more traditional features tend to have the most restrictive attitudes regarding name change.[6]

Religion and Views on Name Change

As in the previous chapter, we once again examine the link between religious views and attitudes toward family life. We return to beliefs about the inerrancy of the Bible, which are often used as a proxy for evangelical Christian beliefs. As we see in figure 7.6, Americans who

Figure 7.5   Views Regarding Name Change, by Race

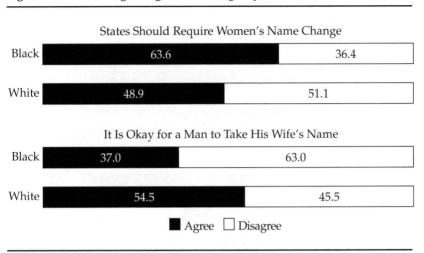

Source: *Constructing the Family Survey* (Powell 2006).

interpret the Bible literally held the most restrictive views regarding name change. They were the most likely to believe that women's name change is better (89.3 percent), to support a legal requirement (71.7 percent), and to disagree that it is okay for men to change their names (66.9 percent). In contrast, those who see the Bible as a book of "fables, legends, history, and moral teachings" had the most liberal views—fewer than half agreed that it is better for women to change their names (47.2 percent), only around one-quarter supported a legal requirement (28.6 percent), and only about one-third disagreed with men's name change (34.2 percent). In other words, as we saw with views about single-parent living arrangements in the previous chapter, absolutist beliefs about the Bible are strongly related to absolutist beliefs about family life—in this case, the issue of women's name change. The least restrictive views about the Bible are linked to greater flexibility in beliefs about gender in family life.[7]

In summary, views about marital name change are closely linked to both traditional demographic characteristics and religious beliefs. Men, those with lower levels of education, older individuals, blacks, parents, and married individuals are the most traditional in their views. Similarly, views regarding the Bible are important for understanding respondents' beliefs about marital name change. Absolutist beliefs about the Bible are associated with more restrictive attitudes toward name

Figure 7.6   Views Regarding Name Change, by Views on the Bible

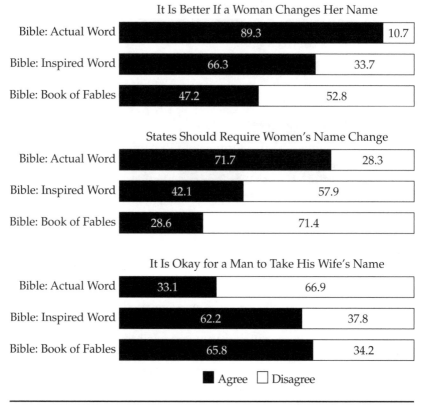

It Is Better If a Woman Changes Her Name

Bible: Actual Word — 89.3 | 10.7

Bible: Inspired Word — 66.3 | 33.7

Bible: Book of Fables — 47.2 | 52.8

States Should Require Women's Name Change

Bible: Actual Word — 71.7 | 28.3

Bible: Inspired Word — 42.1 | 57.9

Bible: Book of Fables — 28.6 | 71.4

It Is Okay for a Man to Take His Wife's Name

Bible: Actual Word — 33.1 | 66.9

Bible: Inspired Word — 62.2 | 37.8

Bible: Book of Fables — 65.8 | 34.2

■ Agree   ☐ Disagree

Source: Constructing the Family Survey (Powell 2006).

change. These patterns indicate that beliefs about name change not only speak to more than the specific issue of names but also reflect key divisions in gender beliefs.

In Their Own Words: Attitudes Toward Name Change

To better understand the rationale for people's attitudes regarding name change, we asked respondents to explain *why* they agreed or disagreed that it is better for a woman to change her name.[8] Answers to this question range from the most strongly held sentiments to more weakly held—even wavering—views. Here we address the most common themes used by advocates and critics of traditional name change practices.[9]

Themes Used by Advocates of Traditional Name Change Practices

As in the previous chapter, gender is at the heart of the explanations that Americans provide for their views on women's name change. Both those who advocate the practice and those who do not indicated that women's name change is an important marker of gender identity. Although "identity" is often thought of as a social-scientific term, respondents frequently invoked this term—both in name and in concept—to explain their beliefs about how gender should be enacted in the family context. Their responses tap into the struggle that women may face in balancing their commitment to others—such as their husbands and children—and their commitment to themselves (Bielby and Bielby 1984). Women often share or are exposed to a belief that their most salient identities should be those of wife and mother and in turn they are expected to give precedence to the needs of their families in ways that are not expected of men (Correll, Benard, and Paik 2007; Hays 1996). In this section, we see that respondents' views about name change are deeply embedded in beliefs about how women should identify—primarily with the marriage and family or primarily with themselves.

Name change advocates prioritize women's identification as wives and mothers and see name change as critical to this process. In fact, close to half of all those who agreed that it is better for women to change their names mentioned the importance of women putting marriage and family first. As one older woman explained: "I know right now everyone likes their own identity, but I believe in the old philosophy of a woman taking her husband's name . . . 'Cause once you marry you're part of this man, you know?" She suggested that women should leave behind some of their independence when they marry, just as they leave behind their last name. A middle-aged male expressed a similar opinion: "It just shows that she's committed, actually committed, and she doesn't want to still be her own person. She wants to be a unified person with her husband." Women should be the ones, he noted, to sacrifice in order to create a merged, family identity. Others were even more explicit on this point. One older male invoked the notion of ownership—that women are the property of their husbands—in explaining why women should change their names: "So that there's a connection there. Just a connection to let you know that she belongs to him."

Name change is seen by some as an important marker of women's choice to identify with the marriage. An older woman explained:

> Simple, if you gonna marry somebody, you take on that name, if that's the God-given name you were sworn to before a minister. . . . A lot of women don't wear wedding bands or rings, but that name change does have a difference, does make a difference.

She suggested that women's name change is the single most important indicator of marriage—more so even than a wedding ring.

While many of these respondents focused on the *marital* identity (that is, on the marriage and a wife's commitment to her husband), others emphasized the importance of a *family* identity. According to one middle-aged man, women should change their names "for identification with the man . . . with the family. It's better for the children if the family all have the same name." Similarly, a young woman believed that women's name change is important because "in written form [name change] is their bond of union. That they share the same name and they share the same family."

These concerns often hinged on the presence of children, suggesting a willingness to reconsider name change under other circumstances. As one middle-aged woman explained:

> It brings unity, a kind of unity if there's children involved. . . . I personally have done it, but I don't feel that it is a bad thing if a woman does not change her name. I only think it is a bad thing if there is children.

Thus, those who focus on a family identity more than a marital identity tended to be more reserved about their support for name change, with roughly one-third as opposed to one-half strongly agreeing that the practice is better.

While many of those who advocate traditional name change practices focused on the *meaning* of women's appropriate gender identity— that is, prioritizing marriage and self above the family—others focused on the *source* of their beliefs about gendered behavior in the family. They emphasized the issue of *who* or *what* should determine marital name change—and thus women's gender identity.

A small group of those who support women's name change (roughly 12 percent) argued that religion should dictate women's role in the family and, consequently, the naming practice. These respondents were among the strongest and most fervent advocates: more than two-thirds of those who mentioned religion strongly agreed that it is better for women to change their names. Often, they turned to the Bible to justify women's name change—even though it is not mentioned in the Bible. In the words of one older man:

We're changing history, we're changing tradition, we're changing the relationship, woman was made out of man, and therefore man is the head of the house. I know the feminine isn't gonna like that, but that's the way the biblical standard is. That doesn't mean the woman is a slave to anybody or anything else, but it does mean just what it says, that the man is the head of the house.

As an older woman indicated: "Well, it's just biblical for them to change their name. I kept my husband's name. We divorced and then he died, but I still got his name."

Another respondent, an older man, linked name change to one of the most infamous biblical stories, despite no real connection between the two. As he noted of the traditional name change practice: "That's the way this country was founded, and I think we should continue, we don't need to follow the ways of Sodom and Gomorrah."

Not all respondents who drew on religion referred to the Bible. One middle-aged man argued that name change comes from Eastern spiritualism, although the two are not related. He explained: "The nature of yin [femininity] is receptive, yang [masculinity] is more dominant, aggressive, and that's the philosophy of energies from the East. So it's an Eastern concept."

The majority of name change advocates focused, however, on tradition and custom. They saw marital name change as a practice that has been in existence "for hundreds of years" or "has been like that forever and a day." In fact, approximately half of all those who agreed that it is better for women to change their names indicated that this practice should remain in part because it is the way things have always been done. As a young man suggested:

> That's what marriage is all about—uniting two people from different backgrounds together. I guess it's just been the common practice for so long—the common thing to do. It's the way we did it. That's the way I think it should be done.

Others were even more eloquent about the centrality of this practice to an American way of life. As an older man noted, women's name change is important "because it has to do with our moral fabric and our values."

Respondents who cited tradition as the main reason for supporting name change were often more measured in their beliefs than those who also cited religion: only about half of these respondents strongly agreed that this practice is better. They often suggested that name change is all they have ever known and something they never really questioned. As an older man elaborated: "There's no real reason or anything. I've lived eighty years, and that's always the way it's been, and that's the way I grew up, and so I guess that's the way I believe." A few respondents, upon reflection, indicated a willingness to reconsider their beliefs. As a middle-aged man reasoned:

> I reckon that's just because that's the way [it's] always been. . . . [I] really hadn't just sat down and [taken] a really good look at it. 'Cause if you really look at it, a man could change his name to the lady's name. I really don't see no, no problem with it, but, you know, I don't know. I reckon it just shot up through generation to generation like that.

A middle-aged woman also worked through the logic behind her original answer:

> Maybe I was raised old school. . . . My personal opinion, I would say my husband's last name. That's out of respect. Even though I like my last name. Then again, now that you're asking these questions, you know, actually these are really good questions at this point of my life. Because, when I think about it, I like my last name, but I think out of respect for your husband, in the old school, you take his name. But nowadays, you can do slash-slash-slash, which I think looks kinda silly.

Although often willing to bend their own beliefs, these respondents warned that there are social and cultural costs to going against tradition. One young woman reported:

> I live in northern Indiana, it's a fairly conservative area. . . . I wouldn't say [not changing your name upon marriage] makes a person a pariah, but it certainly stands out, and [changing your name] is just traditional.

Similarly, a middle-aged woman cautioned: "It is customary in this culture to do so. . . . It's just, if you go against the cultural norm, you can expect some difficulties. Not that you can't do it, just expect to have some problems." These responses suggest that while some individuals may be willing to bend their own beliefs, they would still adhere to cultural norms rather than face social disapproval.

One small group of respondents was even more practical about name change than other advocates. These respondents—about 18 percent of name change advocates—argued that women's name change simply makes things easier. As one older woman noted: "I think for legal reasons it is easier in our system of business. . . . I think it's just easier in our culture." A middle-aged woman explained: "It's been going on for so long. It would be so confusing to change it now." Another, an older man, joked that name change "keeps the mailman from getting confused."

These respondents tended to have the most moderate beliefs of any name change advocates: roughly two-thirds of them only somewhat agreed that it is better for women to change their names. They were less concerned about appropriate gendered behavior or adherence to religious or traditional norms; instead, they focused much more on the outcome—the smooth operation of society. Consequently, they may have been the most open to considering alternative means of achieving the same ends. As one middle-aged man noted: "That was the reason I said 'somewhat [agree']. It's just for name consistency. I don't believe that it matters whether the man or woman changes."

As these examples indicate, those who advocate women's name change tend to focus on the importance of women enacting a gendered identity that prioritizes marriage and family—one that is also understood as integral to religion and tradition. Even those who cite pragmatism as the reason behind their beliefs privilege the interests and needs of larger groups—such as communities and families—over those of individual women. Thus, name change advocates generally have an unambiguous notion of how family life should be structured, the appropriate role of women in creating this structure, and the central function of women's name change. Their comments suggest that advocates may have more restrictive definitions of family that emphasize the centrality of two distinct genders.

In the next section, we turn to the explanations provided by critics of name change in order to understand what their views on name change imply about how they delineate familial boundaries.[10]

Themes Used by Critics of Traditional Name Change Practices

Whereas an overriding theme among those who advocate traditional name change practices is the importance of marriage and family, a recurring theme among those who are critical of women's name change is the importance of the self in defining one's own gender identity. Rather than emphasizing a particular structure of family life that women should accommodate, they focus on individual women's interests and how these might intersect with those of marriage and family. Respondents in this group espoused a range of views—from strongly opposing the name change practice itself to advocating women's choice, whatever that might be. However, in their explanations all of these respondents prioritized the self and emphasized the centrality of the individual.

About one-quarter of critics espoused the most explicit beliefs about name change, arguing that this practice results in a loss of women's own personal identities. A majority of these respondents (56 percent) strongly disagreed with women's name change. As one middle-aged woman explained:

> Because when a woman changes her name, she loses her identity. To me she loses her identity. A lot of the times in the past when a woman got married, she lost her rights as a single person to make her own decisions, so I never agreed with that. . . . I didn't like that.

Another middle-aged woman spoke from experience: "I did change my name when I married my husband, but I'm kind of sorry that I did because I lost my original identity as a person."

To others, the loss of one's name is more than a matter of identity—it is equivalent, they argued, to losing ownership over oneself. As a middle-aged woman explained:

> When you take someone else's name, it almost implies ownership, like you went with a pink slip. . . . It's like the person who has to give up their name is being bought or purchased. It's like, suddenly somebody signed a pink slip form and they became something else. It's not equal.

While more women than men espoused this view, the men who focused on the importance of women's independent identities were particularly fervent. As one older man exclaimed:

> It's unnecessary. How's that? What's the point of that? It's a matter of possession. Do you like to be possessed? I mean, it's almost like ownership, isn't it? That's my feelings of it. Hey, and I'm an old guy. I've never understood that.

A smaller group (about 18 percent) of women's name change critics focused on a particular instance in which a woman's own needs might be at odds with changing her name—that of employment.[11] One middle-aged woman stated:

> I'm a clinical psychologist. So I've been in practice for a very long time.... I would never drop my name; I would simply add on or hyphen a name. I think I've been whoever I've been for this long amount of time. I can't see that I'm suddenly going to become something else. I don't

mind adding something to my life, but I don't think I should have to subtract.

She highlighted the centrality of a professional identity and noted that name change is detrimental to this part of the self.

Others explained that women's maiden names are attached to professional achievements that they should not have to lose. As a middle-aged woman put it:

> She may have professional association, maybe known for her accomplishments, under her own name. And if she changes her name, as for business correspondence, being found in research, and the like, it's like starting over.

One older woman noted that women's professional identities are as valuable as those of men: "Some people have a career and have other interests, and they believe their name has just as much value as her husband's." Perhaps because this issue was more germane to women's own experiences, no men who disagreed with women's name change cited the importance of women's professional identities.

A similar-sized group (18 percent) of those who did not agree that women's name change is better focused less on the meaning of the practice and more on practical reasons for rejecting women's name change. These respondents shared the emphasis on pragmatism of some name change advocates; however, unlike the latter, whose concern was about making things easier for *society*, they typically suggested that by keeping their names individual women make things easier for *themselves*. As a young woman stated:

> It's difficult. It's a little bit . . . it's hard. And if you have certain things in place already, like a mortgage and stuff, and then you change your name, it takes a long time to do everything. . . . It's just a lot of stuff to do it. And sometimes people don't know you have the same name anymore. They don't recognize your name and that person you were before.

Similarly, a middle-aged woman noted:

> What a hassle it would be to change everything, you know. Everything is in my name, so I would have to go about changing everything. Plus, I have a child, and he has my last name.

As this response suggests, family forms are often more complicated than a married couple and their children. When women divorce and/

or remarry, the traditional name change practice can become more than just impractical. As another middle-aged woman explained:

> When I was married to my first husband and I carried his last name, I lost everything when I got divorced. I lost all my benefits, all my credit cards, my credit and everything. . . . When I got married to this husband, and I went down to my social security office, they said that you didn't have to carry your husband's last name. . . . That law was passed a long time ago. . . . You don't have to transfer it to your husband's name 'cause everything goes to your husband.

She saw real economic costs for women associated with name change—and thus practical reasons to avoid it.

Like those who advocated traditional name change practices, a number of critics were less concerned about what women identify with and more about the *source* of that decision. Those who were critical of women's name change, however, did not locate this power in outside entities such as religion and tradition. Instead, these respondents argued that individual women should decide whether or not to change their names—even if they personally reject the practice. This was the most commonly used argument among critics: more than half (56 percent) referred to name change as a woman's own decision. As one middle-aged woman succinctly explained: "I think it's an individual decision. An individual right." A young man made a similar comment: "I think they should have their own opinion on it. And if they want to change their name, then more power to 'em. But if not, you know, more power to 'em there too."

Taking a more muted stance against name change than those who argued that women should develop identities separate from marriage and family, these respondents were evenly split between those who somewhat or strongly disagreed that it is better for women to change their names. In ceding power to individual women, they perceived name change as a private issue, not a public issue of right or wrong. As a middle-aged woman noted:

> I don't try to impose my opinions for what's right for everybody to everybody. I mean, I just think it's a personal choice. I think if you want to keep your last name, you could, or if you hated your last name, maybe your husband could take your last name. Or you could hyphen it.

Some respondents realized that women do not necessarily have the ability to make a free, uninfluenced choice. One middle-aged woman explained:

Name change [is] not a necessity. I think she should have the choice of retaining it or changing it. It shouldn't be something that's such a tradition that it's forced upon us. To me it's a very strong tradition in this country and it's not necessary.

She suggested that tradition makes it difficult for those women who do opt out of marital name change. Yet, despite her own feelings about the practice, she was not willing to say that all women should completely reject name change. Even many of those who argued that name change is damaging to women's own identities were often willing to let individuals make that choice on their own. As an older woman stated: "I think it takes away some of her identity. I think it should be choice, not law."

In sum, those who are critical of women's name change are much more flexible in their beliefs than those who advocate the practice. Because they give precedence to women's own identities, all but those who are most strongly opposed to traditional naming practices recognize the variability in what women want and the circumstances under which women live. At times this requires critics to support the right of women to make choices with which they personally disagree. This limits their ability to protest what they see as an inegalitarian and unequal practice, since they generally do not want to force a different practice on women—that of keeping their names. With their greater flexibility, however, they recognize differences in how gender might be enacted in families, see the roles of women and men as more similar than distinct, and are more open to the notion that not all families look the same. This openness suggests that critics of name change may have more expansive definitions of family, a claim that we test in the next section.[12]

Views Regarding Name Change and Definitions of Family

Up to this point, we have examined differences in individuals' views toward marital name change and explanations for their beliefs. Do these views connect to the key issues of the book? That is, are they related to how families are defined? And in particular, do they have anything to do with whether same-sex couples are counted in or out of these definitions? We see a strong link. Attitudes regarding name change are powerful predictors of whether or not gay and lesbian couples are seen as family, even more so than beliefs regarding parenting and gender. For example, as seen in figure 7.7, only half (49.6 percent) of those who agreed that it is better if a woman changes her name defined lesbian couples with children as a family. In contrast, among

Figure 7.7   Do Lesbian Couples with Children Count as Family? Differences by Views Regarding Name Change

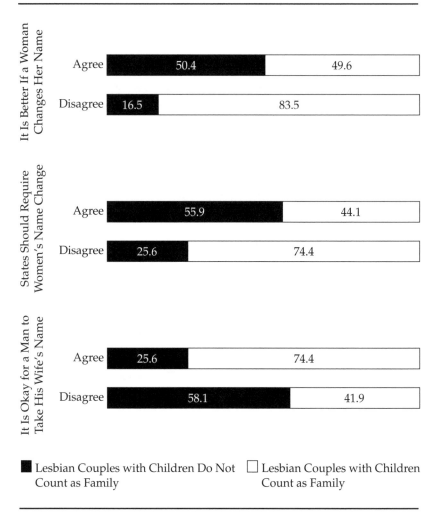

Lesbian Couples with Children Do Not Count as Family   ☐ Lesbian Couples with Children Count as Family

Source: Constructing the Family Survey (Powell 2006).

those who disagreed that women's name change is better, 83.5 percent included lesbian couples with children within familial boundaries. The questions about whether women should be legally required to change their name and whether it is okay for men to take their wife's name also show strong patterns: Americans who have more traditional views were much less likely to define lesbian couples with children as a family than were those with more liberal views.

In figure 7.8, we see that this pattern is even more striking when differentiating between inclusionists, moderates, and exclusionists. While there are similar proportions of moderates among both those who are more traditional and those who are more liberal in their views, there are extremely large divisions between exclusionists and inclusionists by attitude toward name change. Half of Americans who believed that it is better for a woman to change her name (49.6 percent), over half of those who agreed that states should require women's name change (55.1 percent), and nearly three-fifths of those who disagreed that it is okay for a man to take his wife's name (58.1 percent) adopted an exclusionist definition. In fact, only a small percentage of those with traditional beliefs were inclusionists. This difference is most visible when looking at the item regarding male name change: those who do not think it is okay for a man to take his wife's name were over four times as likely to be exclusionist as inclusionist (58.1 percent versus 14.1 percent).[13]

The link between traditional views regarding marital name change and an exclusionist stance regarding family definitions is explicit in the following comments by an older man:

> To me a family is a husband and wife, with or without children. Uh, not live-in, not gay people, not lesbian people. That's not a family, in my opinion. A husband and a wife constitute a family. A husband and a wife and children constitutes a family. See, here's the deal. When a woman marries a man, most cases she changes her name to his in honor, to honor him, and when a man marries a woman, he is honoring that woman. If they're living together, there is no honor.

In contrast, Americans who espouse more liberal views regarding name change were much more likely to be inclusionists than exclusionists. For instance, 53.6 percent of Americans who disagreed that women's name change is better, 41.7 percent of those who did not support a legal requirement, and 45.4 percent of those who believe that it is okay for men to change their names are inclusionists. Only a small proportion of those who are more open to alternative naming options adopted exclusionist views (17.0, 25.6, and 25.1 percent, respectively). These stark patterns further confirm the conclusion reached in the previous chapter: views regarding gender—whether measured through attitudes toward name change or attitudes toward parenting—are strongly related to how Americans understand family and whom they count and do not count as a family.

Figure 7.8   Differences in Family Definitions, by Views Regarding Name Change

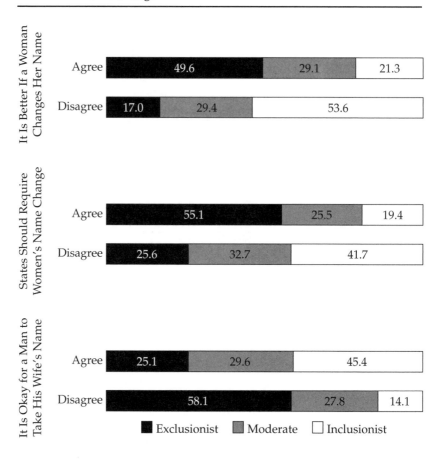

Source: Constructing the Family Survey (Powell 2006).

Conclusion

In this chapter, we have examined how Americans view the practice of marital name change. The issues they raise when discussing women's name change, a traditionally gendered practice, tell us a great deal about their attitudes toward gender. Their views suggest that names are more than just labels—names carry meaning and, in this case, can be used to tap into understandings of how gender should be enacted in family life. Specifically, respondents saw the issue of marital names as symbolic of gender identity. How they approach name change tells us whether or not they believe there is an appropriate gender identity that women should adhere to or whether they are more open to a variety of gendered identities. Their views indicate how they believe women should identify—with a traditional heterosexual marriage and children, or with their own independent needs and desires. In short, attitudes toward name change can tell us how Americans believe women (and men) should organize their private lives, how they should see themselves, and how this relates to the structure of family life.

Yet attitudes toward name change can reveal even more about understandings of family in general. As we have seen in previous chapters, when we think of the debate surrounding who is family, we see that there is a much broader set of items—not just views on homosexuality—that are implicated in how Americans delineate the boundaries between families and nonfamilies. In chapter 5, we saw that people's views about the causes of children's behavior are linked to their definitions of what counts as a family. In chapter 6, we saw that views on parenting and custody are also inextricably tied to definitions of family. In this chapter, we have dealt with a different notion of gender—one that does not deal explicitly with children or parenting, but with the meaning of names. Just as the roles of parent, wife, or husband have gendered meanings, we have learned that views about marital names give us access to beliefs about gender identity that are strongly implicated in who Americans count as family.

Those with the most traditional views about name change—who believe it is better for women to change their names, who support a legal requirement, and who disagree with male name change—tend to have the most restrictive views about family. They believe that women should enact a specific gendered identity that gives precedence to the traditional family structure. This focus on heterosexual marriage and children comes from an adherence to tradition and religion. Name change supporters are thus very specific about the need for two distinct gender identities, and associated roles, within families. In contrast, those with the most liberal views about name change tend to have the most inclusive views about family. They focus more on the interests and circumstances that confront individual women, and many of them allow for greater variability in how women choose to identify. By giving individual women the ultimate authority to decide whether or not to change their names, these respondents are often limited in their ability to oppose the name change practice. Yet most name change critics are consequently more open to diversity in how gender is played out in family life.

Theories of heteronormativity suggest that respondents' views regarding the causes of homosexuality, issues of gender and parental custody, and marital name change should dovetail in predictable and patterned ways, since they reflect a larger worldview on how gender and sexuality should be enacted in family life. However, there are some clear differences. Most notably, some attitudes appear to be changing faster than others. We do not have over-time data on attitudes toward name change, but evidence regarding change in the actual *practice* of marital name change suggests that attitudes may be similarly stalled. For example, the economists Claudia Goldin and Maria Shim (2004) suggest that despite an increase in women's surname-keeping during the early 1970s (an increase that probably coincided with the women's movement), changes in this practice have remained stagnant since the mid-1980s. These authors point to what is, if anything, a slight decrease in recent years in the number of women who choose to keep their own name. Additional estimates confirm that only a minority of American women (roughly 5 to 10 percent) currently do so (Brightman 1994; Johnson and Scheuble 1995). In contrast, in chapter 5, we saw considerable change in attitudes toward the causes of children's behavior— even in the short period between 2003 and 2006.

This comparison should remind us that views regarding the family change at varying speeds. There are reasons why some attitudes shift more quickly than others. For instance, in the years between 2003 and 2006 there was much discussion surrounding gay marriage and gay parenting. The attention that these debates probably brought to the issues of child sexual preference and the gender of parents may have caused some individuals to form or revise their views. Marital name change, however, has not yet come into the public eye. It is not considered politically incorrect to support women's name change, and traditional sentiments toward the practice are viewed as relatively innocuous, if not the norm. As some respondents indicated, name change is simply not an issue they have had to think much about, suggesting an absence of public discussion. Consequently, name change appears to have gone fairly unnoticed as a gender issue. There has been little reason for individuals to reconsider their attitudes regarding the practice, and the majority continue to support women's name change.

Marital name change therefore may represent one issue on which notions of gender difference are particularly anchored. It is important to locate such sticking points where movement toward gender and sexual equality is slowed. These issues remind us that heteronormativity in family life is robust. Movement toward greater inclusiveness in one realm may represent a shift toward social change, yet a more complete change is unlikely when underlying beliefs about the importance of gender difference and complementarity for family functioning remain.

Ironically, there may be considerable benefits to understanding and using slow-to-change attitudinal measures in social-scientific research. A useful contrast that illustrates this point lies in attitudes toward men's and women's work and family roles. Over the past forty years, some of the most commonly used measures of gender and family attitudes have referred to the doctrine of separate spheres, or the notion that women belong in the private sphere of the home while men should be the breadwinners in the public sphere. Questions that tap into gender and work and family roles have become almost standard in social-scientific research—owing in part to their presence on nationally representative, longitudinal surveys (McHugh and Frieze 1997). However, views on women's employment rapidly changed during the last half of the twentieth century as shifting economic and social circumstances made it necessary for women to enter the labor force en masse (Coontz 1992; Wilkie 1991). Today women's share of the labor force is quickly approaching parity with that of men (Chao and Utgoff 2005). Not surprisingly, women's employment is no longer considered a divisive issue but is generally accepted as a practical and commonplace phenomenon.

Because women's employment has become so accepted, items measuring attitudes toward work and family roles no longer have much predictive power. These questions have suffered a "ceiling effect": because the vast majority of Americans believe that it is okay for women to work, these questions can distinguish only the most conservative individuals from the rest. Those with otherwise extremely liberal attitudes cannot be distinguished from those with moderately traditional views. In contrast, because women's name change has been slow to change, individuals are more willing to give conservative responses to questions about it. Consequently, name change questions are more sensitive to a full spectrum of gender attitudes. They also create more room for movement toward egalitarianism in the future, since individuals' gender beliefs often become more liberal rather than more conservative. Thus, the stalled nature of attitudes toward marital name change may make these attitudes particularly useful in the longitudinal study of gender and family.

Attitudes toward name change, as well as the attitudes examined in previous chapters, tell us that views toward family cannot be separated from those about gender and sexuality. It may seem surprising that such seemingly disparate questions, which have experienced such variable levels of change in recent years, should all be so predictive of how Americans define family. Family as an institution, however, is deeply intertwined with beliefs about gender and sexuality; notions of heterosexual marriage, of distinctly gendered identities for wives and husbands, and of parents' roles in gendering and sexualizing their children all speak to this fact. One of our goals in examining such a wide range of attitudes is to demonstrate that views on family are about more than family: they delve into the very fabric of social life. Thus, to fully understand attitudes toward family and definitions of family—and to determine whether same-sex couples count in these definitions—we need to consider more broadly the gender dynamics on which American families are built and in some cases challenged.

═ Chapter 8 ═

Changing Counts, Counting Change: Toward a More Inclusive Definition of Family

FAMILY counts. Few would dispute this statement. Family is assigned a great many responsibilities and in turn is afforded a great number of benefits. It has a profound influence on our lives. But "family" counts too. How "family" is defined determines which living arrangements are expected to perform these responsibilities, which are granted these benefits, and upon which social legitimacy is conferred. Definitions of family—and especially whether same-sex couples should be seen as family—currently lie at the heart of passionate scholarly and public controversy and debate. Whether same-sex couples are counted in or out of this definition, we argue, is a crucial touchstone for understanding family more generally and accordingly is intertwined with views regarding a host of family issues—among them, the relative influence of parenting versus genetic inheritance, gender and parenting, and marital naming practices. Yet we have known little about the boundaries that Americans erect between family and nonfamily—that is, which living arrangements they include as family and which ones they do not. The unique and comprehensive approach taken in this book, however, narrows this gap by explicitly canvassing Americans' views on the definition of family.

In this closing chapter, we revisit the key patterns and themes that emerged from our interviews and discuss what these patterns may indicate about family in American society now and into the future. Despite their disagreements regarding whether same-sex couples should be seen as family and accorded, by extension, marital and other familial rights, "pro-family" and gay rights activists do agree about the centrality of the question of same-sex couples for our understanding of family. The conservative commentator Maggie Gallagher, for example, observes that "gay marriage is not some sideline issue, it *is* the marriage debate" (Gallagher 2003). Since the very first interviews we conducted in 2003, there have been remarkable changes surrounding the debate about same-sex couples and their actual legal status. These changes have not followed a predictably linear path. Rather, they have swung back and forth so much that they have triggered everything from unbridled optimism to devastating despair among both advocates of the extension of family rights to same-sex couples and critics apprehensive about the possible loss of "traditional" families. We have seen gains—or losses, in the view of certain "pro-family" groups—in the rapidly shifting legal and political landscape where the rights of same-sex couples have been advanced. Among these gains are court-initiated legalization of same-sex marriage in Massachusetts, Connecticut, Iowa, and, for a short period of time, California; legislatively approved same-sex marriage in Vermont, New Hampshire, Washington, D.C., and, temporarily, Maine; a publicly supported vote (Referendum 71) in Washington State in favor of expansion of domestic partnership rights and protections for same-sex couples, as well as for senior heterosexual couples[1]; and, at the time of the writing of this chapter, attempts by political leaders to at least tread softly toward extension of some familial rights to same-sex couples (for example, President Barrack Obama's executive order granting hospital visitation rights to same-sex couples) or sometimes to more boldly follow the lead of these states' leads.

At the same time, we have experienced losses—or gains according to traditional "pro-family" groups. Some sharply divided courts, including those with fairly liberal traditions (such as New York's), declined to overturn the long-standing prohibition against same-sex marriage in their states. Often these courts justify their ruling by deferring to the legislature and the will of the people. More than twenty states—representing a cross-section of this nation and wide divergence in political views and geographical locations—have put forth ballot initiatives to outlaw same-sex marriage. Some political commentators contend that this flurry of initiatives played a nontrivial role in the 2004 presidential election and increased support for Republican candidates in state elections: in fact, some pundits maintain that the ballot initiatives in swing states (such as Ohio) were a cynical ploy to secure George W. Bush's reelection. All but one effort passed—many of them decisively. And in Arizona, the one exception, the success was short-lived: voters opposed Proposition 107 ("protection of marriage") in 2006, but in 2008 they cast ballots in favor of Proposition 102, which amended the state constitution to define marriage as a union between one man and one woman. Even in California, one of the most socially liberal states—indeed, a state that several of our respondents labeled as overly liberal or far removed from the American mainstream—voters jettisoned the previously discussed breakthrough court decision when they narrowly voted in favor of Proposition 8, which revised the state constitution to restrict marital status to heterosexual couples.[2] These setbacks often extend beyond the debate regarding marriage. In Arkansas, legislation mainly designed to bar same-sex couples from adopting children or offering a home to foster children also passed.[3]

It is tricky to make predictions about the future of same-sex families, especially given the sheer fluidity of the situation and the intensified public reaction to the debate and to issues regarding sexuality more broadly. Even traditional forms of American entertainment are engaging this issue—from television personalities who advocate for or against same-sex marriage, to contestants in beauty pageants who are asked their views on same-sex marriage, to bloggers who gossip over whether a reality show contestant is gay. Currently, and somewhat surprisingly, some pundits and spokespersons for political parties and advocacy groups act as if the debate is over and proponents of same-sex marriage have prevailed with the American public, or shortly will do so (Waldman 2009). Neither the numbers from our data nor actual votes on initiatives are anywhere near the sufficient magnitude to support the idea that the public is ready to embrace same-sex couples with open arms.[4] To be sure, there still are many Americans who are—in their own words—"appalled," "disgusted," and "repelled" by the very idea of same-sex families and the extension of rights to these groups. Nevertheless, we remain confident that the resistance to same-sex partnerships will dissipate in the not-too-distant future.

Social scientists typically are more comfortable making claims about the past and present, while shying away from forecasting the future. Yet, if we tie together the various pieces of evidence that stand out in the previous chapters, we can make some admittedly cautious but empirically based predictions. We began by identifying and deciphering three distinguishable categories of Americans who vary in the lines that they draw between family and nonfamily: inclusionists, moderates, and exclusionists. These categories have provided a recurring baseline throughout the book that, in turn, is connected to other views about the family. At one end of the spectrum, exclusionists are restrictive in whom they welcome into the realm of family, while at the other end inclusionists are more receptive to living arrangements that exclusionists routinely reject. Moderates may be the most interesting group—or at least most important in terms of the future of American attitudes and beliefs. Moderates are at the very least open to new ways of defining family, but remain more guarded than inclusionists when it comes to granting family status to same-sex couples.

Changing Counts and Recounts

It is telling that even in a short period of time—just three years—we experienced a notable decrease in the percentage of exclusionists and a corresponding increase in the percentage of inclusionists. By 2006 a very clear majority (over three-fifths) of Americans had come to include same-sex couples with children and/or childless same-sex couples under the rubric of "family." This change is all the more impressive given that during that three-year period—from 2003 to 2006— anti-gay-marriage and, more broadly, anti-same-sex-relationships rhetoric reached perhaps its most heated level and arguably was also at its most effective. Although one might question whether this change is merely a blip in one particular data set, the corresponding open-ended comments provided by respondents convinced us that these changes are quite real. Moreover, these patterns are corroborated by a recently added and, in our opinion, most welcome question regarding same-sex marriage provided in the National Opinion Research Center's General Social Survey. Interviewees in the General Social Survey were asked their view regarding same-sex marriage in 2004, 2006, and 2008.[5] Between 2004 and 2006, the percentage of Americans who agreed that "homosexuals should have the right to marry" rose from 29.8 percent to 35.3 percent. Our own survey did not go beyond 2006, but the 2008 General Social Survey suggests that support for same-sex marriage increased further, up to 39.3 percent. Admittedly, these figures fall below any threshold that signals an irreversible tipping point, and therefore they challenge the idea promoted by some pundits that the debate is over. But these figures do indicate that the patterns we report throughout the book are not idiosyncratic to our data. These figures also signify that there is good reason to be confident that views of family and family rights will continue to expand, perhaps with increasing speed.

Had we not listened to the comments that Americans gave to explain the boundaries that they make between family and nonfamily, we might not be as optimistic. The quantitative data give us a picture of the boundaries, but the qualitative data animate the struggles that Americans face in defining family—struggles that should compel them to reevaluate their definitions of family. We do not see much struggle, however, among inclusionists. They believe that love and commitment make a family and bind it together. They embrace a broad definition of family that not only privileges love and commitment but also recognizes the various instrumental and expressive purposes of family and further defers to others' self-definitions of their own living situation. Inclusionists are unambiguous in their views and seem to be impervious to the arguments proffered by those who endorse narrower definitions of family. In fact, we are hard-pressed to envision a scenario in which a large segment of the inclusionist group would reverse itself and rein in its broad-ranging definition of family.

Most exclusionists also do not struggle with their definition of family. Or more precisely, they typically do not wrestle over the question of same-sex couples, although they do face challenges in their views regarding cohabiting heterosexual couples, especially those with children. Regarding same-sex couples, however, exclusionists do not show much potential for change in their views. Exclusionists insist upon heterosexuality, censure homosexuality (sometimes with palpable hostility), rely on interpretations of biblical text that putatively condemn same-sex unions, and emphasize the importance of biological parents—or "blood" relations. These frames may be so powerful that they counteract any attempts to broaden the definition of family, therefore rendering exclusionists unlikely candidates for change.

Still, we see some opportunities for movement even among some exclusionists. Although most exclusionists believe that the structure of families—notably, the presence of marriage—trumps the functions that families provide, some do not. This latter group may be receptive to entreaties to expand the definition of family to those living arrangements in which the needs and functions of family are met by its members regardless of legal documents or sexual orientation. Ironically, the focus on structure—more specifically, the legally endorsed familial structure—may ultimately be an effective strategy to relax exclusionists' resistance to same-sex couples. From our interviews, it is apparent that several exclusionists saw legal marriage as the key ingredient of family status and, in fact, as the only requirement to warrant that status. If legal definitions carry weight with exclusionists who respect legal tradition above all else, then legalization of same-sex marriage in various states may be sufficient to push some exclusionists toward a more moderate, if not inclusionist, stance. Thus, while our overall assumption is that definitions of family precipitate changes in views regarding the extension of legal rights to nontraditional living arrangements, for this group a change in the law might simultaneously shape both their views about same-sex marriage and the line of demarcation they draw between family and nonfamily. Legal changes in the status of same-sex couples, then, may move some exclusionists incrementally toward acceptance of same-sex couples as family.

We see much greater potential for movement among moderates, who—more so than either inclusionists or exclusionists—appear to genuinely struggle as they try to reconcile their traditionalism with their openness to change. This group, however, does not waver on the issue of children: if there is a child in the household, moderates deem the living arrangement to be a family. Given the pivotal role that moderates as a bloc may play in the future of same-sex marriage (and in the extension of other rights to nontraditional family forms), campaigns that emphasize the positive effect that marital rights have on children of same-sex couples may be a winning formula. Moreover, with sophisticated and ever-changing reproductive technologies and increased opportunities for adoption, the number and visibility of same-sex couples residing with their children certainly may increase. From a political standpoint, framing the equality of same-sex couples in terms of "the best interests of the child" may prove to be a successful gateway that, when opened, fosters greater acceptance of same-sex households, along with equal rights and protections.

Still, moderates are hesitant to define childless same-sex couples—and childless heterosexual cohabiting couples—as family. But even here we foresee this reluctance eventually being transformed into steadier or even unwavering support. Surely, we see little evidence that moderates will become more restrictive in their definitions of family. In fact, the arguments that appear most persuasive to exclusionists—for example, pronouncements regarding the immorality of homosexual relations and reliance on biblical text (or particular interpretations of biblical text)—carry little weight among moderates. In contrast, arguments that appeal to inclusionists ultimately may also convert moderates. Given that so many moderates stipulate that the presence of children signals commitment among same-sex and heterosexual partners, the increasing visibility of other signals of commitment may also become a persuasive wellspring of change.

Among these signals is the length of time spent living together—as demonstrated by the sizable number of moderates who agree that a childless same-sex couple who have lived together for ten years constitute a family. Another signal, however, is detected from the functions that partners perform as a unit. Moderates are fully aware that families comprise members who are interdependent in accomplishing shared goals. The more moderates are aware of or actually witness people in loving nontraditional living arrangements carrying out the various emotional and instrumental functions of family, the more receptive they should become to a more expansive definition of family. And this awareness is indeed likely to expand, given the growing number of media representations of loving same-sex families and the greater openness of same-sex couples themselves in schools, work settings, and communities. As moderates reexamine their views regarding same-sex families, social scientists might need to take a fresh look at their own views regarding functional approaches to family.[6] Although functionalism was once the mainstay of much sociological thought, recently it has been summarily dismissed by many social scientists as mere rationalization of the status quo and therefore an unremitting source of conservatism. But our interviews suggest an alternative interpretation: when the functions of families were brought up in our interviews, this topic tended, perhaps counterintuitively, to liberalize individual viewpoints.

Moderates' cognizance of their ambivalence and the inconsistencies in their responses makes us even more convinced of future changes in the boundaries that Americans make between family and nonfamily. In our interviews, moderates often realized that their emphasis on love and commitment, as well as on meeting familial needs, was at odds with their initial exclusion of childless same-sex and cohabiting heterosexual couples from the definition of family. Upon acknowledging their contradictory responses, some asked to change their responses—almost always in the direction of more inclusion. Others did not make this request but clearly felt uneasy with the dissonance in their responses. Some even volunteered that their views might switch or at least soften in the near future. The response of a fifty-year-old moderate woman from Georgia personifies the kind of ambivalence that might give way to a more inclusive view:

I don't . . . I don't know if . . . I don't know, between my religious upbringing and my traditional upbringing, I don't know. I'm still working on this one for myself, and I still don't have one answer. . . . We're not adamant against it [same-sex couples], but like I said, I mean, process is changing. If you call me next year, I might change my mind.

She continued by describing her upbringing and the ongoing process by which she was evaluating her own views:

Well, you know, it's just traditional southern upbringing, where it's not like we knew homosexuals. But you know, it's just, I don't know, it's just . . . it's hard to explain. With my age group we're still learning to consider other—I can't think of the word. I can't think of the word: goodness, it's like once I hit fifty, I forget things! I was brought up one way, but I am slowly changing and considering other options. But I'm not totally, you know, I haven't totally changed some of the things. So, I'm, that's why some of my answers have been like flip-flopping, 'cause I'm not adamant about some of the things. So like I said, this is one of the areas that I am still thinking about. . . . It might be that under the right circumstances I could be convinced that it would be okay.

This respondent might have been apologetic about her lack of clarity or consistency, but her comments spoke volumes about what we be-lieve is an inevitable pull toward greater acceptance of same-sex living arrangements. She exemplifies the many moderates who are poised to ultimately embrace a broader definition of family. A climate of accep-tance is encouraging for those who advocate the extension of familial rights to same-sex couples—and to cohabiting heterosexual ones—but conversely, it is alarming to opponents and may further gird their resis-tance. Some commentators on this subject suggest that defenders of "traditional marriage" realize that there remains only a small window of time in which they can proactively prevent the extension of familial rights to nontraditional living arrangements. This realization could well be the precipitating factor behind the flurry of anti-gay marriage initiatives that were advanced in the past few years. To the dismay of inclusionists, these initiatives have been enormously successful. But even among some exclusionists, we hear resigned recognition that these successes are likely to be short-lived: "In the end I believe all will prevail for the gay community. I will never agree with it. But that will be something I will have to live and die with."

Changing Divisions

This sense of resignation may be due in large measure to exclusionists' appreciation of the vast generational cleavages in definitions of family. Exclusionists realize that youths are no longer living in, as one person puts it, "the *Leave It to Beaver* world anymore." Older respondents were especially attuned to generational differences; in fact, they mentioned these differences more frequently than did younger Americans. The patterns are clear: the younger generation is strikingly more expansive in their definition of family than are their elders, especially those age sixty-five or older. Over 75 percent of adults under the age of thirty view some types of same-sex couples as family, while over 60 percent of adults sixty-five years of age or older refuse to acknowledge any liv-ing arrangement involving gay men or lesbians as family.

Some commentators speculate that youths will outgrow their more liberal views about family. We are less convinced. Instead, generations matter. For example, the members of the baby boom generation es-pouse more liberal views regarding family than would ordinarily be expected, breaking the otherwise smooth linear relationship between age and conservative views on family. This departure in the pattern highlights the powerful influence that a historical climate of tolerance has on individuals as they approach adulthood. Our younger respondents came of age—or are coming of age—at a time when gay issues have been more widely discussed and certainly gays have been less stigmatized. Some mass media have been at the cutting edge in presenting nontraditional families—showing, for example, single-parent and step-parent households at times when out-of-wedlock childbearing and divorce were not generally accepted. The same is true today for media images of gays and lesbians. Contemporary media and other conduits of information are more open about same-sex relations and overall are less heterosexist than they were even just a decade ago. Ironically, even the most virulently negative characterizations of gays and lesbians in public discourse may have the unintended consequence of making a taboo topic less taboo. While one can rightfully critique some images of gays and lesbians in the media (Gamson 1998; Walters 2001), the increased visibility of gays and lesbians in the public domain may be pivotal to the receptiveness of younger adults to a broader definition of family. If trends continue on the same path that they appear to favor, then the replacement of older cohorts by younger ones should invariably reshape the boundaries between family and nonfamily.

Educational differences should create a similar demographic pull toward inclusivity. As also confirmed in past scholarship about social attitudes, Americans with higher levels of education typically are more cosmopolitan in their views. Compared to their peers with lower levels of education, they report greater receptivity to including same-sex couples in their definitions of family. Such increased liberalism is not unexpected. College exposes youths to new ideas and experiences that challenge the often more insular viewpoints they might have had upon entering college. Moreover, college students may know and have contact with gay peers, a pattern that might soften once staunchly held exclusionist positions.[7]

Contact with gay men and lesbians is not limited, however, to the college-educated. Having a gay friend or relative in one's network or even just knowing someone who is gay is related quite strongly to the acceptance of same-sex living arrangements as family. The notable increase between 2003 and 2006 in the percentage of Americans who reported having a gay friend or relative suggests two things. First, gay and lesbian Americans are becoming more open about their sexuality to their friends, relatives, and acquaintances—even during or perhaps because of the heightened negative rhetoric about same-sex couples that took place between 2003 and 2006. Second, heterosexual Americans increasingly acknowledge the presence of gays and lesbians in their personal and professional social networks. These changes parallel the greater visibility of gay and lesbian public figures and, importantly, show no sign of abating. Additionally, current forms of communication (such as blogs, Twitter, and email) all encourage dialogue and openness about sexuality rather than denial of it. In the business world, many companies already offer same-sex benefits and programs, thus perhaps making employees feel more comfortable informing their colleagues about their sexual preference. Taken together, these trends insinuate more openness by the gay community, increasing recognition of gays and lesbians by others, and, in turn, greater receptivity to a broader conceptualization of family.

Earlier in this book, we identified other sociodemographic factors that also are implicated in Americans' definition of family. Regarding gender, women cast a wider net than do men when making decisions about who counts as family. This pattern also foretells a shift toward greater acceptance of various living arrangements as family. Women remain the primary caretakers of children and thus may hold greater sway over what their children come to believe. In a country where divorce and single-parenthood rates remain high, the effects of mothers' views may be especially pronounced. Consequently, children may learn from the example set by their mothers to be more open-minded about other types of families. Women also are as likely as men to vote, if not more so (Carroll and Fox 2006). Thus, as a voting bloc, women may have great sway over future elections and ballot initiative outcomes. Of course, not all women are inclusionists and not all men are exclusionists, but the average pattern is suggestive. Should the majority of women favor a more expansive vision of family, then politicians' hesitation to endorse the same may correspondingly lessen.

This is not to say that men are impervious to change. On the contrary, increased education and contact with gay friends and relatives are at least as liberalizing for men as they are for women. Younger generations of men, not unlike the women of their age cohorts, also are more receptive to inclusionist definitions of family than are their older counterparts. Young men often are portrayed as unrelentingly homophobic, presumably because homosexuality challenges hegemonic ideas of masculinity. But the patterns found in our data challenge the idea that young men constitute the group most resistant to inclusionist visions of family. The patterns also suggest room for future change among men, especially if we listen to how men talk about family. The different frames that men and women use to define family may be useful in campaigns that target male voters. For example, appeals to the responsibilities that are met in the family may provide a winning strategy for gay rights advocates in gaining support among men.

Spatial boundaries also figure into the boundaries that individuals draw between family and nonfamily. Urban-rural and regional schisms in Americans' definitions of family suggest that change will be uneven—with fairly rapid steps taken toward inclusivity in certain areas and nontrivial pushback in others. These differences to some degree explain why, for example, some Americans living in urban areas in the Northeast are so perplexed by strong hostility to same-sex marriage— and more broadly to the idea that a same-sex couple constitutes a family—when they consider it a non-issue, while other Americans living in rural areas of the South are baffled by and even fearful of the acknowledgment of the rights of same-sex couples that is perhaps inexorably under way.

What we already know about attitudes toward interracial couples also may be instructive here. The reader may recall that in chapter 4 we not only showed that age (cohort) and education affect Americans' current definitions of family (that is, whether they are exclusionist) but also noted that these factors closely parallel the age and educational differences in Americans' views regarding interracial marriage several decades ago. The very same survey—the General Social Survey—confirms a huge gap between urban and rural dwellers in 1972, the first year of the survey. In that year, over half (57.4 percent) of rural Americans favored "laws against marriages between (Negroes/Blacks/African Americans) and whites," while over three-fourths (78.9 percent) of respondents living in large cities were opposed to such discriminatory mandates. Although the rural-urban gap never entirely disappeared, over time rural Americans' views drifted closer to those of urban Americans (in other words, became more tolerant). By the mid-1990s, more than three-fourths of rural Americans also expressed opposition to miscegenation laws (76.2 percent in 1994). The very same changes transpired among southerners, although stubborn pockets of resistance in some southern states lingered. These patterns are not atypical: scholars have confirmed that social attitudes—especially innovative and liberal ones—typically spread in the United States from urban to rural areas and from nonsouthern to southern states (Fischer 1978; Firebaugh and Davis 1988). Urban-rural and regional gaps may not entirely disappear, but rural and southern views are more likely to move in the direction of urban and nonsouthern views than the other way around.

Currently, one might characterize the social and political climate regarding familial definitions as one in which pockets of acceptance are scattered. That is, in a small number of states, individuals are more receptive to a broadened definition of family that includes same-sex couples and ultimately promotes the extension of rights and benefits to these couples. The number of such states is small, but if the regional and urban-rural changes in attitudes toward interracial marriage are any indication, the number will continue to grow. Although such growth is likely to encounter additional resistance, this opposition will diminish to the point where only pockets of resistance remain—as we have witnessed with respect to attitudes toward interracial marriage.

Most sociodemographic trends seem to propel us in the direction of a more inclusive definition of family. One influence, however, may stand in the way. Religious ideology and identity—measured in several ways, but most notably by interpretations of the Bible as literal—are powerfully entwined with some Americans' definitions of family. Homosexuality and same-sex relationships are often couched by exclusionists in terms of violating biblical doctrine—as flouting "God's law," "the biblical standard," and "*the* rules." For Americans who resolutely hold on to these positions, it is difficult to envision much movement toward greater inclusivity. The use of these religious frames is so powerful that the greater adherence of some Americans to religious orthodoxy—at least compared to the rest of the Western world—may be a major stumbling block that stands in the way of acceptance of nontraditional groups as families.

Should the number of Americans who subscribe to religiously orthodox or fundamentalist views increase in the future, then we might expect a slowing down or even a reversal in the trend toward a more inclusive definition of family. Whether religious conservatism and fundamentalism in the United States will increase, however, has been widely debated. Some scholars contend that fundamentalism has reached its peak in popularity and is now noticeably on the decline. Instead, they forecast, Americans will become more and more secularized, as indicated by the rise in the number of Americans who indicate that they are agnostic, atheist, or unaffiliated with any particular religion. Others do not deny that religion remains important in the everyday lives of Americans, but they believe that the absolutism associated with fundamentalism is being supplanted by a more expansive religious worldview—an expansiveness that is manifested, for example, in greater concern over global warming and poverty in the developing countries (Bolzendahl and Brooks 2005). The possibility that this greater liberalism will extend to views regarding same-sex relationships is certainly not out of the question. After all, religious messages can and do shift dramatically over time—as witnessed, for example, in the civil rights movement. Many messages in religious texts encourage tolerance above and beyond other values. Relying on these messages, some denominations explicitly welcome gays and lesbians, such as the United Church of Christ and the Episcopal Church (in the United States). Casting religion as an insurmountable and unalterable bulwark holding back the extension of familial definitions and of civil liberties to include gay citizens therefore may itself be too rigid a view.

Changing Accounts

The invocation of "God's will" takes a surprising twist when used to explain the etiology of sexual preference. Ordinarily, we might expect religious reasoning—or, at least, the insertion of "God's will" into causal explanations—to behave in conservative ways. Yet Americans who believe that "God's will" is the principal factor determining sexual preference are surprisingly liberal in their definitions of family. Also unexpected is the age profile of the Americans who are most likely to subscribe to this account: younger adults. These two perhaps jarring patterns do not necessarily imply that religious views per se now automatically convert into liberalism or are on the rise. But they do suggest that some Americans see sexuality as determined not by the individual or the environment, but instead by forces that exist well beyond our understanding. In other words, it is possible to use the concept of "God's will" in a way that reinforces the immutability of sexuality and challenges claims that sexual preference can be changed. Importantly, as comments by the interviewees clarify, this frame may simultaneously appeal to those who are religious and supportive of same-sex families and to those who do not necessarily see themselves as religious (atheists, agnostics, and spiritualists). Just as appeals to "God's will" have been successfully employed in various progressive social causes, the use of this apparent religious frame may be called upon to justify equality for same-sex couples.

Religion and science typically are not thought of as natural allies. Instead, they often are pitted against each other and as such are portrayed as promoting incompatible accounts of human behavior. But here we see a clear exception. Ostensibly religious ("God's will") and scientific (genetic inheritance) explanations of sexual preference share a great deal in common. Paralleling "God's will" explanations, genetic accounts are robustly coupled with a more inclusive definition of family. When Americans attribute sexual preference to genetics—or to "God's will"—they in essence reject the idea that homosexuality is a "lifestyle" choice and therefore is reversible or, in the parlance of gay reparative therapy, "curable." Instead, adherents of genetic accounts—like those who endorse "God's will" explanations—view sexual preference not as a choice, but rather as an intrinsic and immutable trait of individuals.

This view is becoming increasingly popular—as indicated by the growing number of Americans between 2003 and 2006 who selected genetic or "God's will" explanations in the closed-ended questions and correspondingly the declining number who placed responsibility on parenting and parenting practices. Open-ended remarks, especially regarding the extension of marital and other rights to same-sex couples, further demonstrate the resonance of explanations that underscore the genetic or fixed nature of sexual preference. In 2003, the notion that the origins of sexual preference are beyond the realm of individual control rarely appeared in Americans' comments. By 2006, however, Americans had begun to employ this line of reasoning as a compelling factor behind their support of, among other things, gay marriage. Clearly, Americans are hearing and sharing the message promoted by many—but certainly not all—gay rights activists that individuals should not be disparately treated because of a trait that is beyond their control. Should increasing reliance on genetic and "God's will" accounts follow the growth that was witnessed between 2003 and 2006, then support for a more inclusive vision of family should correspondingly accelerate.

These patterns may simultaneously hearten and unsettle social scientists. They certainly should be encouraging to social scientists who advocate expanding familial definitions because they suggest a likely and perhaps unavoidable movement toward inclusivity. But these same patterns also may be disquieting to those social scientists who express serious reservations about the use of genetic accounts of human or social behavior—reservations predicated to a large extent on the historical usage of genetic differences to rationalize racial and gender discrimination. Despite a recent upswing in scholarly ventures that explore the joint influence of social and biological or genetic factors on human behavior, a very large contingency of social scientists remains intransigently opposed to such endeavors, dismissing them as a contemporary rationalization for inequality and unequal treatment.[8] Yet equating genetic frames with a reactionary position is a dangerous oversimplification. As we can see from the responses that Americans give, genetic explanations need not be inherently conservative. Instead, they can be a source of liberalism in some cases. Just as Americans are reevaluating their beliefs about family, many social scientists will need to reconsider their assumptions regarding "nature" and "nurture"—especially in the case of sexual preference, where "nature" currently yields the more liberal response while "nurture" produces the more conservative one.

Unchanging Barriers

The most exclusionist definitions of family come from Americans who believe that parents and parenting practices are primarily accountable for sexual preference. This group sees few limits to parenting—even, or especially, when it comes to sexuality, which they believe can and should be controlled. In listening to Americans' comments regarding the optimal living situation for girls and boys in single-parent households, we come to appreciate how intertwined Americans' views on sexual preference and gender really can be. Americans who believe that boys are better off living with their fathers and girls are better off living with their mothers also are more likely to believe that sexual preference is due to parents and, more importantly, are more likely to take a strongly exclusionist stance when defining the boundaries between family and nonfamily. They do not believe in same-sex couples, but they do believe in the importance of a same-sex parent: fathers for boys and mothers for girls. The same-sex parent is seen as the frontline role model who instills in boys appropriate and desirable masculine traits and behaviors and in girls requisite feminine traits and behaviors. The marked sex differentiation endorsed by Americans may be surprising given the assertions made by many social commentators that gender divisions have loosened greatly. Yet remarks by Americans who highlight the merits of same-sex role models—especially the importance of a male figure in a boy's life as a means to counteract the feminizing influence of women—echo similar arguments made over a century ago. These arguments suggest a sustained fear, disdain, or loathing of feminine qualities in boys—which appears to be coupled with a continuing fear, disdain, or loathing of homosexuality.

But the ongoing durability of gender stereotypes and the power of gender expectations also are seen in the comments by Americans who presume that both boys and girls would be better off living with their mother. This group of Americans is skeptical about fathers' ability to parent and instead perhaps overstates the unique qualifications that women possess in this arena. Clearly, they hold distinct gendered stereotypes regarding parents. Nevertheless, their focus on nurturance and their less rigid differentiation between boys and girls may be critical factors in their greater willingness to include same-sex couples with children as family and may be influential in moving them to even greater inclusivity in the future. That inclusivity may eventually approach that of the group of Americans who believe that a parent's gender and a child's gender are less consequential than the actual quality of the parent-child relationship. Tellingly, members of this group constitute a much smaller percentage than the other two—further evidence of the tenacity of gendered expectations and the wide-ranging effects of these expectations, most notably on definitions of family.

The resiliency of certain gendered assumptions amid a sea of other social changes is clearly on display when Americans discuss their views about marital name change. Nearly three-fourths of Americans agree that it is better for a woman to change her name at marriage, while one-half concur that women should be legally required to change their name at marriage, and almost one-half believe that it is unacceptable for a man to take the name of his wife. These responses not only tell us about Americans' views regarding name practices but also reveal a great deal about their understanding of gender in family life, their openness to a variety of gendered identities, and their receptiveness to a broader definition of family. Despite a clear correspondence between liberal views regarding marital name change and expansive definitions of family, it appears that the rate of change in the latter is much more rapid than in the former. This disparity, we believe, is due mostly to the intensified public attention to the issue of same-sex relations (even in such a short period as 2003 through 2006), in contrast to the virtual absence of public dialogue over marital name change. This pattern also suggests that, ironically, despite the current inextricable link between views regarding gender and sexuality, changes in Americans' views regarding the definition of family may liberalize so swiftly that they may well be decoupled from at least some views regarding gender in the future.

Changing Boundaries

Throughout this book, we have found persuasive evidence that Americans are moving toward a more encompassing definition of family that includes same-sex households. In other words, the boundary between family and nonfamily is being redrawn. For most proponents of equality for same-sex families, this is good news. Still, moving the boundary does not eliminate it. The boundary is simply repositioned. Placing same-sex couples within the category of family does not deny that other living arrangements will continue to be counted out—such as friends living together, nonromantic relationships, and non-exclusive partnerships. Although many of the Americans we interviewed challenged some heteronormative conceptions of "the family," there were limits. For example, over 90 percent—including most inclusionists—categorically dismissed housemates as nonfamily. Would this response have shifted had we focused on the functions of this living arrangement rather than on its form? It is possible, especially for some inclusionists who in their open-ended comments suggested that families can come in a variety of packages that perform familial functions. Still, an unintentional consequence of efforts to include same-sex couples as family—and correspondingly, to recognize same-sex marriage—might be further marginalization of other living arrangements, or "chosen families," that do not enjoy legal recognition and the rights and benefits attendant with such a status.

Two legal scholars, Martha Fineman and Nancy Polikoff, both make arguments along these lines. Fineman (1995, 2004) proposes a more narrow model—or legal definition—of family that expressly privileges relationships between a dependent and his or her caretaker.[9] She also believes that the intimate nature of horizontal relationships between adults should be left out of the question of family and that state-sanctioned marriage should be replaced by private contracts between adult partners. Mirroring Fineman's line of reasoning, Polikoff (2008) critiques the use of marriage as a means of conveying legal and social status. She grants the advantages that legal marital status would provide to same-sex couples, but also is troubled that same-sex marriage would create and strengthen boundaries between the married and nonmarried (see also Ettelbrick 2001; Walters 2001; Warner 1999). According to Polikoff, compelling couples to marry in order to obtain benefits and legal status necessarily results in the exclusion of a number of familial (biological or not) forms that need and deserve protection and benefits under the law, such as adult children taking care of parents, couples who choose not to marry, and cohabiting friends who share a long-standing (though nonsexual) economic and emotional interdependence. Polikoff proposes that marriage be converted to a merely cultural or religious ceremony and that family laws be based on the choices that people make in forming their own family. We bring up Fineman's and Polikoff's positions not because they represent the modal viewpoint currently held among scholars, gay rights activists, or gay men and lesbians (for a detailed description of the various debates within the gay community regarding same-sex marriage, see Hull 2006). But their comments remind us that when efforts to define same-sex couples as family—and relatedly, to legalize same-sex marriage—are successful, the battleground regarding the definition of family will shift, just as it shifted after other barriers to family or marital status were broken.

Counting Change

The United States includes a rich diversity of families whether or not they are officially recognized as such. In fact, "the family," although still invoked far too often in public and scholarly venues, is an increasingly untenable and obsolete concept. Many nontraditional or hitherto transgressive living arrangements—single-parent households, voluntarily childless couples, divorced homes—no longer carry strongly negative connotations or elicit highly judgmental reactions, as in the past. The idea of the legal recognition of interracial marriage, for example, at one time was unthinkable in most parts of the United States. Decades after the Supreme Court ordered the removal of antimiscegenation laws, interracial relations are tolerated, accepted, or even embraced by most Americans.[10]

Despite resistance in some communities to acknowledging a similarity between interracial and same-sex couples, the parallels between the two as highlighted throughout this book are impossible to ignore. The very same sociodemographic cleavages that distinguished supporters and vehement opponents of interracial marriage have reemerged to differentiate between advocates of an inclusive definition of family and critics who take a more exclusionist stance. The discomfort with same-sex couples and, more broadly, contact with gays and lesbians that Americans express closely resembles the discomfort with interracial couples and contact with other races. Arguments to resist the inclusion of same-sex couples as family echo the arguments that were advanced against interracial couples: for example, that these couples are abhorrent, unnatural, and against the law of God. By the same token, the reasons currently offered on behalf of an inclusive vision of family are strikingly similar to the reasons given to support interracial marriage: for example, that love and commitment define the family regardless of its members, that one cannot choose one's sexual preference just as one cannot choose one's race, and that whom one falls in love with cannot be controlled.

But today the fact that interracial relations were legally prohibited not so long ago seems unfathomable, beyond the pale of possibility. Given the cumulative and compelling evidence presented in this book, we envisage a day in the near future when same-sex families also will gain acceptance by a large plurality of the public, the denial of similar rights to same-sex couples will be nothing more than an antiquated memory, and same-sex couples will no longer be counted out.

= Appendix 1.A: = The Study

THE CONSTRUCTING the Family Surveys of 2003 and 2006 are the product of the Sociological Research Practicum (SRP), an annual research project carried out by the Department of Sociology and the Institute of Social Research at Indiana University. This telephone survey of Indiana and U.S. adult residents (712 in 2003 and 815 in 2006) was developed under the direction of Brian Powell (in conjunction with Catherine Bolzendahl, Danielle Fettes, Claudia Geist, and Cher Jamison in 2003, and with Claudia Geist, Laura Hamilton, Yasmiyn Irizarry, Cher Jamison, and Kyle Dodson in 2006) and conducted by the Center for Survey Research (CSR) in Bloomington, Indiana.[1] The purpose of the survey was to gauge public opinion regarding how family is conceptualized. Data were collected on a range of topics, including: definitions of family, birth order influences, the perceived advantages and disadvantages to being older (or younger) parents, family-friendly policies, the relative importance of biological and social factors in the development of child traits, the relative influence of parents and peers, and attitudes about gay and lesbian relationships. Information on sociodemographic characteristics such as education, age, gender, race, religion, and marital status was collected, as was an extensive household roster.

Sampling Procedures

Survey questions were pretested in April 2003 and April 2006. Changes were made to the questionnaire and pretested again in early May of each survey year. Production interviewing began on May 16 in 2003 and on May 11 on 2006 and concluded on July 14 in 2003 and on June 28 in 2006. Interviews ranged in length from 25 to 112 minutes in 2003 and from 13 to 87 minutes in 2006. In 2003, the mean length was 44 minutes and the median was 41 minutes; and in 2006, the mean length was 28 minutes and the median was 24 minutes.

CSR Interviewing Facilities and Procedures

Data were collected by telephone using the University of California Computer-Assisted Survey Methods software (CASES Version 5.3). In 2003, interviews were conducted from 8:45 A.M. to 11:00 P.M. on Mondays through Thursdays, from 4:15 P.M. to 11:00 P.M. on Fridays, from 8:45 A.M. to 4:00 P.M. on Saturdays, and from 12:30 P.M. to 11:00 P.M. on Sundays. In 2006, interviews were conducted from 9:00 A.M. to 1:00 P.M. on Tuesdays and Thursdays, from 12:00 P.M. to 4:00 P.M. on Mondays and Wednesdays, from 6:00 P.M. to 12:30 A.M. on Mondays through Thursdays, from 1:00 P.M. to 5:00 P.M. on Saturdays and Sundays, and from 6:00 P.M. to 12:30 A.M. on Sundays.

The data collection staff included seven supervisors and twenty-six interviewers in 2003 (and four supervisors and thirty-one interviewers in 2006). All interviewers received at least fifteen hours of training in 2003 (and sixteen hours in 2006) on the interview instrument before production interviewing. Interviewers were instructed to use neutral probes and feedback phrases.

Audio and visual monitoring was regularly conducted by the telephone survey supervisors using specialized telephone and computer equipment that did not allow the interviewers to know that they were being monitored. Monitoring was conducted randomly, with each interviewer being monitored at least once during each shift. Because the questionnaire included both closed-ended and open-ended questions, interviews were recorded to audio files, which were then burned onto compact disks. Trained transcribers used these disks to transcribe all open-ended responses, as well as unsolicited responses to closed-ended questions.

All cases with a confirmed valid telephone number were called up to twenty-five times in 2003 and up to twenty-four times in 2006 (mean number of contacts: 5.3) unless the household refused or we had insufficient time before the end of the study. Cases with unknown validity (persistent no answers or answering devices) were called—during the morning, afternoon, evening, late evening, and weekend—a minimum of twelve times in 2003 (and eight times in 2006). The CSR attempts to convert each "refusal" twice. When possible, a conversion attempt is made at the first instance of refusal, and a second is usually made after a few days.

Some Characteristics of the Sample

The telephone numbers were randomly generated by the Marketing Systems Group using the Genesys list-assisted method. The sample was a random selection of households. This method allows for unpublished numbers and new listings to be included in the sample. At each residential telephone number, we randomly selected an adult household member to interview.

Sociodemographic characteristics for this sample were compared to both census data and the General Social Survey. In addition, several questions used in the survey were identical to items in the 2004 GSS, allowing for a comparison of distributions. Differences found in these comparisons were slight, adding confidence in the sample. For example, the distribution of responses to views about the Bible ("Please tell me which of these statements comes closest to describing your feelings about the Bible") in the Constructing the Family (CTF) Survey and the GSS were virtually identical:

A. "The Bible is an ancient book of fables, legends, history, and moral precepts recorded by men." (15 percent CTF; 16 percent GSS)

B. "The Bible is the inspired word of God but not everything in it should be taken literally, word for word." (49 percent CTF; 48 percent GSS)

C. "The Bible is the actual word of God and it is to be taken literally, word for word." (34 percent CTF; 34 percent GSS)[2]

All analyses were conducted with and without sampling weights and yielded very few differences. (Any differences are reported in the text.)

Appendix 1.B:
Constructing the Family Surveys 2003 and 2006: Core Attitudinal Questions

Unless otherwise specified, these questions were asked in 2003 and 2006. Open-ended questions are specified in italics.

Definitions of Family

People these days have differing opinions of what counts as a family. Next, I will read you a number of living arrangements and I will ask you whether you personally think this arrangement counts as a family.

First, a husband and a wife living together with one or more of their children. Would you consider this group of people to be a family?

1. Yes
2. No
7. Depends
8. Don't know
9. Refused

Next, a man and a woman living together as an unmarried couple, with one or more of their children. Would you consider this group of people to be a family?

1. Yes
2. No
7. Depends

8. Don't know

9. Refused

How about a man living alone with one or more of his children? Would you consider this group of people to be a family?

1. Yes

2. No

7. Depends

8. Don't know

9. Refused

What about a woman living alone with one or more of her children? Would you consider this group of people to be a family?

1. Yes

2. No

7. Depends

8. Don't know

9. Refused

Two women living together as a couple with one or more of their children? Would you consider this group of people to be a family?

1. Yes

2. No

7. Depends

8. Don't know

9. Refused

Two men living together as a couple with one or more of their children? Would you consider this group of people to be a family?

1. Yes

2. No

7. Depends

8. Don't know

9. Refused

A husband and wife living together who have no children? Would you consider this group of people to be a family?

1. Yes

2. No

7. Depends

8. Don't know

9. Refused

A man and a woman living together as an unmarried couple who have no children? Would you consider this group of people to be a family?

1. Yes

2. No

7. Depends

8. Don't know

9. Refused

Two people living together as housemates who are not living as a couple and have no children? Would you consider this group of people to be a family?

1. Yes

2. No

7. Depends

8. Don't know

9. Refused

Two men living together as a couple who have no children? Would you consider this group of people to be a family?

1. Yes

2. No

7. Depends

8. Don't know

9. Refused

Two women living together as a couple who have no children? Would you consider this group of people to be a family?

1. Yes

2. No

7. Depends

8. Don't know

9. Refused

In thinking about your answers to the past few questions about what counts as a family, what determines for you whether you think a living arrangement is a family?

Should pets be counted as family members? (Asked in 2006 only.)

1. Yes

2. No

7. Depends

8. Don't know

9. Refused

Rights and Relationships

In the United States, marriage is associated with several rights. Please indicate whether you strongly agree, somewhat agree, somewhat disagree, or strongly disagree that people living in the following arrangements should have certain rights.

A man and woman living together as an unmarried couple who have no children should be able to file joint income tax returns. Do you:

1. Strongly agree

2. Somewhat agree

3. Somewhat disagree

4. Strongly disagree

7. Neither agree nor disagree [volunteered]

8. Don't know

9. Refused

They should have benefits such as health insurance for the partner. Do you:

1. Strongly agree

2. Somewhat agree

3. Somewhat disagree

4. Strongly disagree

7. Neither agree nor disagree [volunteered]

8. Don't know

9. Refused

They should have hospital visitation rights that parents, children, and spouses have. Do you:

1. Strongly agree

2. Somewhat agree

3. Somewhat disagree

4. Strongly disagree

7. Neither agree nor disagree [volunteered]

8. Don't know

9. Refused

They should have inheritance rights similar to a married couple. Do you:

1. Strongly agree

2. Somewhat agree

3. Somewhat disagree

4. Strongly disagree

7. Neither agree nor disagree [volunteered]

8. Don't know

9. Refused

Now we're going to talk about another living arrangement, that of two men living together as a couple or two women living together as a couple, who have no children.

Two men living as a couple or two women living as a couple, who have no children, should be able to file joint tax returns. Do you:

1. Strongly agree
2. Somewhat agree
3. Somewhat disagree
4. Strongly disagree
7. Neither agree nor disagree [volunteered]
8. Don't know
9. Refused

They should have benefits such as health insurance for the partner. Do you:

1. Strongly agree
2. Somewhat agree
3. Somewhat disagree
4. Strongly disagree
7. Neither agree nor disagree [volunteered]
8. Don't know
9. Refused

They should have hospital visitation rights that parents, children, and spouses have. Do you:

1. Strongly agree
2. Somewhat agree
3. Somewhat disagree
4. Strongly disagree
7. Neither agree nor disagree [volunteered]
8. Don't know
9. Refused

They should have inheritance rights similar to a married couple. Do you:

1. Strongly agree
2. Somewhat agree
3. Somewhat disagree
4. Strongly disagree
7. Neither agree nor disagree [volunteered]
8. Don't know
9. Refused

Length of Relationship and Definition of Family (Asked in 2006 Only)

The next series of questions is about *when* a couple becomes a family. Please tell me whether or not you consider each of the following couples to be a family.

From the moment they are married, are a husband and a wife a family?

1. Yes
2. No
7. Depends
8. Don't know
9. Refused

(If no, depends, don't know, refused) What if they have been married for ten years without children—are they a family?

1. Yes
2. No
7. Depends
8. Don't know
9. Refused

From the moment they move in together as a couple, are a man and a woman without children a family?

1. Yes
2. No
7. Depends
8. Don't know
9. Refused

(If no, depends, don't know, refused) What if they have lived together as a couple for ten years—are a man and a woman without children a family?

1. Yes
2. No
7. Depends
8. Don't know
9. Refused

From the moment they move in together as a couple, are two men or two women without children a family?

1. Yes
2. No
7. Depends
8. Don't know
9. Refused

(If no, depends, don't know, refused) What if they have lived together as a couple for ten years—are two men or two women without children a family?

1. Yes
2. No
7. Depends
8. Don't know
9. Refused

We've talked a lot so far about other people's families—and now I'd like you to tell me about your family. When I say the phrase "your family," who do you think of? (Asked in 2006 only.)

Single Parents (Asked in 2003 Only)

In a single-parent household, is a boy better off living with his mother or his father?

1. Mother
2. Father
6. Either
7. Depends
8. Don't know
9. Refused

Why do you feel a boy is better off with his [father/mother]?

In a single-parent household, is a girl better off living with her mother or her father?

1. Mother
2. Father
6. Either
7. Depends
8. Don't know
9. Refused

Why do you feel a girl is better off with her [father/mother]?

Maternal and Paternal Responsibilities (Asked in 2003 Only)

People often have different views about the responsibilities of mothers and fathers when they are parents. Who do you think should have the main responsibility for taking care of a child's physical needs, such as making meals, giving baths, or dressing them? Should it be:

1. Always the mother
2. Usually the mother

3. Both equally [volunteered]
4. Usually the father
5. Always the father
6. Someone else [volunteered]
7. Depends [volunteered]
8. Don't know
9. Refused

Who should have the main responsibility for disciplining the child? Should it be:

1. Always the mother
2. Usually the mother
3. Both equally [volunteered]
4. Usually the father
5. Always the father
6. Someone else [volunteered]
7. Depends [volunteered]
8. Don't know
9. Refused

Who should have the main responsibility for listening to the child's problems—for example, trouble with friends, worries about school, and so forth? Should it be:

1. Always the mother
2. Usually the mother
3. Both equally [volunteered]
4. Usually the father
5. Always the father
6. Someone else [volunteered]
7. Depends [volunteered]
8. Don't know
9. Refused

Causes of Child Behaviors and Traits

The next set of questions is about traits that children develop. For each trait, please tell me whether you think it is influenced mostly by parenting practices, the child's genes or genetic inheritance, the child's friends, the outside environment—including such things as school, media, and so forth—or it is mostly due to God's will.

You may think that all five are important, but we're asking you to decide which are the *most important* (and the *second most important* factors) in the development of each trait.

The first is personality. Is a child's personality influenced mostly by parenting practices, genes or genetic inheritance, the child's friends, the outside environment such as school, media, and so forth, or God's will? (Asked in 2003 only.)

1. Parenting practices
2. Genes or genetic inheritance
3. The child's friends
4. The outside environment
5. God's will
7. Other [volunteered]
8. Don't know
9. Refused

Which is the second most important factor in the development of personality? (Asked in 2003 only.)

1. Parenting practices
2. Genes or genetic inheritance
3. The child's friends
4. The outside environment
5. God's will
7. Other [volunteered]
8. Don't know
9. Refused

Next is aggressive behavior. Is a child's aggressive behavior influenced mostly by:

1. Parenting practices
2. Genes or genetic inheritance
3. The child's friends
4. The outside environment
5. God's will
7. Other [volunteered]
8. Don't know
9. Refused

Which is the second most important factor in the development of aggressive behavior? (Asked in 2003 only.)

1. Parenting practices
2. Genes or genetic inheritance
3. The child's friends
4. The outside environment
5. God's will
7. Other [volunteered]
8. Don't know
9. Refused

Next is a child's weight. Is weight influenced mostly by:

1. Parenting practices
2. Genes or genetic inheritance
3. The child's friends
4. The outside environment
5. God's will
7. Other [volunteered]
8. Don't know
9. Refused

Which is the second most important factor in a child's weight? (Asked in 2003 only.)

1. Parenting practices
2. Genes or genetic inheritance
3. The child's friends
4. The outside environment
5. God's will
7. Other [volunteered]
8. Don't know
9. Refused

What about a child's mental health? (Asked only in 2003.) Is the most important factor:

1. Parenting practices
2. Genes or genetic inheritance
3. The child's friends
4. The outside environment
5. God's will
7. Other [volunteered]
8. Don't know
9. Refused

Which is the second most important factor in a child's mental health? (Asked only in 2003.)

1. Parenting practices
2. Genes or genetic inheritance
3. The child's friends
4. The outside environment
5. God's will
7. Other [volunteered]
8. Don't know
9. Refused

The use of illegal drugs? (Asked only in 2003.) Is the most important factor:

1. Parenting practices
2. Genes or genetic inheritance
3. The child's friends
4. The outside environment
5. God's will
7. Other [volunteered]
8. Don't know
9. Refused

Which is the second most important factor in the use of illegal drugs? (Asked only in 2003.)

1. Parenting practices
2. Genes or genetic inheritance
3. The child's friends
4. The outside environment
5. God's will
7. Other [volunteered]
8. Don't know
9. Refused

Alcohol abuse? (Asked only in 2003.) Is the most important factor:

1. Parenting practices
2. Genes or genetic inheritance
3. The child's friends
4. The outside environment
5. God's will
7. Other [volunteered]
8. Don't know
9. Refused

Which is the second most important factor in alcohol abuse? (Asked only in 2003.)

1. Parenting practices
2. Genes or genetic inheritance
3. The child's friends
4. The outside environment
5. God's will
7. Other [volunteered]
8. Don't know
9. Refused

Intelligence? Is the most important factor:

1. Parenting practices
2. Genes or genetic inheritance
3. The child's friends
4. The outside environment
5. God's will
7. Other [volunteered]
8. Don't know
9. Refused

Which is the second most important factor in intelligence? (Asked only 2003.)

1. Parenting practices
2. Genes or genetic inheritance
3. The child's friends
4. The outside environment
5. God's will
7. Other [volunteered]
8. Don't know
9. Refused

Sexual preference? Is the most important factor:

1. Parenting practices
2. Genes or genetic inheritance
3. The child's friends
4. The outside environment
5. God's will
7. Other [volunteered]
8. Don't know
9. Refused

Which is the second most important factor in sexual preference? (Asked only in 2003.) Is the second most important factor:

1. Parenting practices
2. Genes or genetic inheritance
3. The child's friends
4. The outside environment
5. God's will
7. Other [volunteered]
8. Don't know
9. Refused

Gay Marriage and Gay Adoption

In the last few years there has been a public debate about rights for gays and lesbians. People these days have very different opinions; what we are looking for in this section is *your* personal opinion.

Next, I am going to read a few statements. For each, please tell me whether you strongly agree, agree, disagree, or strongly disagree with that statement.

Gay and lesbian couples should be allowed to marry. Do you:

1. Strongly agree
2. Somewhat agree
3. Somewhat disagree

4. Strongly disagree
6. Depends [volunteered]
7. Neither agree nor disagree [volunteered]
8. Don't know
9. Refused

Why do you think they should be allowed to marry (not be allowed to marry)?

Gay or lesbian couples who have been living in a long-term stable relationship should be allowed to adopt children. Do you:

1. Strongly agree
2. Somewhat agree
3. Somewhat disagree
4. Strongly disagree
7. Neither agree nor disagree [volunteered]
8. Don't know
9. Refused

Marital Name Change (Asked in 2006 Only)

The next few questions are about people changing their last names when they marry. Please tell me whether you strongly agree, somewhat agree, somewhat disagree, or strongly disagree with each statement.

In the past, some states *legally required* a woman to change her name to her husband's name. Do you strongly agree, somewhat agree, somewhat disagree, or strongly disagree that this was a good idea?

1. Strongly agree
2. Somewhat agree
3. Somewhat disagree
4. Strongly disagree
7. Neither agree nor disagree [volunteered]
8. Don't know

9. Refused

It is generally better if a woman changes her last name to her husband's name when she marries. Do you:

1. Strongly agree
2. Somewhat agree
3. Somewhat disagree
4. Strongly disagree
6. Depends [volunteered]
7. Neither agree nor disagree [volunteered]
8. Don't know
9. Refused

Why do you think it's better for a woman to change her name? (Why don't you think it's better for a woman to change her name?)

Under what circumstances would it be better for a woman to keep her own name? (Under what circumstances would it be better for a woman to change her name?)

A woman who changes to her husband's name when she gets married is more committed to the marriage than a woman who does not change her name. Do you:

1. Strongly agree
2. Somewhat agree
3. Somewhat disagree
4. Strongly disagree
7. Neither agree nor disagree [volunteered]
8. Don't know
9. Refused

Couples who hyphenate their last names when they marry are more committed to the relationship than other couples. Do you:

1. Strongly agree
2. Somewhat agree

3. Somewhat disagree
4. Strongly disagree
7. Neither agree nor disagree [volunteered]
8. Don't know
9. Refused

It's okay for a man to take his wife's name when he marries. Do you:

1. Strongly agree
2. Somewhat agree
3. Somewhat disagree
4. Strongly disagree
7. Neither agree nor disagree [volunteered]
8. Don't know
9. Refused

If a woman keeps her maiden name when she marries, what should the last name of the children be? Should it be:

1. The husband's last name
2. The wife's last name
3. A combination of both last names
7. Other [volunteered]
8. Don't know
9. Refused

Comfort with Gay Men and Lesbians (Asked in 2006 Only)

For the next series, please tell me again whether you strongly agree, somewhat agree, somewhat disagree, or strongly disagree with the following statements.

I would be comfortable having a gay man (lesbian) move in next door.

1. Strongly agree
2. Somewhat agree

3. Somewhat disagree

4. Strongly disagree

7. Neither agree nor disagree [volunteered]

8. Don't know

9. Refused

I would be comfortable having two men (two women) living together as a couple move in next door.

1. Strongly agree

2. Somewhat agree

3. Somewhat disagree

4. Strongly disagree

7. Neither agree nor disagree [volunteered]

8. Don't know

9. Refused

I would be comfortable having two men (two women) living together as a couple who have one or more children move in next door.

1. Strongly agree

2. Somewhat agree

3. Somewhat disagree

4. Strongly disagree

7. Neither agree nor disagree [volunteered]

8. Don't know

9. Refused

I would feel comfortable having a gay man (lesbian) as my doctor.

1. Strongly agree

2. Somewhat agree

3. Somewhat disagree

4. Strongly disagree

7. Neither agree nor disagree [volunteered]

8. Don't know

9. Refused

I would feel comfortable if my child's teacher was a gay man (lesbian).

1. Strongly agree
2. Somewhat agree
3. Somewhat disagree
4. Strongly disagree
7. Neither agree nor disagree [volunteered]
8. Don't know
9. Refused

Appendix 2.A Cross-Classification of Living Arrangements Defined as Family

Number of Respondents	Husband, Wife, Children	Man with Children	Woman with Children	Husband, Wife, No Children	Unmarried Man, Woman, Children	Two Women with Children	Two Men with Children	Unmarried Man, Woman, No Children	Two Women, No Children	Two Men, No Children
132	Yes	Yes	Yes	Yes	Yes	Yes	Yes	Yes	Yes	Yes
130	Yes	Yes	Yes	Yes	Yes	Yes	Yes	No	No	No
115	Yes	Yes	Yes	Yes	Yes	No	No	No	No	No
102	Yes	Yes	Yes	Yes	No	No	No	No	No	No
35	Yes	Yes	Yes	Yes	Yes	Yes	Yes	No	Yes	Yes
30	Yes	Yes	Yes	Yes	Yes	Yes	Yes	Yes	No	No
28	Yes	Yes	Yes	No	Yes	No	No	Yes	No	No
19	Yes	Yes	Yes	No	Yes	Yes	Yes	No	No	No
13	Yes	Yes	Yes	Yes	Yes	Yes	Yes	No	No	No
12	Yes	No	No	Yes	No	No	No	No	No	No
10	Yes	No	No	Yes	Yes	No	No	No	No	No
7	Yes	Yes	Yes	No	Yes	Yes	No	No	No	No
6	Yes	Yes	Yes	Yes	No	No	No	Yes	No	No
4	Yes	Yes	Yes	No	Yes	Yes	No	No	No	No
3	Yes	No	No	No	No	No	No	Yes	No	No
3	Yes	No	No	Yes	No	No	No	Yes	No	No

(Table continues on p. 244)

Appendix 2.A (Continued)

Number of Respondents	Husband, Wife, Children	Man with Children	Woman with Children	Husband, Wife, No Children	Unmarried Man, Woman, Children	Two Women with Children	Two Men with Children	Unmarried Man, Woman, No Children	Two Women, No Children	Two Men, No Children
3	Yes	Yes	Yes	Yes	No	No	No	Yes	No	No
3	Yes	Yes	Yes	Yes	No	Yes	Yes	No	Yes	Yes
3	Yes	No	No	No	Yes	No	No	No	No	No
2	Yes	Yes	Yes	Yes	No	Yes	Yes	No	No	No
2	Yes	No	No	No	Yes	No	No	Yes	No	No
2	Yes	No	No	Yes	Yes	Yes	Yes	Yes	No	No
2	Yes	Yes	Yes	Yes	Yes	Yes	Yes	Yes	Yes	No
1	Yes	No	No	Yes	No	No	No	No	Yes	No
1	Yes	No	No	Yes	No	No	No	No	No	Yes
1	Yes	Yes	Yes	Yes	No	No	No	No	No	No
1	Yes	Yes	Yes	Yes	No	No	No	No	Yes	No
1	Yes	No	No	Yes	No	No	No	No	No	No
1	Yes	Yes	No	Yes	Yes	Yes	Yes	Yes	No	Yes
1	Yes	Yes	No	Yes	Yes	No	No	Yes	No	No
1	Yes	Yes	Yes	Yes	Yes	Yes	Yes	No	No	No
1	Yes	Yes	Yes	No	Yes	Yes	Yes	No	No	No
1	Yes	Yes	Yes	No	Yes	Yes	No	No	No	No
1	Yes	Yes	Yes	Yes	Yes	Yes	Yes	Yes	Yes	Yes
1	Yes	Yes	Yes	Yes	Yes	Yes	Yes	No	Yes	No

Source: Constructing the Family Survey (Powell 2003).

Appendix 2.B   Effects of Year (2006 Versus 2003) on Being an Inclusionist, Moderate, or Exclusionist: Multinomial Logistic Regression Estimates (N = 1,371)

	Model 1[a]	Model 2[b]	Model 3[c]	Model 4[d]	Model 5[e]
Inclusionist versus exclusionist					
2006[f]	.28*	.33*	.36*	.48**	.46**
	(.13)	(.14)	(.14)	(.16)	(.17)
Moderate versus exclusionist					
2006[f]	.10	.16	.20	.24†	.32*
	(.13)	(.14)	(.15)	(.14)	(.16)

Source: Constructing the Family Survey (Powell 2003, 2006).

†p ≤ .10, *p ≤ .05, **p ≤ .01

Standard errors are in parentheses.

[a] Model 1 does not include controls.

[b] Model 2 controls for gender, race, age, and education.

[c] Model 3 controls for gender, race, age, education, family structure during youth, marital status, urban residence, and region.

[d] Model 4 controls for gender, race, age, education, family structure during youth, marital status, urban residence, region, and views regarding biblical literalness.

[e] Model 5 controls for gender, race, age, education, family structure during youth, marital status, urban residence, region, views regarding biblical literalness, and adjustment for survey design (ordering of one experimental question).

[f] Reference category is 2003.

Appendix 2.C Effects of Being an Inclusionist, Moderate, or Exclusionist on Attitudes Toward Gay Marriage, Gay Adoption, and Benefits to Gay and Heterosexual Cohabiting Couples: Multinomial Logistic Regression Estimates (N = 633)

	Gay Marriage			Gay Adoption			Gay Benefits			Unmarried Cohabiting Couple Benefits		
	Model 1[a]	Model 2[b]	Model 3[c]	Model 1	Model 2	Model 3	Model 1	Model 2	Model 3	Model 1	Model 2	Model 3
Strongly agreed[d]												
Inclusionist[e]	6.17***	6.13***	6.15***	6.61***	6.50***	6.50***	5.42***	5.66***	5.63***	3.25***	3.46***	3.43***
	(0.65)	(0.66)	(0.67)	(0.65)	(0.65)	(0.66)	(0.54)	(0.57)	(0.57)	(0.38)	(0.40)	(0.41)
Moderate[e]	3.75***	3.72***	3.77***	3.51***	3.47***	3.50***	3.00***	3.11***	3.07***	1.29***	1.37***	1.27***
	(0.62)	(0.63)	(0.63)	(0.51)	(0.51)	(0.52)	(0.51)	(0.52)	(0.52)	(0.32)	(0.33)	(0.33)
Somewhat agree												
Inclusionist	3.70***	3.64***	3.71***	4.67***	4.61***	4.64***	3.30***	3.33***	3.29***	2.89***	3.01***	2.99***
	(0.38)	(0.38)	(0.40)	(0.52)	(0.52)	(0.53)	(0.36)	(0.37)	(0.38)	(0.35)	(0.37)	(0.37)
Moderate	2.41***	2.40***	2.49***	2.70***	2.70***	2.73***	1.96***	1.94***	1.88***	1.05***	1.04***	0.96***
	(0.28)	(0.29)	(0.31)	(0.29)	(0.30)	(0.31)	(0.26)	(0.27)	(0.27)	(0.27)	(0.27)	(0.28)
Somewhat disagree												
Inclusionist	1.28**	1.25**	1.20*	2.86***	2.80***	2.76***	1.56***	1.39***	1.33**	1.29***	1.14**	1.10**
	(0.48)	(0.49)	(0.49)	(0.54)	(0.55)	(0.55)	(0.41)	(0.42)	(0.42)	(0.37)	(0.38)	(0.38)
Moderate	1.30***	1.27***	1.28***	1.65***	1.59***	1.62***	1.10***	1.01***	0.98***	0.52*	0.43†	0.36
	(0.28)	(0.29)	(0.29)	(0.28)	(0.29)	(0.29)	(0.26)	(0.27)	(0.27)	(0.24)	(0.25)	(0.25)

Source: Constructing the Family Survey (Powell 2003).
†p ≤ .10, *p ≤ .05, **p ≤ .01, ***p ≤ .001
Standard errors are in parentheses.
[a] Model 1 does not include controls.
[b] Model 2 controls for gender, age, race, and education.
[c] Model 3 controls for gender, age, race, education, family structure during youth, marital status, region, and urban residence.
[d] Reference category is "strongly disagree."
[e] Reference category is exclusionist.

Appendix 4.A Effects of Sociodemographic Factors on the Likelihood of Being an Inclusionist, Moderate, or Exclusionist: Multinomial Logistic Regression Estimates (N = 1302)

	Inclusionist Versus Exclusionist					Moderate Versus Exclusionist				
	Model 1	Model 2	Model 3	Model 4	Model 5	Model 1	Model 2	Model 3	Model 4	Model 5
Female	0.72***	0.74***	0.71***	1.08***	1.05***	0.10	0.13	0.13	0.31*	0.31*
	(0.15)	(0.15)	(0.15)	(0.16)	(0.17)	(0.14)	(0.14)	(0.14)	(0.15)	(0.15)
Black	-0.29	-0.25	-0.60*	0.25	-0.11	0.05	0.08	-0.07	0.43	0.29
	(0.27)	(0.28)	(0.29)	(0.30)	(0.32)	(0.26)	(0.26)	(0.27)	(0.27)	(0.28)
Other	-0.36	-0.31	-0.50*	-0.10	-0.27	-0.12	-0.09	-0.17	0.05	-0.03
	(0.23)	(0.23)	(0.24)	(0.25)	(0.26)	(0.22)	(0.22)	(0.22)	(0.23)	(0.23)
Age eighteen to twenty-nine[a]	1.99***	1.95***	1.83***	1.80***	1.67***	1.31***	1.29***	1.27***	1.14***	1.12***
	(0.29)	(0.29)	(0.30)	(0.31)	(0.32)	(0.25)	(0.25)	(0.25)	(0.26)	(0.26)
Age thirty to forty-four[a]	1.42***	1.23***	1.33***	1.34***	1.41***	0.68**	0.54*	0.59**	0.55**	0.59**
	(0.26)	(0.26)	(0.27)	(0.28)	(0.29)	(0.21)	(0.22)	(0.22)	(0.22)	(0.23)
Age forty-five to sixty-four[a]	1.21***	1.04***	1.14***	1.09***	1.17***	0.34†	0.22	0.27	0.22	0.26
	(0.25)	(0.25)	(0.26)	(0.27)	(0.28)	(0.21)	(0.21)	(0.21)	(0.22)	(0.22)
Some college[b]		0.31	0.35†	0.28	0.33		0.24	0.22	0.17	0.15
		(0.20)	(0.20)	(0.21)	(0.22)		(0.19)	(0.19)	(0.20)	(0.20)
College[b]		0.80***	0.84***	0.47**	0.55**		0.64***	0.58***	0.39*	0.36*
		(0.17)	(0.18)	(0.18)	(0.19)		(0.16)	(0.17)	(0.17)	(0.17)

(Table continues on p. 248)

Appendix 4.A *(Continued)*

	Inclusionist Versus Exclusionist					Moderate Versus Exclusionist				
	Model 1	Model 2	Model 3	Model 4	Model 5	Model 1	Model 2	Model 3	Model 4	Model 5
Grew up with both parents			-0.59*** (0.17)		-0.55** (0.18)			-0.12 (0.17)		-0.10 (0.17)
Married			-0.56*** (0.15)		-0.54*** (0.16)			-0.22 (0.15)		-0.20 (0.15)
North[c]			0.72* (0.28)		0.35 (0.30)			0.54* (0.27)		0.31 (0.28)
West[c]			0.80** (0.27)		0.55† (0.29)			0.46† (0.27)		0.33 (0.28)
Central[c]			0.21 (0.19)		0.15 (0.20)			0.03 (0.18)		-0.01 (0.18)
Urban residence			0.41** (0.15)		0.36* (0.15)			0.31* (0.14)		0.28* (0.14)
Bible: book of fables[d]				2.99*** (0.27)	2.92*** (0.28)				1.77*** (0.26)	1.71*** (0.26)
Bible: inspired word of God[d]				1.79*** (0.19)	1.72*** (0.20)				1.13*** (0.16)	1.09*** (0.16)
Constant	-0.07	-0.44	-0.30	-2.17	-1.90	0.33	0.05	0.01	-0.88	-0.85

Source: Constructing the Family Survey (Powell 2003, 2006).
†p ≤ .10, *p ≤ .05, **p ≤ .01, ***p ≤ .001
Standard errors are in parentheses.
[a]Reference category is age sixty-five or older.
[b]Reference category is high school or less.
[c]Reference category is South.
[d]Reference category is Bible: actual word of God.

Appendix 4.B Effects of Gay Social Networks on Family Definitions: Logistic Regression Estimates (N = 1299)

	Inclusionist Versus Exclusionist					Moderate Versus Exclusionist				
	Model 1[a]	Model 2[b]	Model 3[c]	Model 4[d]	Model 5[e]	Model 1	Model 2	Model 3	Model 4	Model 5
Gay friend	1.00***	0.92***	0.89***	0.85***	0.78***	0.45***	0.43**	0.40**	0.37**	0.31*
or relative	(0.14)	(0.14)	(0.15)	(0.15)	−0.15	(0.13)	(0.14)	(0.14)	(0.14)	(0.14)

Source: Constructing the Family Survey (Powell 2003, 2006).

$*p \leq .05$, $**p \leq .01$, $***p \leq .001$

Standard errors are in parentheses.

[a]Model 1 controls for gender, age, and race.

[b]Model 2 controls for gender, age, race, and education.

[c]Model 3 controls for gender, age, race, education, family structure growing up, marital status, region, and urban residence.

[d]Model 4 controls for gender, age, race, education, family structure growing up, marital status, region, urban residence, and views regarding biblical literalness.

[e]Model 5 controls for gender, age, race, education, family structure growing up, marital status, region, urban residence, and views regarding biblical literalness.

Appendix 4.C Effects of Indicators of Religiosity on the Likelihood of Being an Inclusionist, Moderate, or Exclusionist: Multinomial Logistic Regression Estimates (N = 1282)

	Inclusionist Versus Exclusionist					Moderate Versus Exclusionist				
	Model 1[a]	Model 2	Model 3	Model 4	Model 5	Model 1	Model 2	Model 3	Model 4	Model 5
No religious preference	1.24*** (0.22)			0.37 (0.25)	0.16 (0.26)	0.87*** (0.22)			0.26 (0.25)	0.18 (0.25)
Religious attendance		-0.45*** (0.04)		-0.37*** (0.06)	-0.27*** (0.06)		-0.31*** (0.04)		-0.27*** (0.05)	-0.21*** (0.05)
Strength of religious beliefs			-0.67*** (0.08)	-0.18† (0.11)	-0.07 (0.11)			-0.44*** (0.08)	-0.08 (0.10)	-0.02 (0.11)
Bible: book of fables[b]					2.24*** (0.30)					1.15*** (0.28)
Bible: inspired word of God[b]					1.42*** (.20)					0.84*** (−0.17)

Source: Constructing the Family Survey (Powell 2003, 2006).
†p ≤ .10, ***p ≤ .001
Standard errors are in parentheses.
[a] All models control for gender, age, race, and education.
[b] Reference category is Bible: actual word of God.

**Appendix 4.D   Effects of Year (2003 Versus 2006) on the Likelihood of
Having a Gay Friend or Relative: Logistic Regression
Estimates (N = 1,366)**

	Model 1[a]	Model 2[b]	Model 3[c]	Model 4[d]	Model 5[e]
2006[f]	.579***	.636***	.679***	.671***	.715***
	(.109)	(.116)	(.126)	(.116)	(.128)

Source: Constructing the Family Survey (Powell 2003, 2006).
***p ≤ .001
Standard errors are in parentheses.
[a]Model 1 does not include controls.
[b]Model 2 controls for gender, race, age, and education.
[c]Model 3 controls for gender, race, age, education, family structure during youth, marital status, urban residence, and region.
[d]Model 4 controls for gender, race, age, education, and views regarding biblical literalness.
[e]Model 5 controls for gender, race, age, education, family structure during youth, marital status, urban residence, region, and views regarding biblical literalness.
[f]Reference category is 2003.

Appendix 5.A Effects of Sociodemographic Factors on Attributions of Sexual Preference: Multinomial Logistic Regression Estimates (N = 1223)

	Genes Versus Parents			God Versus Parents			Other Versus Parents		
	Model 1	Model 2	Model 3	Model 1	Model 2	Model 3	Model 1	Model 2	Model 3
Female	0.44**	0.44**	0.58***	0.72***	0.73***	0.73***	0.19	0.20	0.20
	(0.16)	(0.16)	(0.17)	(0.19)	(0.20)	(0.20)	(0.18)	(0.18)	(0.18)
Black	-0.88**	-0.87**	-0.56	0.18	0.17	0.41	0.16	0.14	0.20
	(0.33)	(0.33)	(0.35)	(0.32)	(0.32)	(0.33)	(0.32)	(0.32)	(0.32)
Other	-0.51*	-0.46†	-0.31	-0.11	-0.13	-0.09	-0.07	-0.07	-0.05
	(0.26)	(0.26)	(0.27)	(0.29)	(0.29)	(0.29)	(0.27)	(0.27)	(0.28)
Age eighteen to twenty-nine[a]	0.22	0.11	-0.25	1.17***	1.20***	1.00**	0.70*	0.71*	0.64*
	(0.29)	(0.29)	(0.30)	(0.34)	(0.34)	(0.35)	(0.32)	(0.32)	(0.32)
Age thirty to forty-four[a]	0.21	-0.02	-0.16	0.71*	0.77**	0.66*	0.32	0.35	0.31
	(0.24)	(0.25)	(0.26)	(0.31)	(0.32)	(0.32)	(0.28)	(0.29)	(0.29)
Age forty-five to sixty-four[a]	0.59*	0.41†	0.30	0.62*	0.67*	0.59†	0.36	0.38	0.36
	(0.23)	(0.24)	(0.25)	(0.31)	(0.31)	(0.32)	(0.28)	(0.28)	(0.28)
Some college[b]		0.40†	0.31		-0.03	-0.12		0.07	0.04
		(0.23)	(0.23)		(0.25)	(0.25)		(0.24)	(0.24)
College[b]		0.84***	0.58**		-0.18	-0.32		-0.10	-0.14
		(0.19)	(0.20)		(0.22)	(0.22)		(0.21)	(0.21)
Bible: inspired word of God[c]			1.38***			0.82***			0.23
			(0.19)			(0.21)			(0.20)
Bible: book of fables[c]			1.60***			-0.08			0.06
			(0.26)			(0.35)			(0.30)
Constant	0.22	-0.13	-0.94	-1.18	-1.15	-1.39	-0.41	-0.40	-0.46

Source: Constructing the Family Survey (Powell 2003, 2006).
†p ≤ .10, *p ≤ .05, **p ≤ .01, ***p ≤ .001
Standard errors are in parentheses.
[a] Reference category is age sixty-five or older.
[b] Reference category is high school or less.
[c] Reference category is Bible: actual word of God

**Appendix 5.B   Effects of Attributions of Sexual Preference on the
Likelihood of Defining Lesbian Couples with Children as
Family: Logistic Regression Estimates (N = 1223)**

	Model 1	Model 2	Model 3	Model 4
Sexual preference: genes[a]	1.73***	1.84***	1.78***	1.54***
	(0.17)	(0.18)	(0.18)	(0.19)
Sexual preference: God[a]	1.20***	1.07***	1.10***	1.05***
	(0.19)	(0.20)	(0.20)	(0.21)
Sexual preference: other[a]	0.40*	0.31	0.32†	0.32
	(0.18)	(0.19)	(0.19)	(0.20)
Female		0.28*	0.28*	0.51***
		(0.13)	(0.13)	(0.14)
Black		0.01	0.03	0.36
		(0.24)	(0.24)	(0.26)
Other		−0.07	−0.05	0.10
		(0.21)	(0.21)	(0.22)
Age eighteen to twenty-nine[b]		1.84***	1.80***	1.59***
		(0.24)	(0.25)	(0.26)
Age thirty to forty-four[b]		1.11***	0.99***	0.99***
		(0.21)	(0.21)	(0.23)
Age forty-five to sixty-four[b]		0.65**	0.56**	0.52*
		(0.20)	(0.20)	(0.22)
Some college[c]			0.19	0.14
			(0.18)	(0.19)
College[c]			0.47**	0.28†
			(0.15)	(0.16)
Bible: inspired word of God[d]				1.19***
				(0.15)
Bible: book of fables[d]				2.14***
				(0.24)
Constant	−0.68	−1.73	−1.90	−2.75

Source: Constructing the Family Survey (Powell 2003, 2006).
†p < .10, *p < .05, **p < .01, ***p < .001
Standard errors are in parentheses.
[a]Reference category is sexual preference: parents and parenting practices.
[b]Reference category is age sixty-five or older.
[c]Reference category is high school or less.
[d]Reference category is Bible: actual word of God.

Appendix 5.C   Effects of Attributions of Sexual Preference on the Likelihood of Being an Inclusionist, Moderate, or Exclusionist: Multinomial Logistic Regression Estimates (N = 1223)

	Inclusionist Versus Exclusionist				Moderate Versus Exclusionist			
	Model 1	Model 2	Model 3	Model 4	Model 1	Model 2	Model 3	Model 4
Sexual preference: genes[a]	2.11***	2.19***	2.13***	1.86***	1.35***	1.49***	1.43***	1.25***
	(0.23)	(0.24)	(0.24)	(0.25)	(0.20)	(0.20)	(0.21)	(0.21)
Sexual preference: God[a]	1.45***	1.26***	1.28***	1.27***	0.94***	0.87***	0.89***	0.83***
	(0.25)	(0.26)	(0.26)	(0.28)	(0.22)	(0.23)	(0.23)	(0.24)
Sexual preference: other[a]	0.45†	0.33	0.34	0.36	0.36†	0.30	0.31	0.30
	(0.26)	(0.27)	(0.27)	(0.28)	(0.22)	(0.22)	(0.22)	(0.23)
Female		0.63***	0.63***	0.96***		0.02	0.02	0.21
		(0.16)	(0.16)	(0.18)		(0.15)	(0.15)	(0.16)
Black		-0.10	-0.08	0.30		0.18	0.19	0.47†
		(0.30)	(0.30)	(0.32)		(0.27)	(0.27)	(0.28)
Other		-0.16	-0.14	0.05		0.04	0.06	0.17
		(0.25)	(0.25)	(0.27)		(0.23)	(0.23)	(0.24)
Age eighteen to twenty-nine[b]		2.34***	2.30***	2.13***		1.48***	1.45***	1.28***
		(0.32)	(0.32)	(0.34)		(0.27)	(0.27)	(0.28)

	1	2	3	4	5	6	7	8
Age thirty to forty-four[b]		1.63***	1.51***	1.59***		0.79***	0.67**	0.67**
		(0.29)	(0.29)	(0.31)		(0.23)	(0.24)	(0.24)
Age forty-five to sixty-four[b]		1.21***	1.11***	1.13***		0.30	0.21	0.18
		(0.28)	(0.28)	(0.30)		(0.22)	(0.23)	(0.24)
Some college[c]			0.12	0.09			0.21	0.14
			(0.22)	(0.23)			(0.20)	(0.21)
College[c]			0.46*	0.24			0.46**	0.29
			(0.18)	(0.19)			(0.17)	(0.18)
Bible: inspired word of God[d]				1.50***				0.95***
				(0.21)				(0.17)
Bible: book of fables[d]				2.78***				1.61***
				(0.29)				(0.27)
Constant	−1.64	−3.38	−3.53	−4.82	−1.10	−1.75	−1.92	−2.53

Source: Constructing the Family Survey (Powell 2003, 2006).
†p < .10, *p < .05, **p < .01, ***p < .001

Standard errors are in parentheses.

[a]Reference category is sexual preference: parents and parenting practices.

[b]Reference category is age sixty-five or older.

[c]Reference category is high school or less.

[d]Reference category is Bible: actual word of God.

Appendix 5.D   Effects of Genetic and "God's Will" Explanations of Sexual Preference and Intelligence on Americans' Definitions of Lesbian Couples with Children as Family: Logistic Regression Estimates (N = 1223)

	Effect of Genetic Explanations[a]		Effect of "God's Will" Explanations[a]	
	No Controls	With Controls[b]	No Controls	With Controls[b]
Attribution of sexual preference	1.66*** (0.18)	1.56*** (0.19)	1.03*** (0.16)	.98*** (0.17)
Attribution of intelligence	0.44† (0.24)	0.58* (0.24)	0.06 (0.19)	−0.01 (0.19)

Source: Constructing the Family Survey (Powell 2003, 2006).
† p ≤ .10, *p ≤ .05, ***p ≤ .001
Standard errors are in parentheses.
[a]Reference category includes parenting, peers, and outside environmental explanations (pooled). Models estimating the effect of genetic explanations also control for "God's will" explanations, while models estimating the effect of "God's will" explanations also control for genetic explanations.
[b]Controls include gender, age, race, and education.

Appendix 5.E Effects of Year (2003 Versus 2006) on Attributions of Sexual Preference: Multinomial Logistic Regression Estimates (N = 1223)

	Genes Versus Parents			God Versus Parents			Other Versus Parents		
	Model 1[a]	Model 2[b]	Model 3[c]	Model 1	Model 2	Model 3	Model 1	Model 2	Model 3
Year 2006	0.56***	0.53**	0.55**	0.69***	0.70***	0.70***	0.55**	0.56**	0.56**
	(0.16)	(0.16)	(0.17)	(0.19)	(0.19)	(0.19)	(0.18)	(0.18)	(0.18)

Source: Constructing the Family Survey (Powell 2003, 2006).
**p ≤ .01, ***p ≤ .001
Standard errors are in parentheses.
[a]Model 1 does not include controls.
[b]Model 2 controls for gender, age, race, and education.
[c]Model 3 controls for gender, age, race, education, and views regarding biblical literalness.

Appendix 5.F Effects of Year (2003 Versus 2006) on Attributions of Weight: Multinomial Logistic Regression Estimates (N = 1223)

	Genes Versus Parents			God Versus Parents			Other Versus Parents		
	Model 1[a]	Model 2[b]	Model 3[c]	Model 1	Model 2	Model 3	Model 1	Model 2	Model 3
Year 2006	−0.29*	−0.29*	−0.28*	−0.61†	−0.60†	−0.55†	0.19	0.18	0.18
	(0.12)	(0.12)	(0.12)	(0.34)	(0.34)	(0.34)	(0.24)	(0.24)	(0.25)

Source: Constructing the Family Survey (Powell 2003, 2006).
†p ≤ .10, *p ≤ .05
Standard errors are in parentheses.
[a]Model 1 does not include controls.
[b]Model 2 controls for gender, age, race, and education.
[c]Model 3 controls for gender, age, race, education, and views regarding biblical literalness.

Appendix 6.A Effects of Sociodemographic Factors on Views Regarding Custody Arrangements: Multinomial Logistic Regression Estimates (N = 585)

	Boy Better Off with Father Versus Either/Depends				Boy Better Off with Mother Versus Either/Depends			
	Model 1	Model 2	Model 3	Model 4	Model 1	Model 2	Model 3	Model 4
Female	-0.64**	-0.75**	-0.60**	-0.71**	-0.36	-0.47*	-0.37	-0.48*
	(0.23)	(0.23)	(0.23)	(0.24)	(0.23)	(0.23)	(0.23)	(0.23)
Black	0.92†	0.89†	0.82†	0.84†	0.57	0.58	0.48	0.52
	(0.50)	(0.50)	(0.50)	(0.51)	(0.50)	(0.51)	(0.51)	(0.51)
Other	-0.14	-0.20	-0.16	-0.21	-0.24	-0.30	-0.25	-0.30
	(0.32)	(0.33)	(0.33)	(0.33)	(0.32)	(0.32)	(0.32)	(0.32)
Age eighteen to twenty-nine[a]	-0.12	-0.28	-0.14	-0.28	-0.43	-0.56†	-0.41	-0.54
	(0.34)	(0.34)	(0.34)	(0.35)	(0.32)	(0.33)	(0.32)	(0.33)
Age thirty to forty-four[a]	-0.19	-0.31	-0.19	-0.29	-0.57†	-0.65*	-0.55†	-0.64*
	(0.33)	(0.33)	(0.33)	(0.34)	(0.31)	(0.32)	(0.31)	(0.32)
Age forty-five to sixty-four[a]	-0.26	-0.41	-0.29	-0.41	-0.80†	-0.87*	-0.76†	-0.85*
	(0.42)	(0.43)	(0.43)	(0.44)	(0.42)	(0.43)	(0.42)	(0.43)
Some college[b]	-0.48	-0.45	-0.42	-0.41	-0.38	-0.37	-0.37	-0.37
	(0.32)	(0.32)	(0.32)	(0.32)	(0.31)	(0.32)	(0.32)	(0.32)
College[b]	-0.97***	-0.81**	-0.89***	-0.78**	-0.77**	-0.66*	-0.73**	-0.64*
	(0.26)	(0.27)	(0.27)	(0.27)	(0.26)	(0.27)	(0.26)	(0.27)

Bible: book of fables[c]		-1.18***			-1.07**	-1.07**		-1.05**
		(0.34)			(0.35)	(0.34)		(0.35)
Bible: inspired word of God[c]		-0.49†			-0.40	-0.24		-0.26
		(0.26)			(0.27)	(0.26)		(0.27)
Sexual preference: genes[d]			-0.51†		-0.34		0.05	0.18
			(0.28)		(0.29)		(0.29)	(0.30)
Sexual preference: God's will[d]			-0.20		-0.14		0.24	0.26
			(0.36)		(0.37)		(0.36)	(0.36)
Sexual preference: other[d]			0.12		0.12		0.56	0.55
			(0.34)		(0.35)		(0.35)	(0.35)
Constant	1.40	1.97	1.56	1.55	1.99	1.98	1.36	1.74

Source: Constructing the Family Survey (Powell 2003).

†p < .10, *p < .05, **p < .01, ***p < .001

Standard errors are in parentheses.

[a]Reference category is age sixty-five or older.

[b]Reference category is high school or less.

[c]Reference category is Bible: actual word of God.

[d]Reference category is sexual preference: parents and parenting practices.

Appendix 6.B   Effects of Views Regarding Custody Arrangements on the Likelihood of Being an Inclusionist, Moderate, or Exclusionist: Multinomial Logistic Regression Estimates (N = 585)

	No Controls Model 1[a]	With Controls Model 2[b]	With Controls Model 3[c]
Inclusionist[d]			
Boy with father[e]	−1.21***	−1.12***	−0.88**
	(0.27)	(0.28)	(0.31)
Boy with mother[e]	−0.55*	−0.55*	−0.33
	(0.25)	(0.27)	(0.29)
Moderate[d]			
Boy with father[e]	−0.47†	−0.49†	−0.37
	(0.26)	(0.27)	(0.28)
Boy with mother[e]	0.01	−0.05	0.07
	(0.26)	(0.27)	(0.28)

Source: Constructing the Family Survey (Powell 2003).
†p < .10, *p < .05, **p < .01, ***p < .001
Standard errors are in parentheses.
[a]Model 1 does not include additional controls.
[b]Model 2 includes controls for gender, age, race, and education.
[c]Model 3 includes controls for gender, age, race, education, and views about the Bible.
[d]Reference category is exclusionist.
[e]Reference category is "either/depends."

Appendix 7.A   Effects of Sociodemographic Factors on Views Regarding
Name Change[a]: Multivariate Regression Estimates
(N = 644)

	Model 1	Model 2	Model 3
Female	0.66***	0.65***	0.86***
	(0.21)	(0.20)	(0.19)
Black	−1.52***	−1.46***	−0.94**
	(0.36)	(0.37)	(0.36)
Other	0.03	−0.12	−0.14
	(0.27)	(0.27)	(0.27)
Age eighteen to twenty-nine[b]	1.65***	1.21***	1.02**
	(0.36)	(0.38)	(0.36)
Age thirty to forty-four[b]	1.39***	1.23***	1.16***
	(0.31)	(0.32)	(0.30)
Age forty-five to sixty-four[b]	1.12***	1.02***	0.94***
	(0.29)	(0.30)	(0.28)
Some college[c]	0.89**	0.77**	0.75**
	(0.29)	(0.28)	(0.27)
College degree[c]	1.56***	1.38***	1.09***
	(0.24)	(0.24)	(0.23)
Married		−0.23	−0.23
		(0.21)	(0.20)
Number of children		−0.21***	−0.11†
		(0.06)	(0.06)
North[d]		0.85*	0.45
		(0.37)	(0.36)
West[d]		1.02**	0.68†
		(0.37)	(0.35)
Central[d]		0.51*	0.40†
		(0.25)	(0.23)
Urban residence		0.37†	0.41*
		(0.20)	(0.19)
Bible: book of fables[e]			2.77***
			(0.32)
Bible: inspired word of God[e]			1.63***
			(0.22)
Constant	4.75	4.94	3.65

Source: Constructing the Family Survey (Powell 2006).
†p ≤ .10, * p ≤ .05, ** p ≤ .01, *** p ≤ .001
Standard errors are in parentheses.
[a]Scale derived from three items: (1) It is generally better if a woman changes her last name to her husband's name when she marries (better); (2) In the past, some states legally required a woman to change her name to her husband's name. Do you strongly agree, somewhat agree, or somewhat disagree that this was a good idea?(legal); (3) It's okay for a man to take his wife's name when he marries (reverse-coded) (man).
[b]Reference category is age sixty-five or older.
[c]Reference category is high school or less.
[d]Reference category is South.
[e]Reference category is Bible: actual word of God.

Appendix 7.B Effects of Sociodemographic Predictors on Views Regarding Name Change, Individual Items: Multivariate Regression Estimates (N = 644)

	Model 1			Model 2			Model 3		
	Better	Legal	Man[a]	Better	Legal	Man[a]	Better	Legal	Man[a]
Female	0.24**	0.17†	0.26**	0.24**	0.17†	0.26**	0.33***	0.24**	0.31***
	(0.08)	(0.09)	(0.09)	(0.08)	(0.09)	(0.09)	(0.07)	(0.09)	(0.09)
Black	-0.29*	-0.53***	-0.60***	-0.30*	-0.51***	-0.58***	-0.13	-0.31*	-0.41*
	(0.14)	(0.15)	(0.16)	(0.14)	(0.16)	(0.16)	(0.14)	(0.16)	(0.16)
Other	0.01	-0.04	-0.05	-0.02	-0.05	-0.06	0.01	0.03	-0.02
	(0.12)	(0.13)	(0.13)	(0.14)	(0.15)	(0.14)	(0.12)	(0.14)	(0.15)
Age eighteen to twenty-nine[b]	0.39**	0.49***	0.74***	0.24†	0.36*	0.60***	0.18	0.30†	0.54***
	(0.13)	(0.15)	(0.16)	(0.14)	(0.16)	(0.17)	(0.13)	(0.16)	(0.16)
Age thirty to forty-four[b]	0.32**	0.43***	0.64***	0.27*	0.38**	0.61***	0.25*	0.36**	0.61***
	(0.12)	(0.13)	(0.14)	(0.12)	(0.14)	(0.14)	(0.11)	(0.13)	(0.14)
Age forty-five to sixty-four[b]	0.27*	0.39**	0.45***	0.25*	0.35**	0.43***	0.22*	0.32*	0.40**
	(0.11)	(0.12)	(0.13)	(0.11)	(0.13)	(0.13)	(0.11)	(0.12)	(0.13)
Some college[c]	0.25*	0.47***	0.20	0.21*	0.43***	0.17	0.20*	0.41***	0.15
	(0.11)	(0.12)	(0.12)	(0.11)	(0.121)	(0.12)	(0.10)	(0.12)	(0.12)
College degree[c]	0.47***	0.66***	0.44***	0.41***	0.59***	0.41***	0.33***	0.50***	0.30**
	(0.09)	(0.10)	(0.10)	(0.09)	(0.10)	(0.10)	(0.09)	(0.10)	(0.10)
Married				-0.13†	-0.03	-0.13	-0.13†	-0.02	-0.12
				(0.08)	(0.09)	(0.09)	(0.08)	(0.09)	(0.09)

Number of children				−0.08*** (0.02)	−0.06* (0.03)	−0.06* (0.03)	−0.04† (0.02)	−0.02 (0.03)
North[d]				0.29* (0.14)	0.36* (0.16)	0.23 (0.16)	0.16 (0.14)	0.25 (0.16)
West[d]				0.21 (0.14)	0.41* (0.16)	0.41* (0.16)	0.11 (0.13)	0.28† (0.165)
Central[d]				0.17† (0.09)	0.16 (0.11)	0.23* (0.11)	0.13 (0.09)	0.12 (0.10)
Urban residence				0.18* (0.07)	0.12 (0.09)	0.08 (0.09)	0.20** (0.07)	0.14† (0.08)
Bible: book of fables[e]							1.04*** (0.12)	0.99*** (0.14)
Bible: inspired word of God[e]							0.53*** (0.08)	0.55*** (0.10)
Constant	1.40	1.78	1.61	1.49	1.78	1.63	1.04	1.32

(final column) Number of children −0.035 (0.03); North[d] 0.13 (0.16); West[d] 0.30† (0.16); Central[d] 0.19† (0.11); Urban residence 0.07 (0.09); Bible: book of fables[e] 0.74*** (0.14); Bible: inspired word of God[e] 0.54*** (0.01); Constant 1.25.

Source: Constructing the Family Survey (Powell 2006).

†p ≤ .10, * p ≤ .05, ** p ≤ .01, *** p ≤ .001.

Standard errors are in parentheses.

[a]Man is reverse coded so that a higher score indicates approval of a man changing his name at marriage.

[b]Reference category is age sixty-five or older.

[c]Reference category is high school or less.

[d]Reference category is South.

[e]Reference category is Bible: actual word of God.

Appendix 7.C   Effects of Views Regarding Name Change on the Likelihood of Being an Inclusionist, Moderate, or Exclusionist: Multinomial Logistic Regression Estimates (N = 644)

	Model 1[a]	Model 2[a]	Model 3[a]	Model 4[a]	Model 5[b]	Model 6[b]	Model
Inclusionist[e]							
Better	1.96***			1.14***	1.80***		
	(0.24)			(0.29)	(0.25)		
Legal		1.49***		0.62*		1.33***	
		(0.21)		(0.25)		(0.22)	
Man[f]			1.97***	1.50***			1.76**
			(0.22)	(0.24)			(0.23)
Moderate[e]							
Better	1.11***			0.54	0.98***		
	(0.25)			(0.29)	(0.26)		
Legal		0.99***		0.66**		0.85***	
		(0.20)		(0.23)		(0.21)	
Man[f]			0.87***	0.58**			0.68*
			(0.20)	(0.21)			(0.21)

Source: Constructing the Family Survey (Powell 2006).
* $p \leq .05$, **$p \leq .01$, ***$p \leq .001$
Standard errors are in parentheses.
[a]Models 1 to 4 do not include any controls.
[b]Models 5 to 8 control for gender, education, age, and race.

del 8[c]	Model 9[c]	Model 10[c]	Model 11[c]	Model 12[c]	Model 13[d]	Model 14[d]	Model 15[d]	Model 16[d]
)9***	1.75***			1.05***	1.33***			0.79**
29)	(0.25)			(0.30)	(0.27)			(0.31)
58*		1.30***		0.57*		0.92***		0.34
26)		(0.22)		(0.26)		(0.23)		(0.27)
34***			1.73***	1.34***			1.50***	1.23***
25)			(0.23)	(0.25)			(0.25)	(0.26)
51	0.97***			0.50	0.66*			0.31
30)	(0.26)			(0.30)	(0.27)			(0.31)
59*		0.84***		0.59*		0.61**		0.44
24)		(0.21)		(0.24)		(0.22)		(0.25)
43			0.67**	0.43			0.49*	0.34
22)			(0.21)	(0.22)			(0.22)	(0.23)

odels 9 to 12 control for gender, education, age, race, marital status, parental status, region, and urban idence.
odels 13 to 16 control for gender, education, age, race, marital status, parental status, region, urban idence, and views regarding biblical literalness.
ference category in multinomial models is exclusionist.
an is reverse coded so that a higher score indicates approval of a man changing his name at marriage.

═ Notes ═

Chapter 1

1. In his thoughtful article, Weigel (2008) explores college students' assessment of the key features and traits they attribute to "family" and their evaluation of particular living arrangements as prototypical of family. For two of the few analyses of adults' conceptualizations of family—one relying on a Swedish sample and the other relying on an Australian sample—see Trost (1990) and Evans and Gray (2005).
2. State of Arkansas, Adoption Act ACA §7-9-107 (2007), written by the Secretary of State. See "Notice of Certification of Sufficiency," November 13, 2007, available at: http://www.sos.arkansas.gov/elections/elections_pdfs/proposed_amendments/2007-293_Adopt_or_Foster_parent.pdf. The status of this ban is in doubt. A circuit judge in Arkansas struck down the law as unconstitutional, although at the time of writing it is likely that this judicial decision will be appealed.
3. For more detail about these interviews, see appendices 1.A and 1.B. Despite claims by many of our interviewees that they would not be able to speak to us for more than a few minutes, they often became so involved in the interview that they spoke for much longer than we had anticipated. The phone interviews ranged in length from 25 to 112 minutes in 2003, with a mean length of 44 minutes and a median length of 41 minutes. We used a more abridged inventory of questions in 2006, resulting in interviews that ranged in length from 13 to 87 minutes (with a mean of 28 minutes and median of 24 minutes).
4. But see Trost (1990). Trost also notes that the use of the term "parent-child unit" instead of "child-parent unit" is a "matter of taste" but could imply to some a hierarchy that places children at a structural disadvantage by relegating them to a lesser status. Some critics, however, might note that Trost expresses less concern over the relegation of nonromantic roommates (and other coresidential arrangements that do not involve a parent-child or a romantic/sexual dyad) to nonfamily status.
5. The sociologists Kathryn Harker Tillman and Charles Nam (2008) offer an insightful look at the policy implications and other implications of varying definitions of family.
6. Still, there is a great deal of variation among members of this group, even

among pro-marriage supporters who have collaborated in their efforts to promote "stronger families." The sociologist Linda Waite and the columnist Maggie Gallagher, for example, take divergent positions regarding same-sex couples; see Waite and Gallagher (2000).
7. For a slightly revised interpretation of family by Coontz, see Coontz (2008).

Chapter 2

1. Such a definition could also include nonbiological children, such as adopted children. The U.S. Bureau of the Census (2001, 71), however, explicitly excludes adoptive families from the category "traditional nuclear family" ("a family in which a child lives with two married biological parents and with only full siblings if siblings are present"), thereby reinforcing the idea that adoptive families are inauthentic or nonstandard. For a discussion of some implications of this definition and for various social-scientific views regarding adoption, see Hamilton, Cheng, and Powell (2007).
2. At the time of writing, same-sex marriage had been allowed or was pending in Connecticut, Iowa, Massachusetts, New Hampshire, Vermont, and Washington, D.C. Recognition of marital status in one's own state does not translate into similar recognition by the majority of states that prohibit same-sex marriage or by the federal government.
3. Preliminary analyses indicate that the ordering of items does not significantly affect patterns of response. Pretesting, along with the open-ended component of our interviews, also indicates that respondents generally understood "two men (women) living together as a couple" as a same-sex (gay-lesbian) couple, although in reference to this living arrangement one person responded, "That's not possible. That doesn't exist in Texas."
4. Indeed, earlier drafts of our interview inventory included a much larger set of living arrangements. However, our pretest phone interviews were so long that we needed to delete several items from our final version of the survey.
5. Some scholars contend that the "benchmark" family may be even narrower than the father-mother-child living arrangement asked about in our interviews. The sociologist Sandra Hofferth (1985) notes that a particular division of labor—with the father employed in the labor force and the mother responsible for the care of the child—further defines the benchmark family. Although Hofferth's depiction is from the 1980s and is not altogether reflective of the changes in women's labor force participation and in familial division of labor that have occurred since then, later in this book (chapter 6) we see that gendered visions of family—in particular, of the roles of mothers and fathers—are still strongly adhered to by a large segment of the American population.
6. To account for the disproportionately high number of certain groups in our interviews (that is, women and senior citizens), the tables and figures in this chapter rely on weighted data. The overall patterns are robust. Patterns based on unweighted data or on data that use alternative weighting ap-

proaches (for example, adjusting for additional socioeconomic factors) are very similar to those presented in this and other chapters.

A small number of respondents expressed an unwillingness or inability to answer our question about one or more of the eleven living arrangements. The patterns presented here are derived from interviewees who responded to each of these living arrangements. In ancillary analyses, we relaxed this restriction and included all responses even if the interviewee did not answer all questions regarding the eleven living arrangements. These analyses do not appreciably alter the patterns discussed in this or other chapters.

7. There are reasons to anticipate a greater receptiveness to a lesbian household with children than to a gay male couple with children: (1) respondents may assume that an inimitable biological mother-child bond confers automatic family status (a connection we discuss in chapter 6); (2) they may use gendered assumptions about women as mothers and homemakers and as being more family-oriented; or (3) they may express greater disapprobation toward gay men with children. That said, although the sample includes a larger number of respondents who saw a lesbian household with children as family than those who viewed a gay male home with children as family, these differences are slight and approach marginal significance only when the 2003 and 2006 data are pooled.

8. Table 2.1 and appendix 2.A exclude "two people living together as housemates who are not living as a couple and have no children" because, as noted earlier, the number of respondents incorporating this living arrangement in their definition of family was quite small. Many respondents agreed that this type of living arrangement is not a family, so much so that any attempt to group this item with the other items creates inconsistencies that detract from understanding the overall patterns in the responses.

9. Since marriage was not a legal option for same-sex couples in the United States in the 2003 survey, all references to married or unmarried couples refer to heterosexual couples.

10. Latent class analysis allows the specification of a categorical latent variable (X). This variable indicates the "ideal types" (in our analysis, the common clusters in defining family) and then calculates the probability that items will fall into these latent categories (ideal types). Respondents are assigned to latent classes using estimates of the model parameters to calculate the probability that latent variable X will take on level t given that the observed items are at particular levels. Latent class analyses were conducted with a statistical package called MPlus. For more detailed discussions of latent class models and their similarities to and differences from conventional factor analysis, see Bartholomew (2002), Hogan, Eggebeen, and Clogg (1993), and McCutcheon (1987).

11. The number of latent classes must be specified prior to obtaining results and fit statistics. By comparing these results, the model fit, and the theoretical implications of the model, we conclude that a model that divides respondents into three latent classes best represents how respondents de-

fined family. Although an examination of Bayesian Information Criterion (BIC) statistics indicates a slightly better fit for a four-class solution, the four-class model produces two classes that are nearly identical in that both see all arrangements as a family. The exception is that in one of these classes respondents were slightly less likely to agree that unmarried couples without children are a family. Auxiliary analyses suggest that pooling these two classes together does not compromise the findings presented in this and subsequent chapters.

12. Admittedly, the labels we assigned to each group may not necessarily correspond with how members of these groups would label themselves. Members of the exclusionist latent class, for example, might prefer the label "traditionalist," although moderates and inclusionists might believe that this term is too benign to represent exclusionists accurately. Similarly, some exclusionists and inclusionists might question whether "moderates" are really moderate and might see them instead as vacillating. Or exclusionists might characterize moderates as too liberal or nearly inclusionist, while inclusionists might describe moderates as too conservative or nearly exclusionist.

13. Shortly after the vote for the constitutional ban, some members of the Oregon state legislature actively promoted the legal recognition of same-sex couples in the form of domestic partnerships. It took a couple of years for this bill to be enacted; when it took effect, Oregon became one of the few states that both ban same-sex marriage and afford many legal privileges of marriage to same-sex couples. For a discussion of the chronology of the debate over same-sex marriage, see Hull 2006. Timelines of the debate over same-sex marriage are available at many websites, among them: Lambda Legal, http://data.lambdalegal.org/publications/downloads/fs_marriage-equality-timeline.pdf; Human Rights Campaign, http://www.hrc.org/justice/resources/justice_timeline.pdf; and Born Gay, http://borngay.procon.org/viewresource.asp?resourceID=000025#20th (all accessed May 18, 2010).

14. Some might argue that the public concerns over same-sex rights accelerated a few months earlier—more specifically, with *Lawrence et al. v. Texas*, the Supreme Court case that struck down an anti-sodomy law in Texas, thus invalidating similar laws that existed in twelve other states as well. The Supreme Court ruling was announced on June 26, 2003, toward the end of our data collection. We were able, however, to compare the responses both before the announcement (approximately 80 percent of the sample) and after (nearly 20 percent). We detected few differences between these two groups. Moreover, in their open-ended responses, only an isolated few in the post-*Lawrence* sample mentioned the case either directly or indirectly, even though we posed several open-ended questions regarding the rights of same-sex individuals and couples. The most notable exception was a middle-aged New Yorker who volunteered: "I support the latest Supreme Court decision that just came down." In other words, although the *Lawrence* case was a turning point for gay rights, the case appears to have

had very little resonance for our sample. In contrast, references to same-sex marriage in Massachusetts were not uncommon in our 2006 interviews.

15. As noted earlier in this chapter, frequency distributions in this and other chapters are based on weighted data that adjust for the overrepresentation of certain sociodemographic groups (by age and gender) in the interviews. Figures 2.2 and 2.3 are derived from weighted data, thereby discounting the possibility that the over-time differences in familial definitions are a function of sample discrepancies in age or gender.

16. As will be discussed in chapter 4, family definitions are shaped not only by age and gender but also by other sociodemographic factors. To account for possible differences between 2003 and 2006 in the distribution of these factors, we conducted additional multivariate analyses that adjusted for these factors and variations in survey design (that is, methodological experimentation involving the order of an open-ended question for a subsample in 2006). These analyses, as seen in appendix 2.B, demonstrate the resiliency of the differences between 2003 and 2006. Regardless of the combination of sociodemographic factors included, the respondents from 2006 were significantly less likely than their counterparts from 2003 to be exclusionist and, correspondingly, more likely to be inclusionist. In fact, the adjustment for sample discrepancies in certain sociodemographic factors results in an even larger difference in family definitions between 2003 and 2006. For example, figure 2.3 suggests a 7.2 percent decline between 2003 and 2006 in the overall percentage of exclusionists. In contrast, predicted probabilities calculated from the last column of appendix 2.B, in which all the core sociodemographic factors are controlled, indicate a 9.1 percent decline. In other words, the magnitude of change in Americans' definitions of family may well be greater than what is shown in figures 2.2 and 2.3.

17. For an alternative and more skeptical view of the impact of public opinion, see Converse (2000), Orloff (1993), Skocpol (1992), Weir, Orloff, and Skocpol (1988), and Zaller (1992).

18. The powerful relationship between membership in one of these latent classes and attitudes toward gay marriage, gay adoption, and benefits to same-sex and cohabiting heterosexual couples is robust. In a series of multivariate analyses, we explored whether this relationship notably decreases or disappears if we also took sociodemographic factors into consideration. Appendix 2.C displays multinomial logistic regression estimates of the effects of being an inclusionist or a moderate (compared to an exclusionist) on these attitudes. For each attitude, we display the bivariate effect of latent class membership, as well as its effect in one of the many multivariate models that we tested, each yielding very similar patterns. This multivariate model includes gender, age, race, education, family structure during youth, and marital structure. An inspection of the regression coefficients confirms that whether one is an inclusionist, moderate, or exclusionist is highly predictive of attitudes regarding gay marriage, gay adoption, and benefits. For example, regarding attitudes on gay marriage, the first coeffi-

cient in the first column, 6.17, indicates that the odds of inclusionists strongly agreeing versus strongly disagreeing that gay marriage should be allowed is *more than four hundred times greater* ($e^{6.17}$ = 478.19) than comparable odds among exclusionists. The addition of the sociodemographic controls does little to alter this coefficient. This observation does not, however, mean that these sociodemographic factors are unimportant. In fact, as detailed in chapter 4, whether one is an exclusionist, moderate, or inclusionist is determined in part by sociodemographic factors.

Chapter 3

1. Nearly all (705 of 712) interviewees in 2003 answered the open-ended question addressed in this chapter. Approximately one-third of the sample were asked the same question in 2006. Of these 287 interviewees, 285 offered an answer. Responses to open-ended questions in this and later chapters were coded and analyzed by our research team. In identifying themes, we used a variety of analytical techniques and approaches, including Atlas.ti, computer software that facilitates the analysis of a large number of qualitative responses. In this and later chapters, we also include some of the unsolicited remarks to our closed-ended questions that seem germane.
2. Because respondents may emphasize more than one theme, the sum of the percentages in this and other figures may exceed 100 percent.
3. As we discuss later in this chapter, responses commonly included many nonverbal utterances (for example, "uh" and "um"). To facilitate the readability of the comments by the interviewees, with one exception later in this chapter, we exclude most nonverbal utterances from the quotes used in this chapter and subsequent chapters.
4. These comments are in line with Kathleen Hull's (2006) discussion of the potential symbolic power of the law in affirming and legitimating the identities and relationships of same-sex couples. Members of the gay community—especially those in academia and advocacy groups—disagree about whether the extension of marital rights to same-sex couples is a step forward (a position consistent with the assimilationist segment of the gay rights movement) or a step backward (a stance promoted by more radical constituencies). Still, the possibility that marriage confers family status, or social legitimacy, on gay and lesbian couples who otherwise might not be granted it is among the reasons why so many of the same-sex couples interviewed by Hull—even some who were ambivalent about marriage or reluctant to consider marriage for themselves—supported the current strategy of the gay rights movement to promote the legalization of same-sex marriage.
5. For other discussions of how adoptive children are seen by the American public, by the legal system, and by social scientists, see Hamilton, Cheng, and Powell (2007).
6. As with exclusionists, only a very few moderates and inclusionists interjected pets into their discussion of families; for example: "Pets count too. Definitely, because I consider my dog like kind of a child. Actually my

child. A family seems to need a third party . . . usually more often than not, a child. It's not to say that a committed couple isn't a family. But to me, to complete a family, there has to be someone [else]. I suppose if you had a dog or a cat, it would count as family as well." Because of these responses, in 2006 we also asked a subsample, "We've talked a lot so far about other people's families—and now I'd like you to tell me about your family. When I say the phrase 'your family,' what do you think of?" In answering this question, approximately one-seventh (13.5 percent) of our interviewees specifically mentioned their pets (with twice as many referring to their dogs as to their cats).

7. It therefore may not be that surprising that in the following year the Palm Beach Community College in Florida decided to offer veterinary pet insurance but not domestic partner benefits to its employees. The disjuncture in these two decisions did not escape notice, as seen in this comment by Deidre Newton of the Palm Beach County Human Rights Council: "While many pet owners consider their dogs and cats part of their families, there is a basic disconnect when an employer will insure an employee's pet but not an employee's partner"; see Travis (2007). After much publicity regarding these decisions, the trustees of the college reversed themselves the following year and voted to grant domestic benefits to same-sex and heterosexual cohabiting couples.

8. Whereas these examples highlight cases in which exclusionists offered more expansive open-ended responses than their closed-ended ones, we also saw some examples of the converse—for example, a middle-aged woman who in her closed-ended responses included cohabiting couples with children as family but in her open-ended responses noted: "Well, I guess I always believe in marriage. Married to me is a man and a woman is married. That constitutes a family."

9. As mentioned in chapter 2, we exclude roommates from this characterization since approximately 10 percent of the sample said that roommates constitute a family. Still, we note that inclusionists were more likely than moderates or exclusionists to see roommates as family.

10. This respondent's use of the word "group" explicitly allowed for the possibility of a family being made up of more than two adults, thereby challenging the importance of an adult dyadic relationship. We examined the responses by all interviewees who used the word "group" in their definition of family and found that they were disproportionately represented among the inclusionists (as also can be seen in figure 3.8). In some cases, the use of the word "group" (and other terms such as "people") connoted a willingness to include a larger number of adults in their definition of family. Still, most of their responses did not necessarily distinguish "group" from "dyad," and some used these terms interchangeably. Instead, the use of "group" often appeared to be intended to avoid the gendered terms associated with dyads (husband and wife, man and woman) or to employ an umbrella term that referred to the various combinations of adult dyadic relationships that they saw as family. In their responses, "group" was occasionally understood to include children as well.

11. For inclusionists, then, whether the couple is heterosexual or homosexual was mostly a non-issue, thus challenging the heteronormative privileging of a heterosexual couple (preferably married with children). Nevertheless, even most inclusionists did not speak at length about sexuality. In fact, they (and most moderates and exclusionists) avoided words that explicitly addressed sexual relations or sexual behavior. It is possible to interpret this omission as a sign that Americans do not see sexual relations as a core requirement of a loving adult dyad. If so, as one reviewer of this book suggested, this implies that they would be amenable to criticisms of the heteronormative family model for excluding couples who are not sexually involved. In listening to and reading through the interviews, however, we came to believe that a more plausible explanation is that the absence of discussions of sexual relations in most of the interviews is a sign of Americans' discomfort in even mentioning sexual relations—especially when discussing same-sex couples, as discussed later in this chapter.

12. The predicted probabilities control for age and gender. Probabilities derived from alternative specifications are very similar to those presented in figure 3.5.

13. One respondent's reliance on WIMTT resulted in her chastising us for asking about such a limited set of living arrangements. After expressing that a family is "a relationship between the people that they consider a family," she volunteered that: "Oh, I think you didn't get all the combinations. There are brothers and sisters that live together that family. There are all kinds of other family arrangements. Well, you know this is Alabama; we have cousins. Yes, [*laughs*] in Alabama we stretch our family way out, extended family."

14. We used tagcrowd.com to create the word clouds in figures 3.6, 3.7, and 3.8. The word clouds exclude words from a custom stoplist and groups some similar words. Upon these exclusions and groupings, we restrict each word cloud to the forty-five to fifty words most commonly used.

15. For discussions of the meaning of nonlinguistic signals and filled pauses such as "uh" and "um," see Clark and Fox Tree (2002), Goffman (1981), and Maclay and Osgood (1959).

16. The survey was randomized so that half of the respondents were asked about their comfort with lesbians while the other half were asked about gay men.

17. For an example of the application of social distance scales to attitudes regarding gays and lesbians, see Gentry (1986).

18. As in figure 3.5, the probabilities in figure 3.9 are adjusted for gender and age. Controls for other sociodemographic variables do not noticeably alter the overall distribution of responses.

19. Exclusionists' reported discomfort with gay or lesbian doctors was shaped by gender: women voiced greater discomfort with lesbian doctors than gay ones, while the reverse was found among exclusionist men.

20. Hull (2006) also discusses another opportunity missed by the many sexuality scholars who theorize about heteronormativity and resistance to mar-

riage without hearing how same-sex couples talk about their relationships
and their views about marriage.

Chapter 4

1. To assess whether the effects of certain factors are reduced or increased
   with the addition of other variables, appendix 4.A presents five models: (1)
   one that includes gender, race, and age; (2) one that adds education; (3) one
   that adds family background, marital status, urban-rural residence, and region; (4) one that includes gender, race, age, education, and religious beliefs (that is, views regarding the literalness of the Bible); and (5) a full
   model that includes all of these items. Multivariate models in this chapter
   are derived from both the 2003 and 2006 data. Additional analyses for each
   year separately confirm the robustness of the patterns, with few exceptions
   (discussed later in this chapter).
2. In our exploration of the literature, we identified hundreds of articles that
   find that American women express more liberal views regarding gender
   than do men. See, for example, Bolzendahl and Myers (2004), Brooks and
   Bolzendahl (2004), Kane (2000), Klein (1984), Manza and Brooks (1999b),
   Plutzer (1988), Rhodebeck (1996), and Schnittker, Freese, and Powell (2003).
   For examples of studies that find gender differences in views on homosexuality, see Andersen and Fetner (2008), Bernstein (2004), Britton (1990),
   Herek and Capitanio (1996), Herek and Glunt (1993), and Loftus (2001).
3. The predicted probabilities presented here are based on models that control for gender, race, age, and education. Of course, predicted probabilities
   vary as a function of the other items included in the multivariate models.
   Figure 4.1 may underestimate the extent to which men and women vary. In
   fact, gender differences in predicted probabilities in this figure are lower
   than those derived from models 4 and 5, which also take into account religious orthodoxy.
4. Sex-specific latent class analysis reveals that responses cluster in the same
   way—although not in the same frequency—for men and women. That is,
   for both men and women there are three latent classes—exclusionists,
   moderates, and inclusionists.

   As mentioned in chapter 2, so few Americans defined housemates ("two
   people living together as housemates who are not living as a couple and
   have no children") as family that this living arrangement is not included in
   the latent class analyses (presented in chapter 2) and their subsequent multivariate analyses. We did, however, conduct logistic regressions that consider the sociodemographic determinants of believing that housemates
   count as family. These analyses confirm that women were significantly
   more likely than men to include housemates under the rubric of family.
5. The lowest degree of gender variation is found among the exclusionists.
   Both men and women with these more restrictive family views based their
   explanations on "traditional" markers—in particular, marriage. The theme
   of marriage, however, was more emphatically used by women than by

men. Exclusionist women also invoked children and religion more than men did, whereas men's discourse was more evenly distributed across a variety of themes.

6. Along with other social scientists, the anthropologist Nicholas Townsend has documented the importance of the provider role to men in families; see Townsend (2002).

7. That said, as seen in appendix 4.A (model 3), the inclusion of marital status, although a significant predictor of the likelihood of being inclusionist, moderate, or exclusionist, does not notably alter the effects of age and cohort. Auxiliary analyses that add parenthood to the model also confirm that the negative effects of age and cohort are not a function of parental status.

8. For this question, the difference between adults over age sixty-four and their younger peers is statistically significant in multivariate models that adjust for the key sociodemographic factors described in this chapter.

9. *The Golden Girls* was a popular American television comedy that aired from the mid-1980s to the early 1990s. The show follows three unrelated older women (along with the elderly mother of one of them) who live together in the same household and see each other as family.

10. After all, very few, if any, of our respondents were old enough to have grown up during times when some people, especially poor people, were unable to establish a marital household on their own and unmarried household servants were included in the definition of the host family, thus giving rise to the idea that neither blood nor romantic relationships are necessary to form a family.

11. To test for the significance and robustness of the baby boom exception, we compared the fit (Bayesian Information Criterion [BIC] and Akaike's Information Criterion [AIC]) of several multivariate models. For example, we found that the addition of the baby boom category results in a significant improvement in fit over models that have fewer age categories. Similarly, the inclusion of a baby boom exception also results in a significant improvement of fit over a model that includes only a linear term for age.

Because scholars can reasonably disagree with our specification of the baby boomer cohort, we ran several sensitivity analyses that used other plausible operationalizations. Some of these alternatives yielded stronger patterns, others slightly weaker ones. Yet all confirmed the presence of a unique baby boom generation effect.

12. The timing of historical events—that is, the fact that the feminist movement preceded the gay and lesbian liberation movement—may explain why some research on feminist identification detects a liberal baby boom effect for respondents who are somewhat older than the group among whom we find disproportionately liberal views. See, for example, Schnittker, Freese, and Powell (2003).

13. It was not uncommon for respondents to ask the interviewers what they themselves thought about definitions of family and, in particular, about same-sex relations. (Interviewers were instructed not to offer their opin-

ions.) The interviewers, most of whom were under the age of thirty, commented that the respondents—especially those with exclusionist positions—apparently assumed that the interviewers were more open to broader definitions of family, as illustrated in the following exchange:

RESPONDENT: Well, if they have children and they're married. I mean, that's a family, but as far as two men or two women living together, a lot of people say that's a family. But then, I'm from the *old age group*, you know. So I don't really believe in that stuff. . . . Don't you think? Well, I guess you don't . . .

INTERVIEWER: I can't give my opinion.

RESPONDENT: Uh, uh. *You're young anyway* (then laughs).

14. It is important to emphasize, however, that the marked changes between 2003 and 2006 in the direction away from exclusionist definitions of family and toward more inclusionist ones (discussed in chapter 2) are not due mostly to changes in age distributions. Instead, we found noticeable movement between 2003 and 2006 to inclusionist positions for each age group. Thus, future changes in Americans' views of family are likely to be due to a combination of cohort and period effects. For a discussion of generational and period influences on the tolerance of homosexuality, see Andersen and Fetner (2008).

15. The multinomial models on which the predicted probabilities are based use educational degree (high school or less, some college, and college degree or greater). Supplementary analyses that rely on number of years of education yield very similar patterns.

16. In fact, the effect of being at least a college graduate is reduced by over one-third when views regarding the Bible also are included in multinomial models. In appendix 4.A, for example, the effect of a college degree on the likelihood of being an inclusionist (versus an exclusionist) is .80 (model 2); with the addition of questions regarding the Bible, the effect is reduced by 41.3 percent, to .47 (model 4).

17. Notably, she distinguished between "boy" and "child." This distinction suggests that even for inclusionists with the highest levels of education, it is very difficult to erase gender completely from conceptualizations of family. We return to this issue in chapter 6.

18. The sociologists Rory McVeigh and Maria-Elena Diaz (2009) offer compelling evidence of the powerful effect of education at the aggregate level. Exploring county differences in state ballot initiatives to ban same-sex marriage, they find that the average level of education at the county level is negatively associated with the county's support for these initiatives.

19. For assessments of the importance of extended and fictive kin in the black community, see Stack (1974) and Sarkisian and Gerstel (2004). As indicated in appendix 4.A, the black-white difference becomes significant only after familial experiences (such as growing up with both parents or being married or widowed) are added to the multivariate models. As shown later in this chapter, these two familial experiences generally are accompanied by more conservative definitions of family. Since African Americans are less

likely than their white counterparts to have had these experiences, the control for these two factors results in a more exclusionist position by African Americans.

20. Evidence of these countervailing effects is seen in models 4 and 5 in appendix 4.A, in which the addition of views regarding the Bible results in a notable reduction—or reversal in the direction—of racial differences.

21. The small number of Asian American, American Indian, biracial or multiracial, and "other" respondents prevents us from doing any meaningful analysis of each of these racial-ethnic groups.

    We also considered the possibility of racial differences in the clustering of responses. Separate latent class analyses, however, show that the three-class model (exclusionist, inclusionist, and moderate) applies equally well for both white and African American respondents.

22. Familial definitions are linked to white and African American attitudes toward same-sex marriage, although supplementary multivariate models suggest that these definitions are more influential for white adults than for their black peers.

23. The potent influence of religiosity on African Americans' attitudes toward same-sex marriage is confirmed in a similar analysis of the General Social Survey; see Sewell and Powell (2009).

24. For a thoughtful discussion of African Americans' reactions to same-sex marriage as well as the various strategies used by African American gay and lesbians to navigate their interactions with the African American community, see Moore (2010).

25. These predicted probabilities are derived from the multinomial logistic regressions reported in appendix 4.A.

26. The literature on homophobia often asserts that single men are the most likely to show resistance to gay men and lesbians. Although it is possible that homophobic behaviors are more likely to be displayed by single young men, who might see their masculinity challenged by the specter of homosexuality, we find no evidence that among men being young or single is implicated in more exclusionary views regarding same-sex couples.

27. Suburbanites, on the other hand, fall between urban and rural residents. That is, they are more exclusionist (41.60 percent) than urbanites and more inclusionist (29.6 percent) than their rural counterparts. These figures, again based on a compilation of responses from the 2003 and 2006 surveys, are a bit deceptive. Indeed, suburban Americans experienced the greatest change in views regarding family between 2003 and 2006: they moved further away from the positions held by rural residents and much closer to those expressed by urbanites.

28. We use the census measure of region. The Northeast includes the New England states (Maine, New Hampshire, Vermont, Massachusetts, Rhode Island, and Connecticut) and the mid-Atlantic States (New York, New Jersey, and Pennsylvania). The South consists of the south Atlantic states (Florida, Georgia, North Carolina, South Carolina, Virginia, West Virginia, Maryland, Washington, D.C., and Delaware), the east-south-central states (Ala-

bama, Kentucky, Mississippi, and Tennessee), and the west-south-central states (Arkansas, Louisiana, Oklahoma, and Texas). The North Central area comprises the east-north-central states (Illinois, Indiana, Michigan, Ohio, and Wisconsin) and the west-north-central states (Iowa, Kansas, Minnesota, Missouri, Nebraska, North Dakota, and South Dakota). The West is made up of the mountain states (Arizona, Colorado, Idaho, Montana, Nevada, New Mexico, Utah, and Wyoming), the West Coast states (California, Oregon, and Washington), and the Pacific states (Alaska and Hawaii, which were not included in this survey).

29. The census definition of region is not without its detractors. The inclusion of Maryland, Washington, D.C., and Delaware in the South, for example, may strike some readers as puzzling. Scholars have argued over the appropriate definition of "the South," with some proposing a more limited geographical span. If we restrict ourselves to the "deep South" (typically seen as South Carolina, Georgia, Alabama, Mississippi, and Louisiana), the regional differences are magnified.

30. As indicated in appendix 4.A, over half of the North-South difference in the likelihood of being an inclusionist is attributable to regional variation in beliefs regarding biblical literalness (0.72 in model 3 versus 0.35 in model 5).

31. Admittedly, this question, which parallels an item regularly used in the General Social Survey, does not explicitly allow individuals who are members of religions that do not rely on the Bible to discuss the inerrancy of their primary religious text. That said, only eleven respondents refused to answer the question or indicated that they were unable to answer it.

   Nearly half of our respondents (49.1 percent) interpret the Bible as the inspired word of God, over one-third (34.3 percent) view the Bible as actual word of God, fewer than one-sixth (14.7 percent) see the Bible as fables, and the remaining few (1.8 percent) chose not to answer the question. These figures are virtually identical to the distribution of responses to the same question in the 2004 General Social Survey (47.9, 34.2, 15.7, and 2.2 percent, respectively).

32. Models 1 to 3 of appendix 4.C show the effects of the three other indicators: (1) no religious preference or affiliation, (2) the frequency of attendance at religious services, and (3) the strength of religious beliefs. In each of these models—which also take into account gender, age, race, and education—the effect of each of these dimensions of religion is strong. Once these three items are included in the same model (with or without views regarding biblical literalness; see models 4 and 5), it becomes clearer that the direct effect of the frequency of religious attendance is stronger than religious affiliation or the strength of religious beliefs.

33. Thomas Pettigrew and Linda Tropp (2006) offer a comprehensive assessment of the empirical work on the contact hypothesis. For an alternative—and less positive—evaluation of the contact hypothesis, the reader is directed to Bramel (2004).

34. These comments typically were given by men. Correspondingly, in addi-

tional multivariate analyses, we find that women were significantly more likely than men to indicate that they had a gay friend or relative. In contrast, Americans who were over the age of sixty-four, who lived in rural areas, and who held literalist views regarding the Bible were significantly less likely than their younger, urban, and less religiously orthodox counterparts to claim that they had a gay friend or relative.

35. The effects of contact with gay friends or relatives are consistently strong, regardless of the additional factors included in the multinomial logistic regressions. For a summary of the effects of contact in several of these models, see appendix 4.B.

36. See appendix 4.D for a summary of the effect of year (2006 versus 2003) on the likelihood of indicating that one had a gay friend or relative.

37. Perhaps it is not coincidental that there also was an increase between 2003 and 2006 in the number of our respondents—from 1.5 percent to 3.2 percent—who reported that they were gay, lesbian, or bisexual. Given the small percentage involved, these changes are not statistically significant. So we remain cautious about overinterpreting, especially because we interviewed a few respondents who appeared to misunderstand the word "heterosexual," even if they understood the words "gay," "lesbian," and "homosexual." When asked their sexual orientation (whether they were heterosexual, gay or lesbian, or bisexual), several women seemed unable (as opposed to being unwilling) to answer the question. For example, in the 2003 survey, one woman responded, "I'm none of these things"; at least two women incongruously responded, "I'm a white woman"; and another women declared, "Well, I'm a woman, and I'm married to a man. So I'm a bisexual?" Some men also had difficulties with this question—for example, "I like women. I like women. Whichever means I like women." Other responses included: "I'm Italian, I like women," and "I'm normal." Although with additional probing we were able to ascertain their sexual orientation, we believe that these responses speak to the problems in self-labels among the unmarked (in this case, heterosexual), a pattern similar to that found in recent scholarship on "whiteness" (see, for example, Frankenberg 1993). Although we cannot discount the possibility of some self-reporting errors, our interviewees who self-labeled as gay, lesbian, or bisexual, as expected, favored moderate and especially inclusionist stances over exclusionist ones.

38. The decrease in the number of young women and men who self-identify as feminist is an example of an apparent return to more conservative views among the young. The sociologists Jason Schnittker, Jeremy Freese, and Brian Powell (one of the authors of this book) (2003) show that younger Americans are much less likely to see themselves as feminist than are their older counterparts, especially those who came of age during the height of second-wave feminism. Still, according to that study, younger Americans continue to subscribe to more liberal views regarding gender overall than do older generations.

39. The sociologist Michael Rosenfeld (2007) offers a more detailed discussion

of *Loving v. Virginia* in his book *The Age of Independence: Interracial Unions, Same-Sex Unions, and the Changing American Family.* In this highly original book, Rosenfeld makes some provocative demographic claims regarding the similarities between interracial and same-sex couples and the marked increase in their numbers in the past few decades.

40. Our analysis regarding biblical inerrancy relies on data from the 1984 General Social Survey, the first year this question was posed.

41. Other Americans do not specifically discuss interracial couples, but their comments show a commonality in their reaction to—or more accurately, antipathy toward—both racial-ethnic and sexuality minorities. In the following remarks, an elderly woman began by explaining why she did not count same-sex couples as couples and pronouncing her aversion to same-sex couples, but then segued into even more heated commentary about Mexicans: "Why, well laws. You know, what they ought to do—now I'm going to tell you—what they ought to do is send them [gay and lesbian couples] to Bush's ranch in Crawford, Texas. Let them live like animals. That's what he should do with Mexicans too: open the ranch and let them all live there. Or any of the other illegals."

Chapter 5

1. Danielle Fettes contributed to this chapter.

2. The feminist biologist Anne Fausto-Sterling (1992, 2000), for example, contends that "objective" science can be heavily biased by unstated assumptions about gender and sexuality that shape research design and, in turn, scientific findings that ostensibly confirm clear differences by gender and sexuality. Unlike some other critics, however, Fausto-Sterling does not embrace a purely environmental (nurture) approach. Instead, she calls for movement away from a binary perspective that pits nature against nurture, as well as for forgoing dualistic approaches that bifurcate gender into a simplistic male-versus-female dichotomy. For other feminist critiques, see Rose and Rose (2000), and Travis (2003). For a critical examination of the racialization of scientific practices, see Duster (2003).

3. We too have been engaged in this debate—in some cases critically assessing genetic or sociobiological-evolutionary accounts of gender and family structure, while in other cases questioning purely environmental explanations of mental illness. See Freese and Powell (1999, 2003), Freese, Powell, and Steelman (1999), and Hamilton, Cheng, and Powell (2007).

4. The diametrically opposed responses regarding the current state of research on this topic are exemplified by the various reactions of sociologists to this chapter. Interestingly, one reader suggested that these divisions have been mostly settled, while another reader in effect encouraged us to further emphasize the differences by being even more critical of research in genetics and of sociological participation that further legitimizes such research. Still another reader expressed concern that sociologists have failed if, as we

show later in this chapter, Americans endorse genetic explanations for sexual preference.

5. Sheldon's *The Agenda* is one of at least three such books with "agenda" in the title—the other two being Ronnie Floyd's *The Gay Agenda* (2004) and Alan Sears and Craig Osten's *The Homosexual Agenda: Exposing the Principal Threat to Religious Freedom Today* (2003).

6. See, for example, www.Godhatesfags.com, the website of the Westboro Baptist Church, which has participated in "33000 such demonstrations since June 1991, at homosexual parades and other events, including funerals of impenitent sodomites (like Matthew Shepard) and over 200 military funerals of troupes whom God has killed in Iraq/Afghanistan in righteous judgment against an evil nation."

7. Although sexual orientation and sexual preference often are used interchangeably, both gay advocates and anti-gay groups contend that these terms have different connotations. Because "sexual orientation" may more strongly suggest that sexuality is fixed, inborn, or immutable, anti-gay groups have decried the use of this term. "Sexual preference," on the other hand, is a term criticized by some gay advocates for implying that sexuality is less fixed, developed, or changeable. We do not take a stance here on which term is preferable in the public discourse of sexuality. Instead, we decided to use the term "sexual preference" in our survey to ensure that we did not overemphasize the fixed nature of sexuality and to offer, in fact, a conservative estimate of Americans' genetic attributions of sexuality. Still, we suspect that the semantic difference between "sexual orientation" and "sexual preference" is slighter than implied by the debate among various interest groups.

We initially expected some of our respondents to have difficulty with the question about sexual preference because we referred to a child's traits. Pretesting and our subsequent interviews indicated that our concerns were unwarranted. In 2006, however, we added a set of questions about the causes of various adult traits and behaviors (including sexual preference). For the question on sexual preference, the response patterns (with genetic explanations being the modal choice) are nearly identical to those regarding children.

8. We also recognize that our survey is not fully inclusive of the various factors that could influence each human behavior we ask about. Pretesting indicated that a more extensive set of questions on this topic was too onerous for our respondents. That said, although our respondents spent quite a bit of time reflecting on the factors that they thought were most important (a sign to us that they were taking this question very seriously), only a handful of our interviewees (fewer than ten) asked whether there were other options (for example, "Are these my only choices?"). The analyses presented in this chapter exclude the few respondents who were unable to choose or who volunteered an alternative; their inclusion would not have appreciably changed the substantive conclusions of this chapter.

9. As described in previous chapters, descriptive statistics are weighted.

10. On beliefs about wealth and poverty, see Hunt (2007); on public explanations of mental illness, see Phelan (2005); on beliefs regarding the cause of homelessness, see Lee, Jones, and Lewis (1990).

11. More specifically, we use multinomial logistic regression models that control for gender, race, age, and education. When specifically mentioned, models also take into account views regarding biblical literalness. These models are displayed in appendix 5.A. Supplementary multivariate analyses included marital status, parental status, region, and urban residence. The effects of gender, race, age, education, and religious ideology are consistently significant, and the predicted probabilities deviate only slightly regardless of the combination of controls. These models used pooled data from the 2003 and 2006 surveys. Auxiliary analyses also evaluated the 2003 and 2006 data separately. With one notable exception, which we discuss later in this chapter, patterns are very similar in both years.

12. Although we restricted our questions on the causes of children's traits and behaviors to closed-ended questions, some respondents volunteered openended responses.

13. As also seen in chapter 4, there is some evidence of a baby boom exception to this linear and negative effect of age: of all age cohorts, adults between the ages of forty-five and fifty-four were the least likely to use parental explanations.

14. As noted earlier, these predicted probabilities control for generational differences in education, along with other controls. If education is not included in the model, the percentage of adults age sixty-five or older who attributed sexual preference to parenting increases from 26.2 to 33.3 percent, and the percentage attributing sexual preference to genes or genetic inheritance decreases from 42.6 to 35.8 percent.

15. The positive association between age and religiosity (measured by selfdescribed religiosity) is confirmed in the Constructing the Family Surveys, and as in additional analyses we conducted of the General Social Survey, that association is stronger than the link of religiosity to gender, education, or income.

16. We mention this possibility because it is in line with the position of some gay scholars and activists who challenge binary and fixed notions of gender and sexuality. Nevertheless, in searching through the transcripts of the interview, we found very little evidence of this stance.

17. The pattern of responses for other racial groups, a very small percentage of the sample, resembles very closely that of whites. The plurality of this group attributed sexual preference to genes and genetic inheritance.

18. The sociologist Matthew Hunt (2004) also offers compelling evidence of African Americans' attraction to "God's will" accounts for wealth and poverty.

19. Admittedly, the number of gay-lesbian-bisexual respondents was quite small—so small that any pattern is suggestive at best—but it is noteworthy that four-fifths (80.2 percent) believed that sexuality is rooted in genetics or "God's will."

20. Appendices 5.B and 5.C show the coefficients from regression models (logistic regression for appendix 5.B and multinomial logistic regression for appendix 5.C) from which the predicted probabilities for figures 5.8 and 5.9 are derived.

21. As with most other figures in this chapter, predicted probabilities are derived from a multivariate regression (in this case, logistic regression) that adjusts for age, gender, race, and education.

22. See appendix 5.D for a summary of the logistic regressions on which these conclusions are based.

23. For a summary of the multivariate models that test for the significance of this change, see appendix 5.E.

24. For a summary of the multivariate models that explore the significance of this change, see appendix 5.F.

25. For a discussion of the linkage between threats to masculinity and homophobia, see Britton (1990), Herek (1986, 2000), Kimmel (2004), and Stein (2005).

26. Indeed, scholars have noted that an essentialist position may make perceived differences between groups even more salient; see Demoulin, Leyens, and Yzerbyt (2006).

27. Some recent evidence confirms that sociologists are increasingly willing to endorse genetic explanations in areas such as sexuality; see Engle et al. (2006).

Chapter 6

1. Several judges have expressed skepticism regarding the evidence that children living in gay or lesbian households are not "harmed." For example, Justice Martha B. Sosman, in her dissenting opinion in *Goodridge v. Department of Public Health*, contended that "attempts at scientific study of the ramifications of raising children in same-sex couple households are themselves in their infancy and have so far produced inconclusive and conflicting results. Notwithstanding our belief that gender and sexual orientation of parents should not matter to the success of the child rearing venture, studies to date reveal that there are still some observable differences between children raised by opposite-sex couples and children raised by same-sex couples." For four excellent reviews regarding the experiences of children in same-sex households, see Berkowitz (2009), Biblarz and Stacey (2010), Patterson (2000), and Stacey and Biblarz (2001).

2. For more detailed accounts of historical changes in custody decisions and the contemporary debates regarding custody, see Artis (1999), Chambers (1984), Maccoby and Mnookin (1992), Mason (1994), Mnookin (1975), Pearson, Munson, and Thoennes (1982), Polikoff (1983), Scott (1992), and Seltzer (1990).

3. Most cases of single fatherhood were not the result of divorce or separation but of widowhood, which was not uncommon given the high maternal mortality rate (Orthner, Brown, and Ferguson 1976; Sugg 1978).

4. Although homosociality and homosexuality are distinct, the sociologist

Dana Britton (1990) astutely links contemporary homosociality and homophobia, arguing that people who are most comfortable in homosocial
settings also are the least comfortable with homosexuality.

5. Fineman's position is not shared consistently by other feminist legal scholars. Some criticize the ambiguity or "indeterminacy" of the "best interests"
standard, but still support the overriding principles behind it and its symbolic meaning. See, for example, Bartlett (1988), Glendon (1986), and Scott
(1992).

6. Although some might expect that female judges would favor women more
readily than male judges, Artis found the opposite pattern. Compared to
older male judges, female judges—and younger male ones—were more
likely to treat the "best interests" standard as a genuinely gender-neutral
standard and more likely to promote gender equality in custody determinations.

7. As in previous chapters, the percentages presented here are predicted
probabilities derived from multivariate regression (multinomial logistic regression) models that account for gender, age, race, and education. Models
that include these sociodemographic factors—by themselves or in conjunction with views regarding biblical literalness and views regarding the
causes of sexual preference—are available in appendix 6.A. Auxiliary analyses demonstrate that the addition of family background, marital status,
region, and urban residence does not alter the key patterns—with, as we
discuss later, the one exception of race.

8. In the models presented in appendix 6.A, the racial difference—with African Americans being less likely than their white peers to believe that the
optimal living arrangement for boys (and for girls) depends less on the sex
of the parent than on the situation—is marginally significant. The addition
of family background results in a more strongly significant difference.

Although most marital differences here are not strong enough to hold
when other sociodemographic factors are taken into account, we do find
that separated and divorced Americans are significantly more likely than
their married or single counterparts to say that the best living arrangement
for both boys and girls depends on the situation.

9. Because the maternal presumption for daughters is so strong, figure 6.3
and subsequent figures highlight views regarding the preferred living arrangement for boys. That said, increasing educational levels result in some
movement away from the maternal presumption for girls and toward a
more gender-neutral stance.

10. Other dimensions of religion and religiosity (for example, denomination,
frequency of attending religious services, and strength of religious beliefs)
exhibit similar effects.

11. The 2006 version of the Constructing the Family Survey included several
questions that address perceived causes of masculinity and femininity. Un-
fortunately, given the length of the 2006 survey, we were unable to repeat
the questions from the 2003 survey that focused on preferred living arrangements for boys and girls in single-parent households.

12. We used a split-ballot approach for several of our open-ended questions,

reducing the number of responses to approximately 175 respondents. Interviewees who responded "either parent" or "it depends" were not explicitly asked to explain their answer, although recordings of these interviews reveal that many respondents offered explanations without being asked.

13. As with our qualitative analyses discussed in previous chapters, responses were coded and analyzed by a research team of professors, graduate students, and undergraduate students. In identifying themes, we used a variety of analytical techniques and approaches, including the use of Atlas.ti, computer software that facilitates the analysis of a large set of qualitative responses.

14. As noted earlier, other respondents also mentioned issues of sexuality as precisely the reason why girls should live with their mothers. Most of these discussions focused on puberty, but a few disturbingly focused on the possibility of sexual abuse by fathers.

15. Pretests indicate that the ordering of questions does not alter the patterns of responses.

16. The choice of the word "Jezebel" by this African American respondent is notable. It belongs to the list of "controlling images"—along with Mammy and welfare queen—that have been used, Patricia Hill Collins (1990) suggests, to dominate African American women. These images are so powerful that some members of the African American community invoke them, as in this case.

17. Americans who believe that the optimal living arrangement for girls is situational also were more likely to be inclusionists (44.0 percent). There was little difference, however, between those who endorsed a maternal presumption for girls and those who advocated paternal custody: the modal category for both groups was exclusionist (50.2 percent and 48.3 percent, respectively).

   But even within the group of respondents who said that the preferred living arrangement for boys is situational, we find considerable variation. Those who explicitly used a gendered logic (for example, the "drunk" father and the "promiscuous" mother) in their open-ended responses were much more likely to espouse an exclusionist definition of family, while those who used an apparently gender-free logic were more likely to advocate an inclusionist definition.

   As seen in appendix 6.B, these patterns are consistent in models that (1) do not include additional controls; (2) adjust for gender, age, race, and education; and (3) also adjust for views regarding biblical literalness. Supplementary analyses confirm that the effects of preferred custody arrangements are consistent even when other factors (family background, marital status, region, urban residence, views about the causes of sexual preference) are taken into account.

18. Although women and men did not noticeably disagree on the question of responsibility for a child's physical needs, women were significantly more likely than men to believe that mothers should be primarily responsible for disciplining a child.

19. This pattern is consistent regardless of the combination of other factors taken into consideration (for example, gender, race, age, education) and holds for both men and women in our sample.

Chapter 7

1. Additional contributor Laura Hamilton is the lead author on this chapter.
2. For some exceptions, see the following analyses of how Americans' view women and/or men who choose nontraditional naming practices: Etaugh 1999; Forbes et al. 2002.
3. On all questions regarding attitudes toward name change, only a small percentage (between 2 and 4 percent) volunteered a response of "depends" or "neither agree nor disagree." Consequently, these responses are not included here.
4. We discuss only those group differences that are statistically significant in bivariate comparisons as well as in multivariate multinomial logistic regression models that control for other sociodemographic factors. These analyses, as seen in appendix 7.A and 7.B, indicate that the group differences we discuss are robust. Appendix 7.A presents multivariate analyses for a name change scale, constructed of the three items noted earlier (whether it is generally better if a woman changes her last name to her husband's name when she marries; whether it is a good idea for states to legally require women to change their name to their husband's last name; and whether it is okay for a man to take his wife's name when he marries). Appendix 7.B includes the same analyses for each separate item. Regardless of the sociodemographic factors and specific name change items included, the patterns generally hold.
5. The attitudes toward name change of those from other racial-ethnic categories were not significantly different from those of whites, perhaps owing to the small number of respondents in these other categories.
6. Although there are significant differences between the married and nonmarried, they are perhaps not as robust as other sociodemographic differences—they appear in some but not all models—and are strongest for the item regarding whether it is better for a woman to change her name.

    Urban residence and region of residence are also strongly linked to beliefs about marital name change. Respondents living in rural areas espoused more traditional views, and those in urban areas more liberal views. Those who lived in the South had the most restrictive attitudes toward name change, and those from the West and the Northeast had the least restrictive.
7. Other religious indicators—frequency of attendance at religious services, self-reported religiosity, and religious denomination—are also related to views about name change. In general, those who attend religious services with the most frequency and report the highest levels of religiosity have the most traditional views regarding name change. Protestants tend to have the most restrictive beliefs about naming practices and Jews the least

restrictive. This is consistent with the item on biblical inerrancy: Protestants are the religious group most likely to espouse evangelical views.

8. We used a split-ballot approach for several of our open-ended questions, reducing the number of respondents to 246.

9. As discussed in previous chapters, responses were coded and analyzed by a research team of professors, graduate students, and undergraduate students. In identifying themes, we used a variety of analytical techniques and approaches, including the use of Atlas.ti, computer software that facilitates the analysis of a large set of qualitative responses.

10. To get at the exceptions to these beliefs, we also asked a subsample of name change advocates under what conditions they did *not* think it is better for women to change their names. The most commonly cited exception, used by half of the advocates, was that of working women. The openness of name change supporters to the issue of women's employment suggests that they did not see employment as being in conflict with establishing a gender identity that prioritizes marriage and family. These respondents focused on identity salience; that is, they recognized that women may have many identities, but believed that women should be most invested in their identities as wives and mothers.

11. In supplementary analyses (not shown in the appendices), we include employment status as a predictor of attitudes toward name change. There is a marginally significant effect of being employed: the employed have more liberal views, and those who are not employed have more traditional views, regarding marital name change.

12. A subsample of name change critics were asked about exceptions to their beliefs—or the conditions under which it might be *better* for women to change their names. Roughly half of these respondents noted that name change is an individual decision, and thus some women may find it better to take their husband's name. This response supports the notion that the women's choice framework logically extends to both opposing traditional naming practices and supporting them.

13. These patterns hold in multivariate models, as presented in appendix 7.C. Inclusionists and moderates consistently had more liberal views toward name change than exclusionists, even when controlling for a number of important sociodemographic factors (gender, age, education, race, marital status, parental status, urban residence, region, and views regarding the Bible).

Chapter 8

1. Referendum 71 offers expanded domestic partner rights to heterosexual couples when at least one of the partners is sixty-two years old or older.

2. At the time of the writing of this chapter, the constitutionality of Proposition 8 has been challenged before the California Supreme Court.

3. Although a state judge overturned the law, some "pro-family" groups have indicated that they likely will appeal this judicial decision.

4. Even in New York, surely among the most consistently liberal states, Governor David Paterson's attempts to bring forth a vote in the New York Senate to legalize same-sex marriage initially were met with a tepid reaction—and in some cases vehement opposition—by New York legislators from both the Democratic and Republican Parties who were leery of reactions from constituents. Although advocates of same-sex marriage were able to bring a marriage equality bill to a full vote, they did not succeed in getting the bill passed.

5. This question also was asked in 1988.

6. For discussions of how an emphasis on familial functions need not bolster conservative visions of family and instead can undercut them, see Fineman (1995, 2004).

7. The liberalizing effect of education has not gone unnoticed by college students. In our undergraduate classes, we routinely ask students to complete the same set of closed-ended questions and to write their open-ended personal definitions of family. Their responses confirm not only a strikingly large percentage who see same-sex couples as family but also an appreciation of the powerful role played in their inclusive conceptualization of family by college and, in particular, their contact with a diverse group of students.

8. Similarly, some gay activists worry that, taken to the extreme, the position that sexuality is fixed and beyond an individual's control could justify disparate treatment of bisexuals, transsexuals, those who change sexual identities later in life, and others who choose not to identify as either "gay" or "straight."

9. Fineman's preferred typology of family is shared by very few Americans who were interviewed in the Constructing the Family Survey. Only 3 percent indicated that only households in which there is a parent-child relationship count as a family. Fineman's definitions of family may be more attractive in other countries, however. After hearing the results of the Constructing the Family Survey, David Reimer, Cornelia Hausen, Irena Kogan, and Markus Gangl from the University of Mannheim and Mannheim Centre for European Social Research led a data collection effort in 2005 in which more than nine hundred Germans who lived in or near Mannheim, an urban area with a strong manufacturing base, were presented with ten living arrangements (the same as those asked in the Constructing the Family Survey, with the exception of housemates) and asked to indicate which living arrangements they believed count as family. Among this German sample, the most common pattern was to define family solely on the basis of the presence of children. Whereas marriage by itself is a decisive factor among Americans, Germans grant more weight to living arrangements that include children—so much weight, in fact, that married couples without children are less likely than same-sex couples with children to be deemed a family. That said, Germans also are less likely than Americans to privilege single-parent households, perhaps because there is a fairly low proportion of single-parent households and because Germany's public pol-

icies and institutional practices especially encourage a two-parent—and in particular, a breadwinner-homemaker—arrangement.

10. This is not to deny the continued disavowal of interracial relationships among a certain segment of the population. Media representations of interracial couples still provoke strongly visceral reactions by some. The cover story in a recent edition of the *St. Louis Post-Dispatch* (Moore 2009), for example, featured an interracial couple kissing, prompting thousands of comments, mostly complaints:

> Haven't read the story but don't like to see blacks and whites kissing.

> . . . The reality here is that the silent majority does not accept interracial [*sic*] behavior and views it as unnatural. Most responsible parents do not allow cross-relationships such as these and for valid reasons.

The parallel with same-sex couples was explicitly brought up by several readers:

> Next year it will be two people of the same sex. Not that there's anything wrong with that....

> It should be two men kissing because those are the morals that the media wants the public to adopt and if you're offended, the liberals tell you it's because only their morals matter and what you want doesn't matter because they're in control and you're a mentally unstable hater.

Appendix 1.A

1. All analyses examine each sample separately, the samples together, and the two samples with appropriate weights. Any differences from these approaches are reported in the text.

2. An additional 2 percent of the Constructing the Family Survey and General Social Survey samples chose not to answer the question.

= References =

Aldous, Joan. 1999. "Defining Families Through Caregiving Patterns." *Marriage and Family Review* 28(3–4): 145–59.

Allen, Katherine R. 2000. "A Conscious and Inclusive Family Studies." *Journal of Marriage and Family* 62(1): 4–17.

Allen, Katherine R., and David H. Demo. 1995. "The Families of Lesbians and Gay Men: A New Frontier in Family Research." *Journal of Marriage and the Family* 57(1): 111–27.

Allport, Gordon W. 1954. *The Nature of Prejudice.* Reading, Mass.: Addison-Wesley.

Alwin, Duane F., and Jon A. Krosnick. 1991. "Aging, Cohorts, and the Stability of Sociopolitical Orientations over the Life Span." *American Journal of Sociology* 97(1): 169–95.

Alwin, Duane F., Ryan J. McCammon, and Scott M. Hofer. 2004. "Studying the Baby Boom Cohorts Within a Demographic and Developmental Context: Conceptual and Methodological Issues." In *The Baby Boomers at Midlife: Contemporary Perspectives on Midlife,* edited by Susan K. Whitbourne and Sherry L. Willis. Mahwah, N.J.: Lawrence Erlbaum Associates.

Amato, Paul R., and Alan Booth. 1997. *A Generation at Risk: Growing Up in an Era of Family Upheaval.* Cambridge, Mass.: Harvard University Press.

Andersen, Robert, and Tina Fetner. 2008. "Cohort Differences in Tolerance of Homosexuality: Attitudinal Change in Canada and the United States, 1981–2000." *Public Opinion Quarterly* 72(2): 311–30.

Artis, Julie E. 1999. "What Makes a Good Parent? An Examination of Child Custody Statutes, Case Law, and Judges." Ph.D. diss., Indiana University.

———. 2004. "Judging the Best Interests of the Child: Judges' Accounts of the Tender Years Doctrine." *Law and Society Review* 38(4): 769–806.

Barrow, Bill. 2009. "House Passes Bill Restricting Birth Certificates for Adoptions by Unmarried Couples." *New Orleans Times-Picayune,* May 12. Available at: http://www.nola.com/politics/index.ssf/2009/05/house_passes_bill_restricting.html (accessed May 3, 2010).

Bartholomew, David J. 2002. "Old and New Approaches to Latent Variable Modeling." In *Latent Variable and Latent Structure Models,* edited by George A. Marcoulides and Irini Moustaki. Mahwah, N.J.: Lawrence Erlbaum Associates.

Bartlett, Katharine. 1988. "Re-expressing Parenthood." *Yale Law Journal* 98(2): 293–340.

Bearman, Peter. 2008. "Exploring Genetics and Social Structure." *American Journal of Sociology* 114(supplement): Sv–x.

Becker, Gary. 1980. *A Treatise on the Family*. Cambridge, Mass.: Harvard University Press.

Berkowitz, Dana. 2009. "Theorizing Lesbian and Gay Parenting: Past, Present, and Future Scholarship." *Journal of Family Theory and Review* 1(3): 117–32.

Bernardes, Jon. 1999. "We Must Not Define 'The Family'!" *Marriage and Family Review* 28(3–4): 21–31.

Bernstein, Mary. 2004. "Paths to Homophobia." *Sexuality Research and Social Policy* 1(2): 41–54.

Bernstein, Mary, and Constance Kostelac. 2002. "Lavender and Blue: Attitudes About Homosexuality and Behavior Toward Lesbians and Gay Men Among Policy Officers." *Journal of Contemporary Criminal Justice* 18(3): 302–28.

Bernstein, Mary, Constance Kostelac, and Emily Gaarder. 2003. "Understanding 'Heterosexism': Applying Theories of Racial Prejudice to Homophobia Using Data from a Southwestern Police Department." *Race, Gender, and Class* 10(4): 54–74.

Bernstein, Mary, and Renate Reimann, eds. 2001a. *Queer Families, Queer Politics: Challenging Culture and the State*. New York: Columbia University Press.

———. 2001b. "Queer Families and the Politics of Visibility." In *Queer Families, Queer Politics: Challenging Culture and the State*, edited by Mary Bernstein and Renate Reimann. New York: Columbia University Press.

Bianchi, Suzanne M., Melissa A. Milkie, Liana C. Sayer, and John P. Robinson. 2000. "Is Anyone Doing the Housework? Trends in the Gender Division of Household Labor." *Social Forces* 79(1): 191–228.

Biblarz, Timothy J., and Judith Stacey. 2010. "How Does the Gender of Parents Matter?" *Journal of Marriage and Family* 72(1): 3–22.

Bielby, Denise Del Vento, and William T. Bielby. 1984. "Work Commitment, Sex-Role Attitudes, and Women's Employment." *American Sociological Review* 49(2): 234–47.

Black, Beverly, Thomas P. Oles, and Linda Moore. 1998. "The Relationship Between Attitudes: Homophobia and Sexism Among Social Work Students." *Affilia* 13(2): 166–89.

Blackstone, William. 1765. *Commentaries on the Laws of England*. Vol. 1. Oxford: Clarendon Press.

Blair, Sampson Lee, and Daniel T. Lichter. 1991. "Measuring the Division of Household Labor: Gender Segregation of Housework Among American Couples." *Journal of Family Issues* 12(1): 91–113.

Bobo, Lawrence, and Frederick C. Licari. 1989. "Education and Political Tolerance: Testing the Effects of Cognitive Sophistication and Target Group Affect." *Public Opinion Quarterly* 53(3): 285–308.

Bodine, Ann. 1975. "Androcentrism in Prescriptive Grammar: Singular 'They', Sex-Indefinite 'He', and 'He or She'." *Language in Society* 4(2): 129–46.

Bogardus, Emory S. 1932. "Social Distance Scale." *Sociology and Social Research* 17(3): 265–71.

Bolzendahl, Catherine I., and Clem Brooks. 2005. "Polarization, Secularization, or Differences as Usual? The Denominational Cleavage in U.S. Social Attitudes Since the 1970s." *Sociological Quarterly* 46(1): 47–78.

Bolzendahl, Catherine I., and Dan J. Myers. 2004. "Feminist Attitudes and Support for Gender Equality: Opinion Change in Women and Men, 1974–1998." *Social Forces* 83(2): 759–89.

Bourdieu, Pierre, with Jean-Claude Passeron. 1977. *Reproduction in Education, Society, and Culture.* Theory, Culture, and Society Series. London: Sage Publications.

Bramel, Dana. 2004. "The Strange Career of the Contact Hypothesis." In *The Psychology of Ethnic and Cultural Conflict,* edited by Juet Ting Lee, Stephen Worchel, Clark McCauley, and Fathali Moghaddam. New York: Praeger.

Brewster, Karin L., and Irene Padavic. 2000. "Change in Gender Ideology, 1977–1996: The Contributions of Intra-Cohort Change and Population Turnover." *Journal of Marriage and the Family* 62(2): 477–87.

Brightman, Joan. 1994. "Why Hillary Chooses Rodham Clinton." *American Demographics* 16(3): 9–10.

Britton, Dana M. 1990. "Homophobia and Homosociality: An Analysis of Boundary Maintenance." *Sociological Quarterly* 31(3): 423–39.

Brooks, Clem, and Catherine Bolzendahl. 2004. "The Transformation of U.S. Gender Role Attitudes: Cohort Replacement, Social-Structural Change, and Ideological Learning." *Social Science Research* 33(1): 106–33.

Brooks, Clem, and Jeff Manza. 1997. *Why Welfare States Persist.* Chicago: University of Chicago Press.

Budig, Michelle. 2007. "Feminism and the Family." In *The Blackwell Companion to the Sociology of Families,* edited by Jacqueline L. Scott, Judith Treas, and Martin Richards. New York: Blackwell.

Burden, Barry C. 2004. "An Alternative Account of the 2004 Presidential Election." *The Forum* 2(4): 1–10.

Burgess, Ernest W. 1926. "The Family as a Unity of Interacting Personalities." *Family* 7(1): 3–9.

Burstein, Paul. 1998. "Bringing the Public Back In: Should Sociologists Consider the Impact of Public Opinion on Public Policy?" *Social Forces* 77(1): 27–62.

———. 2003. "The Impact of Public Opinion on Public Policy: A Review and an Agenda." *Political Research Quarterly* 56(1): 29–40.

Byne, William, Stuart Tobet, Linda A. Mattiace, Mitchell S. Lasco, Eileen Kemether, Mark A. Edgar, Susan Morgello, Monte S. Buchsbaum, and Liesl B. Jones. 2001. "The Interstitial Nuclei of the Human Anterior Hypothalamus: An Investigation of Variation with Sex, Sexual Orientation, and HIV Status." *Hormones and Behavior* 40(2): 86–92.

Cameron, Deborah. 1995. *Verbal Hygiene.* London: Routledge.

Campbell, David E., and J. Quin Monson. 2008. "The Religion Card: Gay Marriage and the 2004 Presidential Election." *Public Opinion Quarterly* 72(3): 399–419.

Carrington, Christopher. 1995. *No Place Like Home: Relationships and Family Life Among Lesbians and Gay Men.* Chicago: University of Chicago Press.

Carroll, Susan J., and Richard Logan Fox, eds. 2006. *Gender and Elections: Shaping the Future of American Politics*. New York: Cambridge University Press.

Carter, J. Scott, and Casey A. Borch. 2005. "Assessing the Effects of Urbanism and Regionalism on Gender-Role Attitudes, 1974–1998." *Sociological Inquiry* 75(4): 548–63.

Carter, J. Scott, Lala Carr Steelman, Lynn M. Mulkey, and Casey Borch. 2005. "When the Rubber Meets the Road: The Effects of Urban Rural Residence on Principle and Implementation Measures of Racial Tolerance." *Social Science Research* 34(2): 408–25.

Cassidy, Margaret L., and Bruce O. Warren. 1996. "Family Employment Status and Gender Role Attitudes: A Comparison of Women and Men College Graduates." *Gender and Society* 10(2): 312–29.

Chambers, David L. 1984. "Rethinking the Substantive Rules for Custody Disputes in Divorce." *Michigan Law Review* 83(3): 477–569.

Chao, Elaine L., and Kathleen P. Utgoff. 2005. "Women in the Labor Force: A Databook." Government report 985 (May). Washington: U.S. Department of Labor.

Cheal, Daniel. 1991. *Family and the State of Theory*. Toronto: University of Toronto Press.

Cheng, Simon, and Brian Powell. 2005. "Small Samples, Big Challenges: Studying Atypical Family Forms." *Journal of Marriage and the Family* 67(4): 926–35.

Cherlin, Andrew J. 2003. "Should the Government Promote Marriage?" *Contexts* 2(4): 22–29.

———. 2004. "The Deinstitutionalization of American Marriage." *Journal of Marriage and Family* 66(4): 848–61.

Clark, Herbert H., and Jean E. Fox Tree. 2002. "Using 'Uh' and 'Um' in Spontaneous Speaking." *Cognition* 84(1): 73–111.

Coleman, James. 1988. "Social Capital in the Creation of Human Capital." *American Journal of Sociology* 94(supplement): 95–120.

Coleman, Marilyn, and Lawrence H. Ganong, eds. 2004. *Handbook of Contemporary Families: Considering the Past and Contemplating the Future*. Thousand Oaks, Calif.: Sage Publications.

Collins, Patricia Hill. 1990. *Black Feminist Thought: Knowledge, Consciousness, and the Politics of Empowerment*. Boston: Unwin Hyman.

Converse, Philip E. 1964. "The Nature of Belief Systems in Mass Publics." In *Ideology and Discontent*, edited by David E. Apter. Glencoe, Ill.: Free Press.

———. 2000. "Assessing the Capacity of Mass Electorates." *Annual Review of Political Science* 3: 331–53.

Coontz, Stephanie. 1992. *The Way We Never Were: American Families and the Nostalgia Trap*. New York: Basic Books.

———. 2008. "The Future of Marriage." Cato Unbound (January 14). Available at: http://www.cato-unbound.org/2008/01/14/stephanie-coontz/the-future-of-marriage/ (accessed May 3, 2010).

Cooper, Joel. 2007. *Cognitive Dissonance: Fifty Years of a Classic Theory*. London: Sage Publications.

Cooperman, Alan, and Thomas B. Edall. 2004. "Evangelicals Say They Led Charge for the GOP." *Washington Post*, November 8.

Correll, Shelley J., Stephen Benard, and In Paik. 2007. "Getting a Job: Is There a Motherhood Penalty?" *American Journal of Sociology* 112(2): 1297–1338.

Davis, James A., and Tom W. Smith. 2009. *General Social Surveys, 1972–2008.* Chicago: National Opinion Research Center.

Davis, Nancy J., and Robert V. Robinson. 1991. "Men's and Women's Consciousness of Gender Inequality: Austria, West Germany, Great Britain, and the United States." *American Sociological Review* 56(1): 72–84.

———. 1996. "Are the Rumors of War Exaggerated? Religious Orthodoxy and Moral Progressivism in America." *American Journal of Sociology* 102(3): 756–87.

DeMillo, Andrew. 2008. "Gay Adoption Ban Cleared for Arkansas Ballot." Cybercast News Service (August 25). Available at: http://www.cnsnews.com/Public/Content/article.aspx?RsrcID=34554 (accessed May 3, 2010).

Demo, David H., Katherine R. Allen, and Mark A. Fine, eds. 2000. *Handbook of Family Diversity.* New York: Oxford University Press.

Demoulin, Stephanie, Jacques-Philippe Leyens, and Vincent Yzerbyt. 2006. "Lay Theories of Essentialism." *Group Processes Intergroup Relations* 9(1): 25–42.

Dion, Kenneth L. 1987. "What's in a Title? The Ms. Stereotype and Images of Women's Titles of Address." *Psychology of Women Quarterly* 11(1): 21–36.

Dion, Kenneth L., and Albert A. Cota. 1991. "The Ms. Stereotype." *Psychology of Women Quarterly* 15(3): 403–10.

Dion, Kenneth L., and Regina A. Schuller. 1990. "Ms. and the Manager: A Tale of Two Stereotypes." *Sex Roles* 22(9–10): 569–77.

Dobson, James. 2001. *Bringing Up Boys: Practical Advice and Encouragement for Those Shaping the Next Generation of Men.* Wheaton, Ill.: Tyndale House Publishers.

Donaldson, Aubrey. 2005. "Risk That More Children Will Become Homosexual Through Learned Behavior." *Indiana Daily Student* (April 27).

Downey, Douglas B., and Brian Powell. 1993. "Do Children in Single-Parent Households Fare Better Living with Same-Sex Parents?" *Journal of Marriage and the Family* 55(1): 55–71.

Durkheim, Émile. 1977. *Suicide.* New York: Free Press. (Orig. pub. in 1897.)

Duster, Troy. 2003. *Backdoor to Eugenics.* 2d ed. New York: Routledge.

———. 2006. "Comparative Perspectives and Competing Explanations: Taking on the Newly Configured Reductionist Challenge to Sociology." *American Sociological Review* 71(1): 1–15.

Ellis, Lee. 1996. "A Discipline in Peril: Sociology's Future Hinges on Curing Its Biophobia." *American Sociologist* 27(2): 21–41.

Engle, Michael, Joseph McFalls, Bernard Gallagher, and Kristine Curtis. 2006. "The Attitudes of American Sociologists Toward Causal Theories of Male Homosexuality." *American Sociologist* 37(1): 68–76.

Epstein, Steven. 2003. "Sexualizing Governance and Medicalizing Identities: The Emergence of 'State-Centered' LGBT Health Politics in the United States." *Sexualities* 6(2): 131–71.

———. 2007. *Inclusion: The Politics of Difference in Medical Research.* Chicago: University of Chicago Press.

Erikson, Robert S., Michael MacKuen, and James Stimson. 2002. *The Macro Polity*. New York: Cambridge University Press.

Ernulf, Kurt E., and Sune M. Innala. 1989. "Biological Explanation, Psychological Explanation, and Tolerance of Homosexuals: A Cross-National Analysis of Beliefs and Attitudes." *Psychological Reports* 65(3): 1003–10.

Etaugh, Claire E., Judith S. Bridges, Myra Cummings-Hill, and Joseph Cohen. 1999. "Names Can Never Hurt Me? The Effects of Surname Use on Perceptions of Married Women." *Psychology of Women Quarterly* 23(4): 819–23.

Ettelbrick, Paula L. 2001. "Domestic Partnership, Civil Unions, or Marriage: One Size Does Not Fit All." *Albany Law Review* 64(3): 905–14.

Etzioni, Amitai. 1968. "Sex Control, Science, and Society." *Science* 161(3846): 1107–12.

Evans, Ann, and Edith Gray. 2005. "What Makes an Australian Family?" In *Australian Social Attitudes: The First Report*, edited by Shaun Wilson, Gabrielle Meagher, Rachel Gibson, David Denemark, and Mark Western. Sydney: University of New South Wales Press.

Fausto-Sterling, Anne. 1992. *Myths of Gender: Biological Theories About Women and Men*. 2d ed. New York: Basic Books.

———. 2000. *Sexing the Body*. New York: Basic Books.

Feagin, Joe R., Hernán Vera, and Nikitah Imani. 1996. *The Agony of Education: Black Students in White Colleges and Universities*. New York: Routledge.

Featherman, David, and Robert Hauser. 1978. *Opportunity and Change*. New York: Academic Press.

Festinger, Leon. 1957. *A Theory of Cognitive Dissonance*. Stanford, Calif.: Stanford University Press.

Fineman, Martha Albertson 1991. *The Illusion of Equality: The Rhetoric and Reality of Divorce Reform*. Chicago: University of Chicago Press.

———. 1995. *The Neutered Mother, the Sexual Family, and Other Twentieth-Century Tragedies*. New York: Routledge.

———. 2004. *The Autonomy Myth: A Theory of Dependency*. New York: New Press.

Firebaugh, Glenn, and Kevin Chen. 1995. "Voter Turnout of Nineteenth Amendment Women: The Enduring Effect of Disenfranchisement." *American Journal of Sociology* 100(4): 972–96.

Firebaugh, Glenn, and Kenneth E. Davis. 1988. "Trends in Antiblack Prejudice, 1972–1984: Region and Cohort Effects." *American Journal of Sociology* 94(2): 251–72.

Fischer, Claude S. 1978. "Urban-to-Non-Urban Diffusion of Opinions in Contemporary America." *American Journal of Sociology* 84(1): 151–59.

Fischer, Claude S., Michael Hout, Samuel R. Lucas, Martín Sánchez Jankowski, Ann Swidler, and Kim Voss. 1997. *Inequality by Design: Cracking the Bell Curve Myth*. Princeton, N.J.: Princeton University Press.

Fisher, Allen P. 2003. "Still 'Not Quite as Good as Having Your Own'? Toward a Sociology of Adoption." *Annual Review of Sociology* 29: 335–61.

Floyd, Ronnie W. 2004. *The Gay Agenda*. Greenforest, Ark.: New Leaf Press.

Forbes, Gordon B., Leah E. Adams-Curtis, Kay B. White, and Nicole R. Hamm. 2002. "Perceptions of Married Women and Married Men with Hyphenated Surnames." *Sex Roles* 46(5–6): 167–75.

Ford, Donna Y., Sonja Feist-Price, Dennese L. Jones, Lynda B. Wright, Marilyn Strutchens, Jessica E. Stephens, and J. John Harris III. 1996. "Family Diversity: Perceptions of University Students Relative to Gender and College Major." *Urban Education* 31(1): 91–106.

Frankenberg, Ruth. 1993. *White Women, Race Matters: The Social Construction of Whiteness*. Minneapolis: University of Minnesota Press.

Freese, Jeremy. 2008. "Genetics and the Social Science Explanation of Individual Outcomes." *American Journal of Sociology* 114(supplement): S1–35.

Freese, Jeremy, Jui-Chung Allen Li, and Lisa D. Wade. 2003. "The Potential Relevances of Biology to Social Inquiry." *Annual Review of Sociology* 29: 233–56.

Freese, Jeremy, and Brian Powell. 1999. "Sociobiology, Status, and Parental Investment in Sons and Daughters: Testing the Trivers-Willard Hypothesis." *American Journal of Sociology* 104(6): 1704–43.

———. 2003. "Tilting at Twindmills: Rethinking Sociological Responses to Behavioral Genetics." *Journal of Health and Social Behavior* 44(1): 130–35.

Freese, Jeremy, Brian Powell, and Lala Carr Steelman. 1999. "Rebel Without a Cause or Effect: Birth Order and Social Attitudes." *American Sociological Review* 64(2): 207–31.

Friess, Steve. 2007. "More Men Taking Wives' Last Names." *USA Today* (March 20).

Gallagher, Maggie. 2003. "The Stakes." *National Review Online* (July 14). Available at: http://article.nationalreview.com/269352/the-stakes/maggie-gallagher (accessed May 18, 2010).

Gamson, Joshua. 1995. "Must Identity Movements Self-Destruct? A Queer Dilemma." *Social Problems* 42(3): 390–407.

———. 1998. *Freaks Talk Back: Tabloid Talk Shows and Sexual Nonconformity*. Chicago: University of Chicago Press.

Gentry, Cynthia S. 1986. "Development of Scales Measuring Social Distance Toward Male and Female Homosexuals." *Journal of Homosexuality* 13(1): 75–82.

Gieryn, Thomas F. 2000. "A Space for Place in Sociology." *Annual Review of Sociology* 26: 463–96.

Gilens, Martin. 1995. "Racial Attitudes and Opposition to Welfare." *Journal of Politics* 57(4): 994–1014.

Glendon, Mary A. 1986. "Fixed Rules and Discretion in Contemporary Family Law and Succession Law." *Tulane Law Review* 60(6): 1165–97.

———. 1989. *The Transformation of Family Law: State, Law, and Family in the United States and Western Europe*. Chicago: University of Chicago Press.

Glenn, Norval D. 1993. "A Plea for Objective Assessment of the Notion of Family Decline." *Journal of Marriage and the Family* 55(3): 542–44.

Glenn, Norval D., Steven L. Nock, Linda J. Waite, William J. Doherty, William A. Galston, John Gottman, Barbara Markey, Howard J. Markman, Gloria G. Rodriguez, Isabel V. Sawhill, Scott M. Stanley, and Judith Wallerstein. 2002. "Why Marriage Matters: Twenty-one Conclusions from the Social Sciences." *American Experimental Quarterly* 5(2): 34–44.

Goffman, Erving. 1981. "Radio Talk." In *Forms of Talk*, edited by Erving Goffman. Philadelphia: University of Pennsylvania Press.

Goldberg, Abbie. 2009. *Lesbian and Gay Parents and Their Children: Research on the Family Life Cycle*. Washington: American Psychological Association.

Goldin, Claudia, and Maria Shim. 2004. "Making a Name: Women's Surnames at Marriage and Beyond." *Journal of Economic Perspectives* 18(2): 143–60.

Goodnough, Abby. 2009. "Pact Is Near on Same-Sex Marriage." *New York Times*, May 15.

Gould, Stephen J. 1996. *Mismeasure of Man*. New York: W. W. Norton.

Greenberg, Aaron, and J. Michael Bailey. 2001. "Parental Selection of Children's Sexual Orientation." *Archives of Sexual Behavior* 30(4): 423–37.

Greenberger, Scott S. 2005. "Gay Marriage Ruling Pushed Voters, Mobilized Bush, Left Kerry Wary." *Boston Globe*, November 7.

Gregory, Derek. 1995. *Geographical Imaginations*. Cambridge, Mass.: Blackwell.

Hamilton, Laura, Simon Cheng, and Brian Powell. 2007. "Adoptive Parents, Adaptive Parents: Evaluating the Importance of Biological Ties for Parental Investment." *American Sociological Review* 72(1): 95–116.

Hays, Sharon. 1996. *The Cultural Contradictions of Motherhood*. New Haven, Conn.: Yale University Press.

Henley, Nancy M. 1987. "This New Species That Seeks a New Language: On Sexism in Language and Language Change." In *Women and Language in Transition*, edited by Joyce Penfield. Albany: State University of New York Press.

Herek, Gregory. 1986. "On Heterosexual Masculinity: Some Psychical Consequences of the Social Construction of Gender and Sexuality." *American Behavioral Scientist* 29(5): 563–77.

———. 1988. "Heterosexuals' Attitudes Toward Lesbians and Gay Men: Correlates and Gender Differences." *Journal of Sex Research* 32(2): 95–105.

———. 1990. "The Context of Anti-Gay Violence: Notes on Cultural and Psychological Heterosexism." *Journal of Interpersonal Violence* 5(3): 316–33.

———. 1998. *Stigma and Sexual Orientation: Understanding Prejudice Against Lesbians, Gay Men, and Bisexuals*. Thousand Oaks, Calif.: Sage Publications.

———. 2000. "The Psychology of Sexual Prejudice." *Current Directions in Psychological Science* 9(1): 19–22.

Herek, Gregory M., and John P. Capitanio. 1995. "Black Heterosexuals' Attitudes Toward Lesbians and Gay Men in the United States." *Journal of Sex Research* 32(2): 95–105.

———. 1996. "'Some of My Best Friends': Intergroup Contact, Concealable Stigma, and Heterosexuals' Attitudes Toward Gay Men and Lesbians." *Personality and Social Psychology Bulletin* 22(2): 412–24.

Herek, Gregory M., and Eric K. Glunt. 1993. "Interpersonal Contact and Heterosexuals' Attitudes Toward Gay Men: Results from a National Sample." *Journal of Sex Research* 30(3): 239–44.

Herrnstein, Richard J., and Charles Murray. 1994. *The Bell Curve: Intelligence and Class Structure in American Life*. New York: Free Press.

Hill, Robert B. 1999. *The Strengths of Black Families: Twenty-five Years Later*. Lanham, Md.: University Press of America.

Hofferth, Sandra. 1985. "Children's Life Course: Family Structure and Living Arrangements in Cohort Perspective." In *Life Course Dynamics: Trajectories and Transitions, 1968–1980,* edited by Glen H. Elder. Ithaca, N.Y.: Cornell University Press.

Hogan, Dennis P., David J. Eggebeen, and Clifford C. Clogg. 1993. "The Structure of Intergenerational Exchanges in American Families." *American Journal of Sociology* 98(6): 1428–58.

Holstein, James A., and Jay Gubrium. 1999. "What Is Family? Further Thoughts on a Social Constructionist Approach." *Marriage and Family Review* 28(3): 3–20.

Hudson, Walter W., and Wendell A. Ricketts. 1980. "A Strategy for the Measurement of Homophobia." *Journal of Homosexuality* 5(4): 357–72.

Hull, Kathleen E. 2006. *Same-Sex Marriage: The Cultural Politics of Love and Law.* Cambridge: Cambridge University Press.

Hunt, Matthew O. 1996. "The Individual, Society, or Both? A Comparison of Black, Latino, and White Beliefs About the Causes of Poverty." *Social Forces* 75(1): 293–322.

———. 2004. "Race-Ethnicity and Beliefs About Wealth and Poverty." *Social Science Quarterly* 85(3): 827–53.

———. 2007. "African American, Hispanic, and White Beliefs About Black-White Inequality, 1977–2004." *American Sociological Review* 72(3): 390–415.

Indianapolis Star. 2005. "Indiana Senate OKs Ban on Gay Marriage." February 22.

Jackman, Mary R. 1981. "Education and Policy Commitment to Racial Integration." *American Journal of Political Science* 25(2): 256–69.

Jackman, Mary R., and Michael J. Muha. 1985. "Education and Intergroup Attitudes: Moral Enlightenment, Superficial Democratic Commitment, or Ideological Refinement?" *American Sociological Review* 49(6): 751–69.

Jayaratne, Toby Epstein, Oscar Ybarra, Jane P. Sheldon, Tony N. Brown, Merle Feldbaum, Carla A. Pfeffer, and Elizabeth M. Petty. 2006. "White Americans' Genetic Lay Theories of Race Differences and Sexual Orientation: Their Relationship with Prejudice Toward Blacks and Gay Men and Lesbians." *Group Processes & Intergroup Relations* 9(1): 77–94.

Jensen, Arthur R. 1969. "How Much Can We Boost IQ and Scholastic Achievement?" *Harvard Educational Review* 39(1): 1–123.

Jensen, Larry, David Gambles, and Joe Olsen. 1988. "Attitudes Toward Homosexuality: A Cross-Cultural Analysis of Predictors." *International Journal of Social Psychiatry* 34(1): 47–57.

Johnson, David R., and Laurie K. Scheuble. 1995. "Women's Marital Naming in Two Generations: A National Study." *Journal of Marriage and the Family* 57(3): 724–32.

Kane, Emily W. 1995. "Education and Beliefs About Gender Inequality." *Social Problems* 42(1): 74–90.

———. 2000. "Racial and Ethnic Variations in Gender-Related Attitudes." *Annual Review of Sociology* 26: 419–39.

———. 2006. "'No Way My Boys Are Going to Be Like That!': Parents' Responses to Children's Gender Nonconformity." *Gender and Society* 20(2): 149–76.

Kane, Emily W., and Else K. Kyyro. 2001. "For Whom Does Education Enlighten? Race, Gender, Education, and Beliefs About Social Inequality." *Gender and Society* 15(5): 710–33.

Kimmel, Michael S. 1987. "Men's Responses to Feminism at the Turn of the Century." *Gender and Society* 1(3): 261–83.

———. 2004 "Masculinity as Homophobia: Fear, Shame, and Silence in the Construction of Gender Identity." In *Feminism and Masculinities*, edited by Peter F. Murphy. New York: Oxford University Press.

Klein, Ethel. 1984. *Gender Politics*. Cambridge, Mass.: Harvard University Press.

Kluegel, James R., and Eliot R. Smith. 1987. *Beliefs About Inequality*. New York: Aldine de Gruyter.

Koerner, Ascan F., and Mary Ann Fitzpatrick. 2004. "Communication in Intact Families." In *Handbook of Family Communication*, edited by Anita L. Vangelisti. Mahwah, N.J.: Lawrence Erlbaum Associates.

Kramarae, Cheris, and Paula A. Treichler. 1985. "Words on a Feminist Dictionary." In *A Feminist Dictionary*, edited by Cheris Kramarae and Paula A. Treichler. Boston: Pandora Press.

Kurdek, Lawrence A. 1988. "Correlates of Negative Attitudes Toward Homosexuals in Heterosexual College Students." *Sex Roles* 18(11–12): 727–38.

Lakoff, Robin. 1973. "Language and Woman's Place." *Language in Society* 2(1): 45–80.

———. 1975. *Language and Woman's Place*. New York: Harper & Row.

LaMar, Lisa, and Mary Kite. 1998. "Sex Differences in Attitudes Toward Gay Men and Lesbians: A Multidimensional Perspective." *Journal of Sex Research* 35(1): 189–96.

Lee, Barrett A., Sue Hinze Jones, and David W. Lewis. 1990. "Public Beliefs About the Causes of Homelessness." *Social Forces* 69(1): 253–65.

LeVay, Simon. 1991. "A Difference in Hypothalamic Structure Between Homosexual and Heterosexual Men." *Science* 253(5023): 1034–37.

———. 1996. *Queer Science: The Use and Abuse of Research into Homosexuality*. Cambridge, Mass.: MIT Press.

Lieberson, Stanley. 1984. "What's in a Name?... Some Sociolinguistic Possibilities." *International Journal of the Sociology of Language* 1984(45): 77–87.

Lieberson, Stanley, and Eleanor O. Bell. 1992. "Children's First Names: An Empirical Study of Social Taste." *American Journal of Sociology* 98(3): 511–54.

Lieberson, Stanley, Susan Dumais, and Shyon Baumann. 2000. "The Instability of Androgynous Names: The Symbolic Maintenance of Gender Boundaries." *American Journal of Sociology* 105(5): 1249–87.

Lieberson, Stanley, and Kelly S. Mikelson. 1995. "Distinctive African American Names: An Experimental, Historical, and Linguistic Analysis of Innovation." *American Sociological Review* 60(6): 928–46.

Loftus, Jeni. 2001. "America's Liberalization in Attitudes Toward Homosexuality." *American Sociological Review* 66(5): 762–82.

Lopreato, Joseph, and Timothy Crippen. 1999. *Crisis in Sociology: The Need for Darwin*. New Brunswick, N.J.: Transaction.

Lott, Trent. 2006. "Hardball with Chris Matthews." MSNBC (June 6). Available at: http://www.msnbc.msn.com/id/13172421 (accessed May 17, 2010).

Low, Setha M. 1996. "The Anthropology of Cities." *Annual Review of Anthropology* 25: 387–99.

Maccoby, Eleanor E., and Robert H. Mnookin. 1992. *Dividing the Child: Social and Legal Dilemmas of Custody.* Cambridge, Mass.: Harvard University Press.

Maclay, Howard, and Charles E. Osgood. 1959. "Hesitation Phenomena in Spontaneous English Speech." *Word* 15(1): 19–44.

Mannheim, Karl. 1952. "The Problem of Generations." In *Essays on the Sociology of Knowledge*, edited by Paul Kecskemeti. London: Routledge and Kagan. (Orig. pub. in 1928.)

Manza, Jeff, and Clem Brooks. 1999a. *Social Cleavages and Political Change: Voter Alignments and U.S. Party Coalitions.* New York: Oxford University Press.

————. 1999b. "Group Size, Turnout, and Political Alignments and the Development of U.S. Party Coalitions, 1960–1992." *European Sociological Review* 15(4): 369–89.

Martin, Karin A. 2009. "Normalizing Heterosexuality: Mothers' Assumptions, Talk, and Strategies with Young Children." *American Sociological Review* 74(2): 190–207.

Martin, Molly A. 2008. "The Intergenerational Correlation in Weight: How Genetic Resemblance Reveals the Social Role of Families." *American Journal of Sociology* 114(supplement): S67–105.

Mason, Karen Oppenheim, and Yu-Hsia Lu. 1988. "Attitudes Toward Women's Familial Roles: Changes in the United States, 1977–1985." *Gender and Society* 2(1): 39–57.

Mason, Mary Ann. 1994. *From Father's Property to Children's Rights: The History of Child Custody in the United States.* New York: Columbia University Press.

Massey, Douglas S. 2002. "A Brief History of Human Society: The Origin and Role of Emotion in Social Life: 2001 Presidential Address." *American Sociological Review* 67(1): 1–29.

McCabe, Janice. 2005. "What's in a Label? The Relationship Between Feminist Self-Identification and 'Feminist' Attitudes Among U.S. Women and Men." *Gender and Society* 19(4): 480–505.

McCutcheon, Allen L. 1987. *Latent Class Analysis.* Newbury Park, Calif.: Sage Publications.

McFadden, Dennis. 2002. "Masculinization Effects in the Auditory System." *Archives of Sexual Behavior* 31(1): 99–111.

McHugh, Maureen C., and Irene Hanson Frieze. 1997. "The Measurement of Gender-Role Attitudes." *Psychology of Women Quarterly* 21(1): 1–16.

McPhee, Laura. 2005. "Recruited by the Homosexual Agenda." Nuvo (February 16). Available at: http://www.nuvo.net/archive/2005/02/16/recruited_by_the_homosexual_agenda.html (accessed May 3, 2010).

McVeigh, Rory, and Maria-Elena D. Diaz. 2009. "Voting to Ban Same-Sex Marriage: Interests, Values, and Communities." *American Sociological Review* 75(6): 891–915.

Miller, Bonnie. 2008. "Adoption Ban Targets Gay Couples, Critics Say." *Los Angeles Times*, December 4. Available at: http://articles.latimes.com/2008/dec/04/nation/na-gay-adopt (accessed May 3, 2010).

Miller, Casey, and Kate Swift. 1976. *Words and Women.* New York: Doubleday.

Miller, Nathan. 1927. "Some Aspects of the Name in Culture-History." *American Journal of Sociology* 32(4): 585–600.

Mnookin, Robert H. 1975. "Child-Custody Adjudication: Judicial Functions in the Face of Indeterminacy." *Law and Contemporary Problems* 39(3): 226–93.

Mohler, R. Albert, Jr. 2007. "Is Your Baby Gay? What If You Could Know? What If You Could Do Something About It?" (March 2). Available at: http://www.albertmohler.com/2007/03/02 (accessed May 18, 2010).

Moore, Doug. 2009. "Black Men Kissing White Woman Causes Stir," *St. Louis Post-Dispatch*, April 10. Available at: http://interact.stltoday.com/blogzone/a-conversation-about-race/general-news/2009/04/black-man-kissing-white-woman-causes-stir (accessed May 18, 2010).

Moore, Mignon R. 2010. "Black and Gay in L.A.: The Relationships Black Lesbians and Gay Men Have with Their Racial and Religious Communities." In *Black Los Angeles: American Dreams and Racial Realities*, edited by Darnell Hunt and Ana-Christina Ramon. New York: New York University Press.

Moore, Robert J. 2004. "Managing Troubles in Answering Survey Questions: Respondents' Uses of Projective Reporting." *Social Psychology Quarterly* 67(1): 50–69.

Morgenstern Leissner, Omi. 1997. "The Name of the Maiden." *Law Journal* 12(2): 253–99.

Murdock, George P. 1949. *Social Structure*. New York: Macmillan.

Nelkin, Dorothy, and M. Susan Lindee. 2004. *The DNA Mystique: The Gene as a Cultural Icon*. Ann Arbor: University of Michigan Press. (Orig. pub. in 1995.)

Nicolosi, Joseph, and Linda A. Nicolosi. 2002. *A Parent's Guide to Preventing Homosexuality*. Downers Grove, Ill.: InterVarsity Press.

Nilsen, Allen Pace. 1977. "Sexism as Shown Through the English Vocabulary." In *Sexism and Language*, edited by Haig Bosmajian, Alleen Pace Nilsen, H. Lee Gershuny, and Julia P. Stanley. Urbana, Ill.: National Council of Teachers of English.

Odum, Howard W. 1945. "The Way of the South." *Social Forces* 23(3): 16–26.

Odum, Howard W., and Harry E. Moore. 1938. *American Regionalism*. New York: Henry Holt.

Omi, Michael, and Howard Winant. 1994. *Racial Formation in the United States: From the 1960s to the 1990s*. London: Routledge.

Orloff, Ann Shola. 1993. "Gender and the Social Rights of Citizenship: The Comparative Analysis of Gender Relations and Welfare States." *American Sociological Review* 58(3): 303–28.

Orthner, Dennis K., Terry Brown, and Denis Ferguson. 1976. "Single Parent Fatherhood: An Emerging Family Life Style." *The Family Coordinator* 25(4): 429–37.

Page, Benjamin I., and Robert V. Shapiro. 1983. "Effects of Public Opinion on Policy." *American Political Science Review* 77(1): 175–90.

———. 1992. *The Rational Public: Fifty Years of Trends in Americans' Policy Preferences*. Chicago: University of Chicago Press.

Parsons, Talcott. 1954. "The Kinship System of the Contemporary United States." In *Essays in Sociological Theory*, by Talcott Parsons. New York: Free Press.

———. 1955. "The American Family: Its Relations to Personality and the Social Structure." In *Family, Socialization, and Interaction Process*, edited by Talcott Parsons and Robert F. Bales. Glencoe, Ill.: Free Press.

Parsons, Talcott, and Robert F. Bales.1955. *Family, Socialization, and Interaction Process*. Glencoe, Ill.: Free Press.

Pascoe, C. J. 2007. *Dude, You're a Fag: Masculinity and Sexuality in High School*. Berkeley: University of California Press.

Patterson, Charlotte J. 2000. "Family Relationship of Lesbians and Gay Men." *Journal of Marriage and the Family* 62(4): 1052–69.

Pauwels, Anne. 1998. *Women Changing Landscape*. London: Longman.

Pearson, Jessica, Paul Munson, and Nancy Thoennes. 1982. "Legal Change and Child Custody Awards." *Journal of Family Issues* 3(1): 5–24.

Penfield, Joyce. 1987. "Surnaming: The Struggle for Personal Identity." In *Women and Language in Transition*, edited by Joyce Penfield. Albany: State University of New York Press.

Pettigrew, Thomas F., and Linda R. Tropp. 2006. "A Meta-Analytic Test of Inter-Group Contact Theory." *Journal of Personality and Social Psychology* 90(5): 751–83.

Pew Research Center for the People and the Press. 2006. "Less Opposition to Gay Marriage, Adoption, and Military Service." Pew Research Center report (March 26). Available at: http://people-press.org/reports/pdf/273.pdf (accessed May 18, 2010).

Pharr, Suzanne. 1988. *Homophobia: A Weapon of Sexism*. Little Rock, Ark.: Chardon Press.

Phelan, Jo C. 2005. "Geneticization of Deviant Behavior and Consequences for Stigma: The Case of Mental Illness." *Journal of Health and Social Behavior* 46(4): 307–22.

Pinker, Steven. 2002. *The Blank Slate: The Modern Denial of Human Nature*. New York: Viking Press.

Plutzer, Eric. 1988. "Work Life, Family Life, and Women's Support of Feminism." *American Sociological Review* 53(4): 640–49.

Polikoff, Nancy D. 1983. "Why Are Mothers Losing? A Brief Analysis of Criteria Used in Child Custody Determinations." *Women's Rights Law Reporter* 7(3): 235–43.

———. 2008. *Beyond (Straight and Gay) Marriage: Valuing All Families Under the Law*. Boston: Beacon Press.

Polimeni, Anne-Maree, Elizabeth Hardie, and Simone Buzwell. 2000. "Homophobia Among Australian Heterosexuals: The Role of Sex, Gender Role Ideology, and Gender Role Traits." *Current Research in Social Psychology* 5(4): 47–62.

Popenoe, David. 1993. "American Family Decline, 1960–1990: A Review and Appraisal." *Journal of Marriage and the Family* 55(3): 527–55.

Powell, Brian. 2003. *Constructing the Family Survey 2003*. Bloomington: Indiana University Institute of Social Research.

———. 2006. *Constructing the Family Survey 2006*. Bloomington: Indiana University Institute of Social Research.

Powell, Brian, and Douglas B. Downey. 1997. "Living in Single-Parent Households: An Investigation of the Same-Sex Hypothesis." *American Sociological Review* 62(4): 521–39.

Rahman, Qazi, Veena Kumari, and Glenn D. Wilson 2003. "Sexual Orientation–Related Differences in Prepulse Inhibition of the Human Startle Response." *Behavioral Neuroscience* 117(5): 1096–1102.

Reardon, Jennifer. 2004. *Race to the Finish: Identity and Governance in an Age of Genomics*. Princeton, N.J.: Princeton University Press.

Rhodebeck, Laurie A. 1996. "The Structure of Men's and Women's Feminist Orientations: Feminist Identity and Feminist Opinion." *Gender and Society* 10(4): 386–403.

Risman, Barbara J. 1987. "Intimate Relationships from a Microstructural Perspective: Men Who Mother." *Gender and Society* 1(1): 6–32.

———. 2001. "Calling the Bluff of Value-Free Science." *American Sociological Review* 66(4): 605–11.

Rose, Hilary, and Steven P. R. Rose. 2000. *Alas, Poor Darwin: Arguments Against Evolutionary Psychology*. London: Jonathan Cape.

Rosenfeld, Michael J. 2007. *The Age of Independence: Interracial Unions, Same-Sex Unions, and the Changing American Family*. Cambridge, Mass.: Harvard University Press.

———. Forthcoming. "Nontraditional Families and Childhood Progress Through School." *Demography*.

Rossi, Alice S. 1965. "Naming Children in Middle-Class Families." *American Sociological Review* 30(4): 499–513.

Ryan, Maura, and Dana Berkowitz. 2009. "Constructing Gay and Lesbian Parent Families 'Beyond the Closet.'" *Qualitative Sociology* 32(2): 153–72.

Santrock, John W., and Richard A. Warshak. 1979. "Father Custody and Social Development in Boys and Girls." *Journal of Social Issues* 35(4): 112–25.

Sarkisian, Natalia, and Naomi Gerstel. 2004. "Kin Support Among Blacks and Whites: Race and Family Organization." *American Sociological Review* 69(6): 812–37.

Savic, Ivanka, Hans Berglund, and Per Lindström. 2005. "Brain Response to Putative Pheromones in Homosexual Men." *Proceedings of the National Academy of Sciences* 102(20): 7356–61.

Savic, Ivanka, and Per Lindström. 2008. "PET and MRI Show Differences in Cerebral Asymmetry and Functional Connectivity Between Homo- and Heterosexual Subjects." *Proceedings of the National Academy of Sciences* 105(27): 9403–8.

Schiappa, Edward, Peter B. Gregg, and Dean E. Hewes. 2005. "The Parasocial Contact Hypothesis." *Communication Monographs* 72(1): 92–115.

Schnittker, Jason. 2008. "Happiness and Success: Genes, Families, and the Psychological Effects of Socioeconomic Position and Social Support." *American Journal of Sociology* 114(supplement): S233–59.

Schnittker, Jason, Jeremy Freese, and Brian Powell. 2000. "Nature, Nurture, Neither, Nor: Black-White Differences in Beliefs About the Causes and Appropriate Treatment of Mental Illness." *Social Forces* 78(3): 1101–32.

———. 2003. "Who Are Feminists and What Do They Believe? The Role of Generations." *American Sociological Review* 68(4): 607–22.

Schuman, Howard, Lawrence Bobo, and Maria Krysan. 1992. "Authoritarian-ism in the General Population: The Education Interaction Hypothesis." *Social Psychology Quarterly* 55(4): 379–87.

Schuman, Howard, Charlotte Steeh, Lawrence Bobo, and Maria Krysan. 1997. *Racial Attitudes in America: Trends and Interpretations*. 2d ed. Cambridge, Mass.: Harvard University Press.

Scott, Elizabeth S. 1992. "Pluralism, Parental Preference, and Child Custody." *California Law Review* 80(3): 615–72.

Scott, Jacqueline. 1998. "Generational Changes in Attitudes to Abortion: A Cross-National Comparison." *European Sociological Review* 14(2): 1–14.

———. 2000. "Is It a Different World Than When You Were Growing Up? Gen-erational Effects on Social Representation and Child-Rearing Values." *British Journal of Sociology* 51(2): 355–76.

Sears, Alan, and Craig Osten. 2003. *The Homosexual Agenda: Exposing the Princi-pal Threat to Religious Freedom Today*. Nashville: Broadman and Holman.

Seltzer, Judith A. 2000. "Families Formed Outside of Marriage." *Journal of Mar-riage and the Family* 62(4): 527–42.

———. 1990. "Legal and Physical Arrangements in Recent Divorces." *Social Science Quarterly* 71(2): 250–66.

Settles, Barbara H. 1999. "Definitions of the Family Professional and Personal Issues." *Marriage and Family Review* 28(3–4): 209–24.

Sewell, Abigail, and Brian Powell. 2009. "Race, Gender, and Attitudes Toward Homosexuality." Unpublished paper. Indiana University.

Sheldon, Louis P. 2005. *The Agenda: The Homosexual Plan to Change America*. Lake Mary, Fla.: Frontline.

Skocpol, Theda. 1992. *Protecting Soldiers and Mothers: The Political Origins of So-cial Policy in the United States*. Cambridge, Mass.: Harvard University Press.

Smith, Dorothy E. 1993. "The Standard North American Family: SNAF as an Ideological Code." *Journal of Family Issues* 14(1): 50–65.

Sniderman, Paul M., and Thomas Piazza. 1993. *The Scar of Race*. Cambridge, Mass.: Belknap Press of Harvard University Press.

Stacey, Judith. 1996. *In the Name of the Family: Rethinking Family Values in the Postmodern Age*. Boston: Beacon Press.

Stacey, Judith, and Timothy J. Biblarz. 2001. "(How) Does the Sexual Orienta-tion of Parents Matter?" *American Sociological Review* 66(2): 159–83.

Stack, Carol B. 1974. *All Our Kin: Strategies for Survival in a Black Community*. New York: Harper & Row.

Stanley, Julia P. 1977. "Paradigmatic Woman: The Prostitute." In *Papers in Lan-guage Variation: SAMLA-ADS Collection*, edited by David L. Shores and Carol P. Hines. Tuscaloosa: University of Alabama Press.

———. 1978. "Sexist Grammar." *College English* 39(7): 800–11.

Stannard, Una. 1973. *Married Women v. Husbands' Names: The Case for Wives Who Keep Their Own Name*. San Francisco: Germainbooks.

Stein, Arlene. 2001. *The Stranger Next Door: The Story of a Small Community's Battle over Sex, Faith, and Civil Rights*. Boston: Beacon Press.

———. 2005. "Make Room for Daddy: Anxious Masculinity and Emergent Ho-mophobia in the Twenty-first Century." *Gender and Society* 19(5): 601–20.

Stimson, James A., Michael B. MacKuen, and Robert S. Erikson. 1995. "Dynamic Representation." *American Political Science Review* 89(3): 543–65.

Stouffer, Samuel. 1955. *Communism, Conformity, and Civil Liberties.* New York: Doubleday.

Sue, Christina A., and Edward E. Telles. 2007. "Assimilation and Gender in Naming." *American Journal of Sociology* 112(5): 1383–1415.

Sugg, Redding S., Jr. 1978. *Motherteacher: The Feminization of American Education.* Charlottesville: University Press of Virginia.

Sullivan, Maureen. 2001. "Alma Mater: Family 'Outings' and the Making of the Modern Other Mom (MOM)." In *Queer Families, Queer Politics: Challenging Culture and the State,* edited by Mary Bernstein and Renate Reimann. New York: Columbia University Press.

Tillman, Kathryn H., and Charles B. Nam. 2008. "Family Structure Outcomes of Alternative Family Definitions." *Population Research and Policy Review* 27(3): 367–84.

Townsend, Nicholas W. 2002. *The Package Deal: Marriage, Work, and Fatherhood.* Philadelphia: Temple University Press.

Travis, Cheryl Brown, ed. 2003. *Evolution, Gender, and Rape.* Cambridge, Mass.: MIT Press.

Travis, Scott. 2007. "Gay Rights Group Is Upset Over College's Pet Insurance." *South Florida Sun-Sentinel* (November 24).

Trost, Jan. 1988. "Conceptualizing the Family." *International Sociology* 41(3): 301–8.

———. 1990. "Do We Mean the Same by the Concept of Family?" *Communication Research* 17(4): 431–43.

Tuch, Steven A. 1987. "Urbanism, Region, and Tolerance Revisited." *American Sociological Review* 52(4): 504–10.

Udry, J. Richard. 1995. "Sociology and Biology: What Biology Do Sociologists Need to Know?" *Social Forces* 73(4): 1267–78.

———. 2000. "Biological Limits of Gender Construction." *American Sociological Review* 65(3): 443–57.

U.S. Bureau of the Census. 2001. "Living Arrangements of Children: Household Economic Studies, 1996." *Current Population Reports.* Washington: U.S. Department of Commerce.

Waite, Linda, and Maggie Gallagher. 2000. *The Case for Marriage: Why Married People Are Happier, Healthier, and Better Off Financially.* New York: Doubleday.

Waldman, Paul. 2009. "We've Already Won the Battle over Gay Marriage." *The American Prospect* (April 14). Available at: http://www.prospect.org/cs/articles?article=weve_already_won_the_battle_over_gay_marriage (accessed May 3, 2010).

Waller, Willard. 1938. *The Family: A Dynamic Interpretation.* New York: Cordon.

Walters, Susana Dunata. 2001. *All the Rage: The Story of Gay Visibility in America.* Chicago: University of Chicago Press.

Warner, Michael. 1999. *The Trouble with Normal: Sex, Politics, and the Ethics of Queer Life.* New York: Free Press.

Watkins, Susan C., and Andrew S. London. 1994. "Personal Names and Cultural Change: A Study of the Naming Patterns of Italians and Jews in the United States in 1910." *Social Science History* 18(2): 169–209.

Weigel, Daniel J. 2008. "The Concept of Family: An Analysis of Laypeople's Views of Family." *Journal of Family Issues* 29(11): 1426–47.

Weinberg, George. 1972. *Society and the Healthy Homosexual.* New York: St. Martin's Press.

Weir, Margaret, Ann Shola Orloff, and Theda Skocpol, eds. 1988. *The Politics of Social Policy in the United States.* Princeton, N.J.: Princeton University Press.

Weitzman, Lenore J. 1981. *The Marriage Contract: Spouses, Lovers, and the Law.* New York: Free Press.

West, Candace, and Don H. Zimmerman. 1987. "Doing Gender." *Gender and Society* 1(2): 125–51.

Weston, Kath. 1991. *Families We Choose: Lesbians, Gays, Kinship.* New York: Columbia University Press.

———. 1997. *Families We Choose: Lesbians, Gays, Kinship.* 2d ed. New York: Columbia University Press.

Wilcox, Clyde, and Robin Wolpert. 2000. "Gay Rights in the Public Sphere: Public Opinion on Gay and Lesbian Equality." In *The Politics of Gay Rights,* edited by Craig A. Rimmerman, Kenneth D. Wald, and Clyde Wilcox. Chicago: University of Chicago Press.

Wilkie, Jane Riblett. 1991. "The Decline in Men's Labor Force Participation and Income and the Changing Structure of Family Economic Support." *Journal of Marriage and the Family* 53(1): 111–22.

Wirth, Louis. 1938. "Urbanism as a Way of Life." *American Journal of Sociology* 44(1): 1–24.

Wood, Peter B., and John P. Bartkowski. 2004. "Attribution Style and Public Policy Attitudes Toward Gay Rights." *Social Science Quarterly* 85(1): 58–74.

Yang, Alan S. 1997. "The Polls-Trends: Attitudes Toward Homosexuality." *Public Opinion Quarterly* 61(3): 477–507.

Zaller, John R. 1992. *The Nature and Origins of Mass Opinion.* New York: Cambridge University Press.

Zimmerman, Eric. 2008. "Two Takes on Gay Marriage Jurisprudence." *New Republic* (October 10). Available at: http://www.tnr.com/blog/the-plank/two-takes-gay-marriage-jurisprudence (accessed May 3, 2010).

.

═ Index ═

Boldface numbers refer to figures and tables

abortion, 108
academic family definitions, 6–13, 16
adoptive families, 41, 50, 268*n*1. *See also* same-sex adoption
African Americans: controlling images of women, 2+86*n*16; extended family or fictive kin, 3, 84–86; family definitions, 84–86. *See also* racial differences
age and cohort differences: child custody views, 145; family accounts and definitions, 75–81, 97, 208–9; family name change views, 181, **182**; feminist identification, 280*n*38; religiosity, 283*n*15; sexual preference explanations, 113–15, 131
The Agenda: The Homosexual Plan to Change America (Sheldon), 108
aging process, 78–79
Alabama: interracial marriage ban removal, 99
Allen, Katherine, 10
Alliance Defense Fund, 17
Alliance for Children and Families, 17
Allport, Gordon, 92
American Civil Liberties Union, 174
American Heritage Dictionary, 16
American Sociological Association, 105, 106
American Sociological Review, 105
Andersen v. King County, 138–39
anti-gay language, 43–44, 54

antimiscegenation laws, 99–101, 217–18
anti-sodomy statutes, 125
Arizona: marriage protection ballot initiatives, 202–3
Arkansas: adoption restrictions for same-sex and cohabiting couples, 4, 203; same-sex marriage ban, 28
Artis, Julie, 141
attribution research, 134

baby boomers, 79–81, 208–9, 283*n*13
Baehr v. Lewin, 27
Bailey, J. Michael, 108
Baker v. Nelson, 26
Bales, Robert, 46
ballot initiatives, 3–4, 202–3
Baptists, 282*n*6
Baumann, Shyon, 175–76
The Bell Curve (Herrnstein and Murray), 107
"benchmark" family, 268*n*5
benefits, extension to same-sex families, 31–33, 202, 208, 210, **246**
Bernstein, Mary, 11–12
"best interests of child" standard, 140–41
Biblarz, Timothy, 10, 142–43
Bible, views on: and child custody views, 146–47; and family name change views, 182–84, 186–87; and inclusionist, moderate, or exclusionist likelihood, **250**; literal

309